SMALL CHILDREN : BIG DREAMS

SMALL CHILDREN
Big Dreams

KHURSHID DABDI

KALPAZ

Small Children Big Dreams

ISBN: 81-7835-791-1

Reprinted in 2012 in India by
Kalpaz Publications,
C-30, Satyawati Nagar,
Delhi-110 052
E-mail: kalpaz@hotmail.com

Printed at: Chawla Offset Printers, Delhi

Contents

Gratitude

On 11th November '04, before going to bed, in a silent prayer, I poured out my anxieties about Sunbeam to my guru, "Baba, in 1997, being a mother and a friend to the first batch of 18 children was in itself a big responsibility. Today, 7 years hence, my role has undergone a radical change. Being a mentor and a friend to the 25 field staff and the 6 Functional Heads is overwhelming. The pressure and emotional strain of playing that role is immense, considering the deep concerns regarding the high staff turnover, because they are the individuals under whose care are placed our hundreds of child beneficiaries."

The very next morning my dear guru appeared in my dream and made the most unexpected request of me. Friends, let me share with you my dream of 12th November '04 that inspired me to write this book:

Baba was on the stage with a few people seated next to Him on either side. Somewhere in the last row, I sat among the crowd of devotees gathered for His 'darshan'. Distance didn't pose a problem and nothing blocked my view of my beloved guru. Turning to the men seated next to Him on both His sides, Baba asked them something which they couldn't answer. So He turned to His devotees and addressed us thus, "Can any one of you help me explain to the rest of the people gathered here as to how children should be treated?" Surprisingly, no one had anything to say, and to my utter disbelief and joy, I found Baba turn His gaze towards me and ask me if I had anything to share on the topic! Stunned by the faith He had reposed in me, I answered in the affirmative. In order to be able to reach Him from my current position in the last row, it seemed like an impossibly long distance to cover. Yet, not one to be discouraged, I resolved to cross the entire stretch while actually doing His bidding – sharing with His devotees my perspective on how children should be treated. Instead of directly addressing the masses, I adopted a strange method to convey my message. Using a sharp metal instrument as a pen, I began carving out my thoughts on the ground that I covered, one step at a time. The writings got clearly engraved into the ground, leaving no scope for anyone to wipe them away.

I took a step at a time in His direction, all the while walking on my knees or bending in order to be able to inscribe my thoughts, feelings, opinions and expressions on a subject so dear to me. To my delight, I eventually managed to reach His lotus feet and the dream ended.

Now I felt it evident that Baba wished me to bring out a book on children, one with a sharp focus on how they should be handled. Hence, this is a special Volume dedicated to my guru and to our child beneficiaries at Sunbeam.

In this book, I've narrated my experiences and learnings, shared about my own evolution as a human being during my journey with our child beneficiaries at Sunbeam. While yet in the process of writing, I thought of Pearl, my niece, and wondered if I could add a chapter on my experiences with her, and also if I could add on a small chapter on my experiences as a teacher at a convent school. With the passage of time, my convictions on including these chapters in this book, though they are not directly linked to our Sunbeam beneficiaries, became stronger, because children are the same the world over. From my own decade long experience with children, I've come to realise that their fundamental needs in life are the same, whether they happen to be children from affluent families or are slum-dweller/ street children. As you'll read through the pages, you'll notice that their outward attitudes and behaviour in dealing with tough situations in life can vastly differ though.

Even though my guru had made this request of me almost 1½ years ago, it's only between April – June '06 that I got down to actually writing this book (and updated it in January '09). This is because of my extremely comprehensive role at Sunbeam, which doesn't leave me with enough quality time to pursue any other assignment. I deem it a great blessing conferred upon me by my guru – to be given this opportunity to write on a subject so sacred and I sincerely hope that I've been able to do justice to the work He has assigned to me.

Preface

Small Children : Big Dreams is essentially a book with a sharp focus on how children - of whatever background they might be - should be treated. It comprises case-stories about them, especially about those who belong to the lesser privileged sections of society, particularly the ones with whom Sunbeam works. Sunbeam is a registered Public Charitable

Trust, whose mission is to transform the lives of underprivileged Indian children through education.

This book carries articles on children, discussing various areas of interest:

- Their reasonable expectations from adults
- Their unique ways of expressing love
- The way they flower under the umbrella of unconditional love and acceptance
- Their right to be treated with dignity, and of having their individual identities acknowledged.

The non-fiction work is specifically targeted towards three categories of individuals:

- The parents - they form the first school of an infant. Their impression is an everlasting one on its mind.

- The teachers - who form a second home for students. Child and student counselors would also find the literature beneficial in navigating the depths of a child's mind.

This book also shares experiences and learnings of one's own evolvement when one journeys with children. It paints a picture of the life as it is seen through the eyes of a child who has been deprived of the sheer pleasures of childhood.

When making ends meet is the priority, education takes a back seat. It is tough to change mind sets of elders when one wishes to initialize a revolution, even if that might be on a small scale. The problem gets aggravated when girl-children are involved. Yet, a difference can be made in the presence of a strong will.

Lastly, the book reveals that academic excellence in isolation does not constitute progress; that growth and change don't end there. Almost every incident mentioned therein captures and embodies the basic universal principles and values that our children have grown up with. The spirit of Sunbeam holds out a promise - that of grooming each Qf them into committed, caring and responsible citizens in the years to come.

Acknowledgements

I gratefully acknowledge the love, support, guidance and faith so generously given me as I penned this book. On this occasion, I would like to express my deep appreciation to my Divine Parent and to each of my dear friends who have made 'Scriptures of the Sunbeam world' possible.

- I am indebted to my dear guru, for trusting my ability to write on the sacred topic of 'how to treat children'.
- Special thanks to mum, dad and Nargis Aunty, whose belief in my work made me continue writing despite my misgivings about my ability to do justice to this unique assignment.
- Particular gratitude is owed to Aban Bharucha, my dearest friend and Zaineb Lokhandwala, Communications Manager at Sunbeam, who, so lovingly opened their hearts to me and meticulously edited the book in the spirit of love of God.
- Deep appreciation is owed to Vivek Gour, my dear friend, who, with his wealth of insights enriched the book and helped me bring it to its present level.

- Thanks to Jasmine Vakharia (my sister) and to my dear friends, Pervin Varma, Janaki Venkat, Leena Koticha and Shanta Koli for their consistent encouragement.
- Very special gratitude to God for having sent me timely help in the form of Ganesh, one of our child beneficiaries, who assisted me in keying in a part of the data and with taking printouts of the book.

Introduction

I dedicate this book to our child beneficiaries at Sunbeam, who have nourished my soul and filled my life with opportunities to experience them as the angels that they are. They have taught me lessons in faith, courage and triumph and thus, have been my role models in life. Through their selfless acts of love, they remind me how necessary it is for me to keep the child within me alive at all times and to let that reflect in my actions. For this, I remain eternally indebted to them.

Sunbeam is a registered Public Charitable Trust, the mission of which is to transform the lives of underprivileged Indian children, giving them an opportunity to realise their potential. We do so by overseeing their holistic development and also by motivating and empowering the community to be responsible for the welfare of their children.

In everything that I do at Sunbeam, I hope to reflect the values I've learned from my children. They've been my best teachers in life. More importantly, they've helped me grow spiritually.

In majority of the cases of our child beneficiaries, I've watched their dreams come true – partly because of Sunbeam intervention, but largely as a result of their own ability to meet life's challenges with a smile and their persistent efforts towards achieving their modest goals.

I view our children as God's most precious gift to me. Hence, this book on children is an opportunity to put down on paper, all the feelings that have raced through my heart and mind; it is a safe place to vent my fears, joys, sorrows, anguish and the many more emotions that I've felt while handling Sunbeam.

This book carries articles on children - their expectations from adults, their unique ways of expressing love, the process of their flowering to full bloom under the umbrella of unconditional love and acceptance, as well as on their right to be treated with dignity and to be acknowledged for their individual identities. This book will, hopefully, also bring out the reality of how much meaningful, rich and fulfilling a life can the presence of a child make, for us adults.

I dream of a day when not a single one of our 1000+ child beneficiaries would be deprived of a normal childhood. I also dream of a world for them where they would experience adults as caring, nurturing individuals, whose company makes them feel secure. Moreover, I dream for adults to experience children as I've experienced them. Ultimately, I wish to see our Sunbeam intervention resulting in all of our beneficiaries growing up to be responsible, contributing members of society. As I remember, ponder over and record our children's case stories, I sense within myself a growing sense of gratitude for the wonderful opportunity to share the same with you.

1

A Small Beginning with Children

My Life Prior to Sunbeam

Friends, let me share with you in brief my childhood and also my life prior to Sunbeam.

I hail from a middle class Parsi family of 5. Dad, a selfless soul, has been my ideal all my life. Mum is a loving person who built upon my self-esteem during my childhood. Dad worked in the Bombay Dyeing Mills as a Training Officer and, after retirement, served the Banajee Charitable Trust for 13 long years as Secretary of the Trust. (This organisation catered to the education and medical funding needs of the underprivileged.) It's only last year that Peshotan, my brother, and I coaxed him into retiring as, at 73, his failing health might not have allowed him to carry on much longer, given the stress that went with the responsibility of running an entire organisation.

Peshotan was employed with Godrej, then with Larsen and Toubro and later with J.K. Cement, in marketing. As of now, he is running his own business and doing well in life. With his family, he is currently based in Jaipur. He has been a big moral and financial support to my parents and me. Jasmine, my dear sister, is with the State Bank of India Capital Markets Ltd. Yezdi, her husband, serves in ICICI Bank. Their adorable children, Pearl and Jehan, especially Pearl, are the apple of my eye.

I did my schooling and Junior College at the Byramjee Jeejeebhoy Parsi Charitable Institution and graduated from the Hinduja College in 1985. Often, during school days, at the back of my mind was a set of street urchins, dwelling on the footpath opposite the Byramjee School near Charni Road station, and I wondered at the unfair circumstances - while I studied, the kids begged for a living; while I had a roof over my head, they had to make do without one even during the monsoons. My parents provided me with emotional security besides all the other kinds of assurances that the presence of loving parents in a child's life brings whereas my counterparts on the streets were left to fend for themselves, despite their parents being around.

By opting for Commerce I believed I had chosen the wrong field. So, I gladly grabbed the opportunity to join a convent school that offered me the post of a primary class teacher for a year. Thereafter, for reasons that I can't recall or place my finger on, instead of doing a D.Ed. or a B.Ed. diploma, I chose to do a secretarial diploma from J.J. College. For the next two years I served in different organisations till 1989 when I got to know of a vacancy at CRY – Child Relief and You (now renamed Child Rights and You), an NGO (Non Government Organisation) working for the underprivileged children of India. I served CRY as the secretary to Rippan Kapur, Founder Trustee of CRY. I confess, I can't say that there was no turning back.

The first time I quit CRY was as early as 1990, to join IBP (Indo Burma Petroleum) that offered me better remuneration. But the job satisfaction was missing, and, within 8 months I was back at CRY. For the next few years I was privileged to continue to work under Rippan, to see the world through the eyes of an individual who had dedicated his life to serving the underprivileged children of India.

Then came the Divine calling in May 1993. Giving in to the call, I spent 10 months at the ashram of my guru. Let me share with you, dear readers, a few of His teachings to me, rather, His expectations of me. Serving God meant also to serve Him in mankind. He had made me aware that I had to balance my life of prayer and meditation with service to mankind. I would gladly accept whatever work He chose to assign to me. Hence, I resolved to continue to put to use all His teachings even after my return to Mumbai. I would be back in the world fulfilling – not shirking my duties towards humanity. I would offer all my acts to Him.

Once again I went by His will and rejoined CRY in June'94. By then, Rippan had passed away. For the next 7 years or so, I worked in the different divisions of CRY – Production, Administration, and, eventually, HRD in which I stayed for a few years until I quit CRY permanently in May 2001.

My Experiences as a Teacher at a Convent School (Academic Year 1985 – 1986)

June 19, 1985 was my first working day at the Convent School. As I entered the classroom, 60 pairs of twinkling, mischievous eyes followed me. I felt strange. They were indeed adorable little darlings – 7 year olds, a bunch of pure-hearted fresh buds. As a teacher, my desire was to treat them as friends in order to be able to understand them and to relate to them better, and so, I always attempted to make the lessons as interesting as possible.

Homework was often left undone, yet I could never dream of raising my hand on the little ones or punishing them in other ways such as giving remarks in the calendars. Initially, my leniency was misinterpreted as my weakness and the children boldly continued to come to school with incomplete homework. Not wanting them to take advantage of my nature, I found a new, successful plan to make them enthusiastic enough to give priority to their homework. One day I declared, "It is our good fortune that the library cupboard, full of fairy-tales, is kept in our class-room. Since you all are such studious children, I have decided to read you a story every day, during the last 15 minutes of the final period, depending on your home-work." They stared at me and then at each other, as if to make sure that they had heard correctly. Then, there were broad smiles and before I knew what was happening, one little girl from the last bench came running up to me, hugged me tight, motioned me to bend, and planted a kiss on my cheek! The others were all clapping away happily. The teacher next door rushed to inquire what the commotion was all about, spanked a few children and everyone became silent. Turning to me, she said sharply, "You better learn to control your class." These harsh words had an unimaginable effect on the young minds. They had taken an instant liking towards me and didn't appreciate anyone being rude to me. After the other teacher had left, they all sat with their heads bent low; then, in a chorus, said "Sorry, teacher" with a miserable look on their faces that brought tears to my eyes.

My plan worked. They did their homework, and I kept my word by telling them a story daily.

"Children, did you like today's story?" "Yes teacher." "What have we all learnt from this story?" "Teacher, we should help others." "Would you really like to help your friends?" "Yes teacher." "Come then, let's start at it by changing the seating arrangements." They were all dismayed to hear that. I had observed in the past few days that the intelligent ones sat huddled together in the front benches, whereas the kids who had fared poorly in their 1st unit test sat at the back. Not wanting an inferiority complex to set in, which could make them shy away and withdraw into their shells or, alternatively, make them very mischievous (which was their way of covering up their embarrassment), I decided to change their seats (in rotation during the year). They were made to sit in such a way that each average student or a poor performer had a brilliant one by her side. It took them time to accept the idea.

Children possess a heart of gold and it is up to us, teachers, to mould them into fine human beings and contributing members of the society at large. 'Each one - teach one' became the rule and friendships among the little darlings flourished as they extended a helping hand to each other.

Mahi (name changed), a fair, thin girl, with short curly locks, seemed forever withdrawn from the rest of the students. Her grasping power, it appeared, was below normal. But I wanted to go deeper into the matter before drawing any conclusions. From whatever little she spoke to me of her life at home, I gathered that she needed more of love and attention, given which, her academic performance was sure to improve.

One day, I found her classmate teasing her and calling her dull and lazy. Later, I called the naughty one aside and asked her, "Do you like Mahi?" "No teacher, she is so boring. She rarely joins us in our games. Besides, she is an extremely lazy student, or else why would she not complete her homework?" "Well, my child, who helps you with your homework?" "Mum," pat came the reply. "What do you do upon reaching home every evening?" "Mum gives me milk and things that I love to eat. Then she takes me to the park to play. On our return we study for an hour. Mummy loves me." Kids generally co-operate when you talk to them in their language – the language of love and complete honesty, so I explained to her in a tender voice, "Now let me reveal to you why Mahi appears to be lazy, or for that matter, why she is so quiet." "I don't care to know," she said, with a defiant lift of her shoulders. I made her sit on my lap and then on, she listened attentively till the end. "My child, Mahi is not lazy. She is sad and lonely. She is not dull; she does not have anyone to teach her at home. Yes, she too has a mother who loves her but one who has to go to work; and her work place being very far, she reaches home very late in the evening. Mahi has no choice but to spend her long evenings all by herself at her neighbour's house. There is no one to give her a glass of milk or take her to the park. Even when her mother returns home, she is too busy preparing dinner for the family to be able to spare any time to help her with her homework. So don't make fun of her. Be friends with her, help her with her studies. I am positive that if you give her a chance, you will know that she is good, enjoyable company." Two large tears rolled down the little one's cheeks. The next minute she ran out to where Mahi sat all alone, and hugged her. They became the best of friends. In the months to follow, I came to know what a deep impact my words had had on the child who had otherwise seemed so naughty. She had not only started giving Mahi the much-needed company during lunch, but also spared some time for teaching her Maths during the rest of the lunch break.

Shruti (name changed), a charming little ever-smiling angel, had won my heart. She was intelligent, loveable and one of my favourite students (not that I liked the rest any less or that I was partial towards a few). She was one of the top rankers. Unaware of the situation at her home-front, once, I reprimanded her for talking too much during classes, and told her that if she was again found disturbing other students, it would compel me to give her a remark in the calendar that she would have to get signed by her mother. I had not intended to terrify her.

A few minutes later she sought my permission to go to the toilet (it was the last period for the day) and it didn't occur to me that she had not returned. It is only after school hours, when I started with the tuition classes, that I found her missing and inquired on her whereabouts. One of the children chirped,

"Teacher, she has run away." "Can one of you do me a favour? Do you mind calling her? She stays in the next building." "But teacher she has not gone home. She has run away from school as well as home, leaving her school bag here," said another child in a singsong way! I gazed at that innocent face, aghast.

The incident is still etched in my memory. I remember meeting up with her mother and telling her in a barely audible voice that her daughter was missing from school, and as per her friend's report, she had run away from home as well. My hands were cold and stiff. What if something untoward were to happen to her on the way? Would she be found?

Incredulously, the mother was totally indifferent about the disappearance of her child. With a serene look on her face and a smile that had me scared all the more, she dismissed my concerns and queries by saying, "You don't have to worry about that child of mine. She must have run away to Vile Parle, to her granny's place. Not having money on her, I'm sure she must have travelled without a ticket. If I know her well, from there on, she will hire an auto to reach her destination and granny will pay the charge for the same." So saying, she took the child's bag and left! The next minute she returned only to tell me, "You must be wondering as to how I can be so sure on my child's whereabouts. Well, this is not the first occasion that she has run away. Hence, neither of us should worry for her." I found the mother's behaviour indeed strange and insensitive towards her child's well-being.

It was, I suppose, natural that I should feel guilty; after all, hadn't I scared the child with my threat of the calendar remark? Had I been aware of the kind of life she led at home, neglected and ill-treated by her mother, I'd never have uttered those words.

The next morning she was back in her seat. I had to use tact with her. She loved maths, and though it was not the

Maths period, I started the day with that subject. "So, who would like to come and solve this problem on the board?" I asked. Some hands were raised but Shruti's was not among them. "What about you, Shruti? I am sure you can solve this one." She looked at me uncertainly for a long time, then slowly got up from her seat, came and stood in front of me with outstretched hands and open palms, as though prepared for a thrashing. I feigned ignorance and, pretending as though she was asking for a chalk, handed over one to her. It was then that she said in a feeble voice, "Won't you beat me, teacher? Won't you punish me for running away yesterday?" "No, no." I exclaimed, and my eyes filled with tears. The next moment her tiny arms went around my waist. "Teacher, O teacher, then, it's I who misunderstood you. But now I know you still love me. I know that even if no one else cares for me, at least you do." Suddenly she turned around and pulled up her uniform blouse slightly to reveal the marks on her back that were indicative of how mercilessly she had been beaten up. Those were visible marks; the invisible, emotional scars she disclosed to me in her own innocent way – by holding my hand and placing it on her chest. "Teacher, can you hear the heartbeat? I can hear my heart beating so fast. It happens every time I am frightened."

After listening to her words, I could well imagine the things still unsaid, and I immediately went on my knees, and held her tight. She cried for a long time and, amidst sobs, told me her sad tale - "Teacher, yesterday when you assumed I was disturbing others in the class, not allowing them to concentrate on studies, actually I was relating to them my story. The evening before yesterday, my parents had a quarrel and I was a witness to the abuse dad heaped upon mum, who took it all in silence. After dad left, I embraced her and asked her not to cry, in response to which, I was caned. She didn't even help me with my Marathi homework. Next morning, still angry with me, she expected me to pack my bag myself. In the hurry, I left my calendar at home. When the Marathi teacher found my homework incomplete, she asked for the calendar, and, for not being able to provide it, I was taken to the Principal and made to kneel down in front of her cabin for the next 3 periods. Didn't you miss me, teacher? My knees hurt a lot. Since the Maths period was about to commence, I sneaked away and into the class, and was telling my friends about it when you asked for the calendar. This was the first time you scolded me. During the past months, I had received only love from you. So, your threat broke my heart. O teacher, I had always believed that you are the only other person, besides granny, who loves me!"

I spent the next 15 minutes reassuring her that, indeed, I loved her and, that her mother too cared for her and loved her equally, but caught up in her own sorrows, she was perhaps unable to express it. Beyond that, I didn't have the courage to do anything to rectify the situation in her life. Matters might have gone out of hand had I taken the step to speak to Shruti's mother, who would not have liked external interference in her personal matters.

This incident acted as an eye-opener for me. It helped me understand that though Shruti hailed from a well-to-do family, she was a mere child; very, very fragile, vulnerable, insecure in her own home, seeking that love and security in her teacher. This episode made me extra cautious in my speech with the children, to be careful not to break the trust that they had placed in me with any harsh steps, and to correct them firmly, yet lovingly, if they erred.

Friends, another extremely touching incident occurred during my tenure as a primary school teacher: To my confusion, in the unit test, one of the top rankers in the class had fared miserably in her favourite subject, though she had scored the highest marks in the other papers. Soon after the results were declared, during my class, her mother barged in, pulled out the child from her bench, dragged her all the way up to my table and threw her at my feet! This kind of insensitive and unacceptable behaviour rendered all of us shocked and speechless. I broke the silence by gently helping the weeping child to her feet and reprimanded the parent, "I object to your disturbing the class in this manner." "You are responsible for my child's failure in this particular unit test," she retorted in a shrill voice.

She probably gauged my confusion at her peculiar manner, yet she offered no explanation. This forced me to demand for one. In turn, she yelled at the child to speak up. The little girl astounded me by looking me straight in the eye and saying, "Teacher, I didn't attempt to solve any questions in that particular subject though I knew all the answers, because I love you very much." Staring at her askance, I asked her to clarify her incomprehensive reply. She complied. "If I failed, I'd have to repeat the class which would mean an opportunity to spend another year with you! But if I were to be promoted to the 4th standard, Ms. Nanda (name changed) would be my class teacher. So often I have seen her bash her students."

The angel, in all her innocence, had put forward her argument – one, that to her mind, was good enough to risk repeating another year in the same class. I had no answer forthcoming. At least at that point in time, she was too scared of the other class teacher to listen to my good counsel, so, I decided to deal with her differently. I whispered soothingly, "My child, the final exams are approaching and I am disclosing a secret to you so that you may pass with good marks. Next year, I am to be appointed as the 4th standard class teacher." She looked astonished. The message got through and she smiled; a smile that illuminated her tear-stained face. Later, I felt guilty and realised that I had to be honest with her or else she would never be able to trust anyone again. After her final exams, I spared the time to talk to her at length, "My child, as much as you love me, I too love you. Forgive me because I lied to you.

As a teacher I don't want to set a wrong example. You are a disciplined and a brilliant student, and no teacher will ever beat you. Besides, I'm going to be around, and you can always come and meet me in my class whenever you feel like it." After almost a minute, she asked me to bend low, and planted a kiss on my cheek. This was her way of conveying to me that I had been granted pardon!

Before I come to the end of my chapter at the Convent School let me relate to you the way in which my sixty little students, on the occasion of Teachers' Day, demonstrated their love for me :-

A day prior to 'Teachers' Day', my students requested that I forego my tuition class after school. Unaware of the sweet little plot brewing in their minds, I granted them respite from the same. As I reached the main gate of the school, I remembered that my drawer had been left unlocked. So, I retraced my steps to the classroom, where, heart pounding, I feared that the kids were up to something. The scene that met my eyes, made it clear that they were decorating the class with festoons for the next day. Being so tiny, their hands wouldn't reach high. Hence, they had placed one bench over the other and were busy sticking the colourful balloons on the walls and the crepe paper ribbons from one end of the room to the other-with cello tape. My presence would have disappointed them because they wanted to surprise me on Teachers' Day, so, I quietly left the room without any of them noticing that I had been around.

The next day they showered me with precious little gifts such as a lunch box, sweets, and the like, which I couldn't refuse for fear of hurting their sentiments. There were a number of bouquets of all sizes that covered my entire table. None of the other rooms in the school were decorated with festoons as mine was. One of the teachers who passed by my class addressed the children with a tinge of sarcasm in her voice, "Is there a birthday party going on? Ah! What is that on your teacher's table? Is it her birthday today?" "It's Teachers' Day," they replied in chorus.

I thanked them all profusely and gently explained to them that the monitor of the class or any other child could present a rose or a bouquet to each of the other teachers in the school, from amongst those many bouquets and roses. Initially, they didn't approve of the idea, and one of them wailed, "O teacher, but these are meant for you alone because we all love you." "Dearies", I said, "if you love me then all the more reason that you should do that which brings me happiness. Show every class teacher the respect due to her. Go and give a rose to each of them as a token of love and respect on behalf of our class, and to the Principal hand over this large, beautiful bouquet." They finally did obey me.

2

On Sunbeam's Evolution 1997 - 2009

Sunbeam - as it Evolved in CRY (end 1996 – 1998)

One fine day, towards the end of 1996, Satnam, from the administration division of CRY, announced, "I think all of us here have been doing our bit for the children from the adjacent construction site. I've seen some of you hand over a biscuit packet to a child, and others giving them crayons and drawing books. Why don't we get together and brainstorm on what we can do to give our work a structure and a name?"

Thus started 'CRY Neighbourhood Project', a small initiative, of which I too became a part. (That's what Sunbeam was known as in those days.) I confess that my involvement was limited to Rs. 50/- per month like most of the employees at CRY. "It is Satnam's baby, so why do I have to go out of my way to do anything more than necessary?" is what I reasoned with myself.

One morning, in 1997, Laxmi (7) walked up to me, demanding as to why their midday meals and playgroup classes had come to a halt. Shame engulfed me as I thought of how very limited my involvement had been. I had not realised that, since the past month, with Satnam in hospital after having a near fatal accident, there was no one to take care of the project kids, or seek financial support from us for their midday meals or their part-time teacher's remuneration. "Well, after all it means giving just about 10 to 15 minutes of my time on a daily basis after office hours and once a month going around collecting funds from CRY colleagues. So why don't I take it on? Perhaps, it is God's will that I be more involved with these children," I thought, reassuring myself that I wasn't taking on more than I could handle.

And that was the beginning of what became my life in the decade to follow – my life with children.

Words can never do justice to the support that I received from CRY as an organisation and from all of my CRY colleagues, right up to the management committee level. Yet, I attempt to acknowledge CRY - it's my way of cementing the memories of those lovely, fun-filled days, though full of struggles even then:-

Parvati (7) would walk into our office with her 6 month old sibling, Kavita, cradled in her arms. Kavita, being the youngest of the 12 to 15 kids in the project, was the favourite. Her toothless smile had won the hearts of all of us at CRY.

- If Leela (from Communications) gave Kavita a scrub in our washbasin, and Sangeeta (from the same division) allowed Parvati and others to have their midday meals at her table and patiently cleaned up the mess, there were many others who too were equally involved.
- Raman (our Production Head) would, day after day, carry along nourishing homemade meals prepared by his wife.
- Sumrati Chachi, who served tea to CRY employees, took up the assignment of boiling milk and distributing it to our children.

It was as though the CRY Communications department had turned into a creche!

- One incident that remains imprinted in my heart is of the day when, during the HYM (half yearly meeting) at CRY, Parvati placed Kavita on Pervin's lap. (Pervin was then a member of the Managing Committee of CRY and later became the CEO of the organisation). After a little while of cooing and smiling at Pervin as though she understood all of what Pervin was saying (not to her but to us gathered at the meeting!), Kavita fell fast asleep. Pervin sat in the same position for 3 hours so as not to disturb the little one!

- When Padma (12) was diagnosed with malaria, it was Parul (from Resource Generation) and her family who sponsored her hospital expenses, and Aban (from Resource Generation), Sonali (from Youth Wing), and other CRY staff members took turns to stay with her.

- When Ramu's foot had to be operated upon, and post surgery, he had to be taken to the hospital every alternate day for dressing; Sashikant (our office assistant) carried him, in his arms, from the construction site and took him to the hospital in a cab.

- Maria (Communications Exec.) enrolled the kids into a municipal school near the CRY office.

- Vanita (CRY Administration Head) sponsored the salary of our part-time teacher, who spent two hours a day with our children.

Not knowing what I was in for, I had taken the responsibility of being in charge of the project. One day, I thought of checking it out with the children whether they enjoyed their daily sessions with their teacher. "Didi, we all love her dearly," said one. "Ask us why?" quipped in another. Before I could frame my question, a third replied, "Because she doesn't come more than once a week and none of us have to put up with mastering the boring alphabet!" That's when I made a promise to myself and kept it - "If my colleagues at CRY are giving me their contributions in full faith, it's my duty to see to it that their funds are properly utilized, also, that the classes are made more interesting." That involved more work, regular monitoring, guidance and direction to our part-time teacher.

Funding for the neighbourhood project had begun with our Mumbai branch employees but soon extended to the CRY branches all over India. I just had to ask for funds and they shelled out whatever they could from their salaries:-

- Puja (HRD Manager) was a dear friend of all our kids, and her relocation to Delhi in 1998 in no way made the children feel distanced from her, because most of them, especially Nirmala, wrote lovely letters to her and Puja in turn, remained in touch with them. Her notes to me, actually meant for HRD work, inadvertently ended with statements like, "Do send me a list of things we need for the project, we'll try to source them here, in Delhi."

- Bondi (heading CRY Delhi branch) made her way into the children's hearts by being their Santa Claus, whose arrival they eagerly awaited. She personally selected and brought along clothing for all of them from our CRY Materials Bank at Delhi, each time that she visited Mumbai for the Managing Committee meeting.

- Sandeep (heading Finance Dept. of Mumbai branch), a dear friend of mine, patiently taught me the basic accounting principles and helped me maintain updated and accurate accounts. That kind of transparency brought credibility to our little project.

- After the registration of our project, for years at end, Sharad (Accounts Assistant at CRY), helped with internal audit of our accounts.

- There was yet another special friend of our children, Ingrid, whose faith in our work took many forms. She never hesitated to recommend Sunbeam to anyone interested in directly supporting a small grass-root level project. At a personal level too, her family has been supporting Sunbeam financially till date.

Whenever I needed CRY's assistance at different levels, I sought the prior permission of the Managing Committee, be it for anything - using the CRY kitchen and gas stove for our children's midday meals program, the CRY van for taking the children on excursions, or the xerox machine or computer for our quarterly newsletters. The management was always obliging and supportive.

The CRY Neighbourhood Project was funded by the CRY staff members and never by CRY as an organisation. Also, I ensured from the first, not to approach a single CRY donor. However, Ashish Sheth, a CRY donor, upon getting to know of our Neighbourhood Project, offered to help. We accepted his support for our project in cash and kind after due permission from the management of CRY. Moreover, it wasn't at the cost of his support to CRY.

Friends, you may wonder where the children's study classes were being conducted. As Rajashree, our first full-time teacher will vouch for: Initially, the kids would sit on the steps of the CRY office, two on each step, in neat rows, - with the teacher at the bottom of the stairs. At times, they were even taught on the CRY office terrace! Later on, we took permission from the builder to allow the classes to be conducted in the building under construction, opposite CRY office. When the construction work came to an end, I wondered where I'd shift the children. Just then, in the true spirit of CRY, Raman (Production Manager) offered a part of their room for the children's study classes - a room that had been taken on rent by CRY for their cards production jobs. Soon it was time for CRY to hand over the possession of that room too to the owners, as the lease agreement had come to an end. Once again, my CRY colleagues saw to it that our kids were given another shelter – this time a permanent one, for their study classes to continue. Thanks to Alpana Tandon (Manager - Resource Generation) who offered to sponsor a major part of the deposit and rent for the premises. The rest too pitched in. That became Sunbeam's first full-time education center.

Beginning from 1999, one education center at Arthur Road and 15 children, we've now (i.e. in 2009) grown to 2 education centers in rented rooms in BMC schools / private premises, and our outreach is 1000+ child beneficiaries. (Of course, the interim period wasn't easy. We conducted our classes from wherever we managed to get suitable space - the construction sites, the temple grounds or from within the slums.)

Sunbeam required my presence beyond 6 p.m. to 8.30 p.m., the time that I spent with the children and their families. This I realised after my visit to the Phoenix Mills Education Center one afternoon: The teacher wasn't aware of my presence in the class. During the Maths class, a 9 year old boy requested for relief from homework, as his evenings were meant for earning dinner for his entire family. Otherwise he would have to discontinue with Sunbeam and the formal schooling.

The teacher behaved as though she hadn't heard his plea, and carried on with her Maths lesson. Within minutes, another child, a girl of 11, stood up to share a problem that needed immediate attention, "Didi, my dad had taken a heavy loan from someone. In order to repay it, I am employed at a nearby hotel where I daily go to wash the dishes in the evenings, after study classes. Today, however, I'm scared to go there. I've been ordered to stay the night at the hotel with the owner. Can you help me?" The teacher had nothing to offer, neither a solution nor a word of assurance of investigating the matter. (Later, upon being questioned by me, she shared that she was too shaken to react in any way.)

That's when I made up my mind - Sunbeam's focus area might be formal education, but what about the children's emotional and psychological well-being? What about their security? What about community development and changing the mindsets of the adults in the family? I couldn't possibly carry on with my job at CRY and stay satisfied with collecting and disbursing funds for the Neighbourhood Project and join the children only on weekends. I could no longer leave it to the teachers to handle the project, especially so since they saw their role limited to academics alone. Hence, from the next day itself, I decided to work only part-time at CRY, and the management agreed to let me do so. Eventually, I quit CRY in May '01 to be full-time with Sunbeam.

In the interim period i.e. for the time that I worked part-time with CRY, however, if I had managed to meet my targets of the Key Focus Areas set for me, both at CRY and at Sunbeam, then, it's Maxy who made it possible for me. Maxy Anthony was my colleague in the HRD department of CRY. He saw to it that I could switch to working part-time without feeling guilty at not being able to complete my assignments. Very willingly he shouldered part of my duties by staying back late evenings in order to complete the work. Furthermore, since, at that point in time, I didn't have a single office level staff at Sunbeam, he shared my load at Sunbeam as well. While I worked at the field level, he took on the responsibility of answering donors' emails, responding to their queries, and also corresponding with the few volunteers who used to support our project then. "Khurshid, I don't want you to lose out on any of your donors or volunteers. Busy as you are at the field level, if you do not respond to them in time, they might get the impression that their support is either not required or not valued. But you can always count on me for any assistance in that area. That's my way of contributing to Sunbeam," he answered whenever I thanked him.

Had I not received unstinted support from the CRY management and colleagues, I would not have had the courage to embark on the extremely challenging (though equally fulfilling) journey with our children. A child once remarked, "My parents are construction labourers and they help in making buildings that enable others to live in comfort. But we never get an entry into them, let alone an opportunity to live there. This office is the one place that has opened its doors to us where each one is welcome and made to feel special." Dear readers, this is the spirit with which Sunbeam continues to befriend children till date, always gifting them the much-needed sense of belonging, unconditional love and acceptance, an identity and a hope for a better future.

Sunbeam has been an experience that has enriched my life; given me a greater understanding of myself and a surer sense of purpose. Via Sunbeam, my fate has taken me on a different journey - a route where God continues to manifest Himself in the form of the children we reach out to. My journey with children from 1997 till January 2009 is what I've shared with you in this book. In my attempts at nurturing our fledgling organisation, I've been at the receiving end of Divine Grace at every step.

Mission & Objectives

Mission

To transform the lives of underprivileged Indian children, giving them an opportunity to realise their potential.

Objectives

- To oversee the holistic development of underprivileged children – their physical, psychological and educational needs.
- To motivate and empower the community to be responsible for the overall development of their children.
- To make Sunbeam intervention a programme of transformation rather than service delivery – with clarity

on withdrawal strategy, so that the community can become independent and self-reliant.

Sunbeam Activities

Education

More than just the ability to read and write, education gives children self-confidence and a better future. With space generously donated by the Education Officer in BMC schools and private rooms taken on at a nominal rent, we conduct our formal education classes for children between 5 to 15 years. Beyond that, up to graduation, we sponsor 50 % of their college and private coaching class fees. The 2 major areas that we cover are Worli (where we have 600 + children) and Bandra (East) (where we reach out to 400+ children). We began with 25 – 30 migrant labourers' children in around 1997. Later on, we shifted our focus to children living in the slums and chawls. They comprise of domestic workers' children or their parents are employed as temporary mill workers, drivers, security guards or fruit and vegetable vendors.

Bridge courses are conducted for children who are of age group 5 to 10 but those who've never had an opportunity to attend formal schools or, ones who have attended schools, yet are not up to the desired levels in academics. Appropriate training is imparted to enable them to join the mainstream by ensuring direct admissions to classes based on their age and aptitude.

Today, we are proud to share that over 90 % of our children are attending the formal schools where they have managed to reach the academic levels of the respective classes that they are studying in. Our syllabus is identical to the one followed in these schools. Besides, we also ensure that they come to Sunbeam for the extra coaching before or after their formal school timings. If they attend the school in the mornings, then they come to Sunbeam in the afternoons, and vice versa. This, we believe, will reinforce and consolidate what they have already learnt in the formal schools. Apart from this, we want our children to imbibe the right ideals and principles and hence conduct regular sessions on value education.

Healthcare and Nutrition

This covers the aspects of nutrition, health awareness and counseling the parents on the same. When we started in 1997, healthcare was never a priority with the parents. Now they are empowered enough to take the responsibility of their children's health. These communities avail of the medical facilities available at the government clinics / hospitals. Majority of them also provide nutritive meals to their children. Hence, our midday meals program sponsored by Ratna Nidhi Charitable Trust is limited only to 175 children at our Bandra education center.

Recreation

Earlier on in the project we realised the importance of this aspect. Homework would be completed doubly fast, with the brighter ones coaching, coaxing and even scolding those who had trouble in catching up. So, we regularly take the children on excursions to places of interest or parks and for overnight camps. Besides being a channel for entertainment, we believe that recreation can also be instructive. So we arrange to take our children on exposure visits as well. We've also been fortunate to have services of individual donors who sponsor our overnight outstation camps.

Community Development

Over a period of time, we have realised that Sunbeam would have achieved little without the support of the parents. In order to understand the children, their motivation and their behaviour, it is important for us to build a rapport with the parents. Contrary to the popular belief, they are very concerned about their children's welfare and would like to give them the best opportunities. They want to be a part of this positive change that is taking place in their children's lives. Therefore, we have introduced community meetings once a month to give them an opportunity to share their thoughts with us. Here it must also be mentioned that they willingly contribute part of the expenditure incurred on each child. There has been a steady decline of dependency levels on Sunbeam.

Counselling

At Sunbeam, school work and academic progress do not alone constitute the term 'Education'. A report card that is replete with 'A's is not our only yardstick to measure success. We also pay equal attention to the finer nuances that help mould character and personality. Our aim is to provide a holistic system of education that would eventually enable the kids to face the world with confidence and a growing sense of self-esteem. Hence, value education and counselling form crucial components of our curriculum. Children are encouraged to share their hopes, aspirations, doubts, fears, misgivings; anything that will dispel uncertainties and bring about clarity in their thoughts, words and actions.

From December'05, full-time child counsellors were appointed at each of our education centers. These individuals have been with Sunbeam for over 2 years and are not only completely in tune with Sunbeam values, principles and expectations but also the psychological and emotional needs of our child beneficiaries. Hence, they are best suited for this fundamental yet critical assignment. Children learn best by example and they are bound to benefit by having the right exposure and meaningful, timely guidance. Based on the feedback obtained from the beneficiaries across the organisation, we conduct individual counselling sessions on a case to case basis or alternatively class-wise fortnightly counselling sessions with them.

Sunbeam's Growth 1997 to 2009 (and its short-term Future Plans)

The purpose of this chapter is to give you a glimpse into the past years of Sunbeam regarding its growth, the progress of our beneficiaries and the Human Resource with their roles changing to meet the equally fast changing goals of the organization year after year. It also speaks of the selfless service without which it would have been next to impossible to meet the objectives of the organization or to fulfill its mission.

It goes without saying that the children have covered a long way and yet I believe that this is just the beginning. I would like to see them take wings and soar high beyond school to careers of their choice and moreover to see them as independent contributing members of the society.

Let me share with you about Sunbeam as it evolved from 1997 with 50 beneficiaries to 2009 and 1000 + child beneficiaries: 1997 - 2000

Our beneficiaries then:-

In 1997, we started off with 10 to 15 kids who had no direction in life and would spend their days playing in the heaps of sand and cement at the construction sites where their parents worked. They were listless and with an extremely unkempt appearance.

- An 8 year old Parvati was a surrogate mother to her 6 month old sibling.
- A 10 year old boy, Venkat, at the compulsion of the parents, washed dishes at the roadside tea stall to supplement the family income.
- 5 years old Jagdevi, was being taught all the household chores by her mother who insisted that she was training her up to face the harsh realities of life after marriage that would most probably come about as early as at the age of 12 to 13 years. She may as well have started learning everything that she would need to know after she went to live with her husband.
- 12 years old Tuljamma who took care of her 3 siblings and did all the household chores while her mother worked 2 shifts a day at the construction site.

- 12 years old Ajay burst into tears when he was offered a second helping at the midday meals provided by Sunbeam. He worked at a restaurant close by and was the one who served the customers. He would also have to bear with the beating he got from the owner if any loss or breakage occurred because of him. Being served instead of being the one to serve overwhelmed him so much that he shared all about himself through his uncontrollable tears.
- 9 years old Priti was once found missing and we had to rush to remand homes in a frantic search hoping to find her in one of those lonely places.

Our Human Resource and their Role then :

Mother, friend, mentor, role model, leader, ... to be a field staff at Sunbeam one had to be all of this and more. And yet we've been blessed with individuals who think nothing of slipping in and out of each role with ease. To quite a few of them, Sunbeam isn't a job. It's a passion.

Sharing about our staff and what all they handle can range from non-formal and formal education, to healthcare, to nutrition. It stretches on to roaming from one remand home to another in search of our dear missing children. It also includes visits to the court-room of a remand home fighting the case of one of our kids held there because of misconduct ranging from travelling without a ticket to begging on the streets. Beyond all this, the role moves on to a hospital visit till a child's emergency operation is over and the parents can now manage on their own. More importantly, it includes giving our children adequate amount of time to inculcate in them a set of values that become a way of life. Another equally important role that these dedicated team of staff play is that of being active participants in community meetings in order to bring about a change in the thinking pattern and attitude towards their own children. The role continues to stretch itself and our staff are also found eagerly joining in the games of a screaming, shrieking bunch of kids at the sports grounds. Even accompanying an enthusiastic group of kids to an overnight outstation camp that includes activities such as trekking, rappling, etc. And the list goes on .....

The above job description of our staff would have given you a fair idea of the most challenging role that a staff of Sunbeam was expected to play till 2000. It's only w.e.f. 2001 that we could afford to have a whole set of professionals to handle their respective roles – that of teachers, community workers or child counsellors.

Our Goal then :

We were mainly focused at giving these children a direction in life. The parents being too busy with making two ends meet, Sunbeam didis filled that void by being the emotional anchor for the children. They concentrated mainly on non formal education, limited to ensuring that the children could read and write and also gave them a lot of incentives. This was done in order to win their trust that Sunbeam is one place where they could experience a sense of belonging. The children were provided with midday meals to make up for the lack of nutrition. Activities like drawing, craft and sports were carried out regularly to increase their attendance and gradually their interest level in education.

2001 - 2003

Our beneficiaries then :

By this period, both, the parents and the beneficiaries had understood the importance of formal education and, cooperated well with the Sunbeam didis. The mothers carried out the household chores before and after their duty hours. This enabled the children to have more time at hand to attend Sunbeam classes and then the formal schools. After regular counseling sessions with the fathers, they began to reduce their intake of alcohol. They became more sensitive towards the needs of their wives and children, especially the girl child. They also started contributing towards the income of the family so that the burden of generating income to keep the household running did not rest on the wives alone. The parents now started providing the children with the much required nutrition. Not only that, the concern for the children's academic progress and overall development and also involvement in the same increased on part of the parents.

Academics :

The children comprised of 3 to 4 academic categories. On one hand there were children in the age group 5 to 10, who had never been to a formal school and, also those who were a part of the formal schools but in no way were anywhere close to the levels of the classes that they were in (who we call as the bridge course children). On the other hand, there were an equal number of children who were up to the mark in academics, be it in the primary or the secondary section of the school that they studied in.

Our Human Resource and their Role Then :

The small family of social workers cum non-formal education teachers was always on the move – on the pavements, in the slums and chawls of Mumbai, creating awareness amongst the community members on education and other child welfare related issues. While some teachers were busy going by the formal school syllabus with the general batches of students, others worked hard at bringing the bridge course children up to desired levels in academics.

2003 - 2006

Our beneficiaries then :

Attendance at Sunbeam classes had increased both in number and regularity. The children were now completely focused on formal education and the percentage of children who attended the bridge course classes have gone down from 60 % to 20 % over the years. Children were now promoted based on merit and because they earned the promotion and not because of the rules that the BMC adhere to. Out of the first batch of 70 + students who had joined Sunbeam in as early as 1999, just about 20 + odd children had managed to reach up to higher secondary school. But we could manage to convince the parents of the 800 + children who had been taken into the fold of Sunbeam in the later years to allow their children to not only complete school education but to continue letting their children study in college as well.

Our Human Resource and their Role then :

Though the core social workers still existed under the umbrella of the community development and child counseling team, Sunbeam's need of recruitment had entirely taken a new turn. We now had professional teachers i.e. D.Eds for the primary and secondary and B.Eds for the higher secondary section Sunbeam education classes. Besides, Sunbeam also took on a team of equally dedicated individuals to head the functions of Education, Resource Generation, Finance, Administration and Community Development. However, the staff turnover at the levels of teachers as well as managers has been quite high given that some individuals cannot devote more than a year or two of their time and others find it difficult to fit into an NGO culture.

2007 - 2009

Our Beneficiaries and their Academic Status :

We are proud to share with you our modest achievements. Cent percent of our 1000 + beneficiaries are into formal schools. They are progressing well and they have decided not to let anything make them drop out of school or Sunbeam classes. The members of the community which Sunbeam reaches out to, are empowered and motivated enough to not only attend the parent – teacher meetings, but to contribute up to 50 % towards the fees of the private coaching classes where Sunbeam enrolls the children to prepare them for their board exams.

Beyond this, what we are focusing our attention on now is the importance of our children learning the English language. It took some convincing on the part of the teachers and Education Managers for the children to settle with the idea of learning how to speak English. This was a Herculean task for the children to achieve. They found learning English very boring – but now when some of their classmates, who are more enthusiastic about learning the language, are able to say a few lines in English, the remaining too are following suit.

It is already too late for those children who have passed out of school and are currently in Junior / Degree College and trying to cope up with the change in medium of instruction from Hindi / Marathi to English. So that the same problem does not occur with our remaining 1000 + beneficiaries, we have appointed 9 full time English teachers. This will ensure that the child is exposed to English from as early as the 3rd std at Sunbeam classes.

Our Human Resource and their Role :

From the secondary to the higher secondary divisions, the teachers don't have to now face the frustration of teaching bridge course students as far as the vernacular medium studies are concerned. The children are scoring well – be it in Maths, Science, Social Studies or their own languages. Now a new phase has begun at Sunbeam where the English teachers have to deal with every single child who is at the bridge course level for English. We are positive that within a span of a few years we will be able to achieve 0 % children being in the bridge course even as far as English is concerned.

2010 - 2013

For the next 2 – 3 years, we will not be taking on any new batches of students. Consolidation of our programs (and not expansion) will be our focus.

As and when we start taking on new batches of students, we plan to begin with the primary section English Medium BMC school children as against the Hindi and Marathi medium that we have done till date.

For our current 1000+ beneficiaries, we will ensure that they complete their schooling.

After Junior College, we believe, while the majority of them will complete their graduation, the rest of the children will attend specialized degree courses of their choice and those based on their aptitude.

For those children whose circumstances at home do not permit them to go to college because they are required to supplement their parents' income, we'll make arrangements to enroll them into Vocational Training courses.

In the years to come, our aim will be that all of our girls who are currently in school remain a part of the mainstream, even complete their college education and if possible, take up careers of their choice to ensure that they stand independently on their feet and do not succumb to the derogatory norms of society.

Above all, Sunbeam hopes to create and bring forth individuals, who are not only academically intelligent but also those who will grow up to be selfless, responsible and contributing members, serving society in the true spirit of altruism.

CONSOLIDATED ACADEMIC PROGRESS REPORT

I. General Batches of Students:

Education Center	*Level*		*Of*	*Performance*		
		(No.	*Of*	*Children)*		
	Poor Upto 35%	*Average 36% - 60 %*	*Good 61% - 74 %*	*Excellent 75 % & Above*	*Absent*	*Total*
Worli	112	317	117	27	35	608
Bandra	118	182	23	20	10	353
Total	**230**	**499**	**140**	**47**	**45**	**961**
Percentage	**24 %**	**52 %**	**14 %**	**5 %**	**5 %**	**100 %**

II. Bridge Course Batches of Students:

Education Center	*Level*	*(No.*	*Of*	*Of*	*Performance*	*Children)*
	Poor Upto 35%	*Average 36% - 60 %*	*Good 61% - 74 %*	*Excellent 75 % & Above*	*Absent*	*Total*
Worli	0	0	0	0	0	0
Bandra	30	26	14	9	14	93
Total	**30**	**26**	**14**	**9**	**14**	**93**
Percentage	**32 %**	**28 %**	**15 %**	**10 %**	**15 %**	**100 %**

3

Glimpses into the Lives of Our Little Sunbeams

Introduction

Friends,

Each day at Sunbeam brings us new learnings from the unique world that our beneficiaries inhabit. Not all the learnings are simple and straightforward - some are tough, others heartbreaking and, still others, frustrating. But all of them open us to new insights and encourage us to new approaches.

It's these lessons that have helped me chart the course of Sunbeam; helped us grow our outreach and touch the lives of hundreds of children in Mumbai. These lessons that have also helped me improve my life and have made me a better person.

Allow me, then, to share with you my experiences with children over the past many years. I hope it helps you perceive the amazing grit and grace, the spirited humour and the touching innocence of our children.

An academic progress report chart of our beneficiaries across the organisation is prepared on a half-yearly basis and circulated to the entire Sunbeam family – trustees, donors, volunteers, well-wishers and community members. This is how we measure our success against the goals that we set for ourselves. Yet, to my mind, it does not seem to give a complete picture of Sunbeam's interaction at deeper levels with its beneficiaries, nor does it provide the readers with an understanding of our children's lives. Hence, from time to time I've included a couple of case stories in our regular updates to the donors. We cannot simply focus on numbers and neglect many of the key factors that can't be measured – factors such as the deep impact our intervention has had on the hearts and minds of our students, and the intangible forms in which it has transformed their lives.

No doubt, it is tempting to ensure that every child beneficiary joins the mainstream; I look forward to children completing their schooling and moving beyond - making a career for themselves. Certainly, these are wonderful and obvious things to anticipate, given that our main activity is education. Yet, if I were to focus too much on formal education alone, chances are I'd end up feeling disappointed because I'd be missing out on the incredibly special ways in which Sunbeam can, and has, touched their lives. A small number of these children may have dropped out of school, but even they would always carry with them sweet memories of their experiences during the short span of time that they spent with Sunbeam; happy memories of unconditional love and support, total acceptance for what they were, trust from adults and a sense of belonging.

Upon really examining the intangible but lasting impact on their lives, I realise that Sunbeam has indeed achieved its goal to a great extent. It's time for me to share with the larger family (via this book) the subtle change coming about in the life of each Sunbeam beneficiary.

The children's love has been sublime, inviting me into a world of innocence so rarely visited by adults. They have helped me discover the goodness existing in this world despite the chaos all around us. They never fail to inspire me and to uplift my spirit. Let me take you through case stories of children through the following pages, hoping to capture the magical moments in words.

Those which follow are the stories of some of the children who could not be a part of Sunbeam for long, and also of few of those who managed to teach me some of the most important lessons in life.

Warm regards,

Khurshid

Tulja's Way of Reciprocating Love

In the company of children, moments of experiencing unexpected gifts come to me quite often – moments when I feel deeply moved, moments when time seems to stand still, so that I may cherish His mysterious ways of communicating through children.

It was only a fortnight ago (in 1998) that my chubby little Tulja, (6), had joined Sunbeam. Smiling invitingly and bubbling with delight, he had introduced himself to me (via a translator, since he could speak just Telugu, his mother tongue, a language alien to me). Today, the same child stood before me to bid me farewell.

I can vividly recall that extremely touching parting that had taken place almost 5 years ago. Tulja, with his little fingers rummaging through his shirt pocket, whispered something urgently to Sujata, who explained, "Didi, Tulja had come to Mumbai to spend a few weeks with his parents, who are labourers at our construction site. He had visited our classes quite often. Each time he was offered to join our midday meal program. But all that he accepted was a glass of milk. Today, he is leaving for his village, where he stays with his granny. He claims that on a few of his visits to you at the CRY office, he has seen you order a cup of tea from the LIC canteen next door. As a parting gift, he wants to offer you a cup of tea from the three rupees that he has saved for you."

Tulja was eagerly looking at my face. As the shining coins slid into my palm from his outstretched hand, all anguish at him having to leave Sunbeam vanished. No longer did I believe that in the short span of period that he had been with us, we had failed to touch his life in any meaningful way. He was taking back with him happy memories, and not without returning our love, manifold!

Sunbeam has given me limitless opportunities to give and receive. Often we learn most from whom we teach, to which I am no exception.

Chandu Finds a True Friend in Sunbeam

While dealing with a child's issues, especially his desperate need for acceptance, we have to keep in mind the adverse environment faced by him at home and in a society that's completely indifferent to his existence on the streets. All outward appearances suggest that our street children have not merely survived but overcome their tragedy of living below the poverty line - homeless and abandoned, to fend for themselves. But what about the core? Sometimes, I can clearly sense that the pain in their eyes won't recede until we undo that utter neglect and apathy that they have had to face in life, beginning with their own parents and extending to the society at large. I can understand their caution in trusting strangers, even the well-meaning ones like us, after what they have been through in life - exploited in every possible manner.

"Didi, didi, are you on your way home? Come here. Have a bite." That came from Chandu Kharwa, who rarely attended our class because he didn't like to be reminded about having a haircut or being told to pay attention to personal hygiene. With an impish grin, he offered me the last bite of the 'vada-pav' that he had been eating with unwashed hands. He preferred to go without a bath for days at end. The moment I accepted it, he turned to his friend (whom I was meeting for the first time), and was beside himself with joy, "Ha, ha! You lost the bet. Didn't I tell you that she will eat our food? Give me Rs.10/-. Now would you like to join her school?"

It was absolutely worth having to go through the worst kind of stomach upset in order to hear those words and experience the satisfying results of one more child being able to trust another human being who accepts him for what he is, and, in the process, to enter a different world – Sunbeam.

Chandu himself never joined the mainstream. But he gave up begging and joined his parents in weaving and selling flowers, and visited Sunbeam whenever he felt like assuring himself that his presence still mattered to us. None of the Sunbeam didis ever disappointed him.

In 2002, he met with an accident and lay in the hospital. One or the other didi from Sunbeam stayed with him at the cost of leaving an entire class of regular attendees in the care of a proxy teacher because Chandu was equally dear to them.

Total bonding with the child is the paramount thing; without which there can be no real relationship. To be true friends to our children, we need to appreciate what it must be like for them to grow up with the pressures of poverty and the exploitation that accompanies it. Hence, before offering opportunities of formal education, we make sure to provide them with the emotional support and acceptance that they so desperately seek. Sunbeam is blessed with a dedicated team of staff who stand by our children in their hour of need.

Over the years, we lost touch with Chandu, as he had decided to let go of studies completely. He dwelled on the streets and had begun planning to earn a living for himself instead. There were numerous instances when I used to wonder about his whereabouts and his life post-Sunbeam. As luck would have it, he crossed my path once more in life – in October '08:-

I was at an 'Energy Booth' with Shanta (Community Development Head), when a youth, around 19 years of age, walked up to me and inquired, "Do you recognize me, didi?"

I was completely taken by surprise. After all these years, I was at a loss for placing his identity in memory. Chandu introduced himself and revealed that he had gotten married, and was now a 'family man'. However, unable yet to acquire decent accommodation, he still dwelled on the streets, with his wife. Flower-weaving remains his profession, though now he makes them on large orders.

Here's an instance in which the child himself was adamant against being educated. He had, of his own will, given preference to leading his life the way it was. True it is, Sunbeam reaches out to children in need, but it isn't able to transform every life that comes its way. There are instances when circumstances just get the better of motives, however sound the latter might be.

Impact of Kokila and Anil's Innocence on Sunbeam Visitors

Proximity with children taught me many things. One of them was that it was imperative that I listen, really listen, to what they wished to convey to us - adults. Each of us at Sunbeam, stay alert and open to listening with our hearts, so that we can deeply understand our children from their frame of reference.

I can vividly recall one classroom scene: Three foreigner ladies had come to know of Sunbeam and so, fixed a date for a visit to our children, well in advance. The kids, all pavement dwellers, sang songs and cuddled up to them. The latecomers, as usual, quietly took their seats and joined in. But Kokila Kharwa (11), found the presence of the visitors amusing. She stopped short at the gate with a stunned expression on her face. Her hand flew to her mouth. With her other hand pointing out to them, she asked me the reason of the visit from white people (as she called them) and then laughed outright. I could sense that my child was laughing not at them but in an attempt to conceal her own embarrassment at not being dressed properly, because she, like her other classmates, had not been informed by us about this visit despite it being planned in advance. Kokila's strange behaviour brought forth the question I was dreading, "What is she saying? Why is she laughing at us?" they exclaimed. My clarification had the desired effect and more. "We're so touched by the integrity of your organisation. You didn't feel it necessary to prepare the kids for our visit? That's amazing. Thanks."

Kokila could not understand a word of our conversation (which was in English), but was visibly worried that her natural expression of amazement might have hurt the sentiments of the visitors. Wanting to make up for her error, she held out a string of flowers, and said, "Didi, I had brought these to adorn the frame of Ma Ambe. But may I offer it to them instead?" Without waiting for my response, she hurried up to them and placed it in the hand of the lady nearest to her. A spirit of love and reverence seemed to engulf the visitors, our staff and myself – reverence for Kokila's display of innocence as well as maturity, and appreciation for her act of courage borne out of humility.

The same day, in the same classroom, in the presence of the visitors, another lesson was in store for me - another equally moving insight that a child was to offer me.

The visitors distributed eatables and gifts to the children. As a Sunbeam momento, we offered each of the visitors a beautifully painted diya - the product of a talented volunteer's effort. Looking at me pointedly, Anil Ogania, (8), thundered, "Are you ashamed of me?" I didn't have the vaguest idea of what was really going on in his mind. "No," is all I could say. Besides the anger, I could hear the agitation in his voice as he continued, "Then why did you offer these ladies the diyas painted by the volunteer and not the ones we had painted? Is it that the diyas that we have painted are not as beautiful as those made by the volunteers? I think you are ashamed of our work. Am I right?"

Despite the error of hurting his sentiments, the trust and friendship between us was strong enough for him not to find it hard to open up with me. He felt it safe enough to expose his feelings to and challenge my intentions, thereby giving me an opportunity to rectify the situation.

"I'm sorry, I mean it. Come, come and offer your diya to them." He jumped from his seat, dived at the storage unit, and brought out the precious diya. My boy gleamed like the brightly coloured diya that he offered to our well-wishers, whose hearts he had touched deeply. All present in the room were witness to the self-confidence and pride with which Anil offered the priceless gift to Sunbeam friends in return for the equally priceless treasure that Sunbeam had given him – a high sense of self-esteem.

Payal's unique way of coping with a loved one's loss

Unknown to me, the nursery kids at the Phoenix Centre craved for my attention. One afternoon, during my fortnightly visit, I sat chatting with the primary children, virtually ignoring the little ones waiting to be cuddled by me. I justified my inattentiveness to the little darlings by attributing it to my hectic schedule for the day because I didn't believe that tiny kids could communicate as effectively.

"Didi, didi," chirped Payal Bhadkumbhe, (3½), as she darted into our classroom and placed herself onto my lap. "Do you mind coming over to my place?" she asked in an urgent tone. I obliged. Making me sit on the floor, in the open space outside her hut, she looked at me intently, and gently, but firmly, asked me to sit still for a while. What she did next, amused me greatly. "Ah, there you are," she gurgled delightfully as she proudly displayed to me the grey hair that she had plucked out from my head. Now she went round me in circles, dancing merrily. "My child, why did you have to do that?" I asked confused. She appeared not to have heard me, wrapped up as she was in her own world. "Didi, now I don't need to worry any more. The grey hair is gone!" she exclaimed with relief. Then, in an extremely sad tone she added, "My granny is not to be seen anymore. I miss her a lot. My parents tell me that because all her hair had turned grey, she moved on to a distant land where I can't follow her. The only other person whom I love utmost is you." There was a pause. "Didi, now you will always keep coming back, you will, you will," she added, feeling jubilant at her own feat of having managed to do away with my grey hair. Clapping her hands in glee, she stood beaming with joy. The next moment she gave me a bear hug. Her parents were always working late hours at the construction site, and, with her older siblings busy with their studies, my little one was starved for love and affection. At that moment, I was playing her late granny's role and felt extremely touched that my presence in her life mattered so much to her, despite my inability to spend quality time with her on a more regular basis.

Payal had taken me by surprise, both by her words and her unique way of expressing her love for me. No other child had managed to touch me the way she had. My tears were a mixture of joy and sadness; I could not thank God enough for His precious gifts to me in the form of children.

Yellamma's gift to be Treasured

Somehow, the past year (1999) had brought not only successes, but some failures as well – kids who slipped through the cracks.

Yellamma Kaikade was too busy playing surrogate mother to her 3 younger siblings, with the youngest being 1 ½ years old. Had we really made any difference in the lives of children like Yellamma, who could never join the mainstream? I wondered. But not for long.

At Sunbeam, in those days, when our focus was on informal education, we had evolved some unspoken ground rules. One of them was to keep the door open for every single child regardless of his / her interest level and attendance in regular classes. So, Yellamma would attend classes whenever time permitted her.

One evening after Sunbeam classes, she walked up to me and declared, "I have a gift for you." Just the idea of being able to offer something to me seemed to give her a happier countenance. But suddenly, she seemed to be in two minds. She gulped hard, then again extended her hand, the gift in her clenched fist still not visible to me. "Sorry," she said quickly, as she beat a hasty retreat, only to return, this time determined to hand it over to me. "Didi, you use hankies, don't you? I had a, a, ...," she stuttered and seemed to falter over her words but then finally mustered enough courage and made a hurried speech - "From one of my dresses, I have made out a few hankies for each of you who teach us at Sunbeam. Don't get me wrong. I washed the dress clean and first cut off the torn portions. Only where I found that the material had no tear in it, I properly cut it out into pieces which can now be used as hankies. Will you accept my gift?" "Yes, and I'll treasure it forever," I replied.

Yellamma ran off to play, unaware of the impact her gesture of love had had on me. Through my child's eyes the world looked so different. Circumstances in life never allowed her to join either the non-formal classes or the mainstream, (some of her friends have reached the secondary section by now), and yet, Sunbeam has not failed her completely. At the end of it, what matters most is that we have touched her life in a way she'll always remember. Her most precious gift to me has been the knowledge that I need not feel too guilty for not being able to make a difference in her life, the way I'd have loved to in other visible ways.

Tina Lit the Candle of a New Definition of Love

In my children lay my dream. Giving them a sense of belonging within their families, the community and society, giving them opportunities to enjoy their childhood and to fulfil their physical, emotional and educational aspirations formed an integral part of my dream. As the person who led Sunbeam, I had a key role to play in making this dream come true. With the support of my dedicated team of staff, I knew that I was delivering this dream - Sunbeam had made a real difference in the lives of the children it reached out to. But for the new entrants it was still a long way to go. We always had to take a number of steps towards them before they started taking the step of trusting our intentions and accepting what we had to offer them – hope for a better future. My thoughts ran on these lines on the way to Aksa beach where we had booked the children's camp and where I was to spend 3 days in the company of my little darlings. This particular trip turned out to be an eye-opener for me.

Friends, let me share with you one of my sacred experiences with an extraordinarily selfless child - Tina Satadia. It will give insights into the kind of mutual love and affection between our staff and our children, and also into the kind of challenges / problems faced by them while living on the streets. These are children who still haven't become disillusioned - they continue to offer selfless love and affection to one and all.

Eight year old Tina, a pavement dweller in Mumbai, had joined Sunbeam a month ago and was one of the 55 kids on their journey to Aksa on 29.4.2002. She cuddled up to me, the festering wound on her elbow brushing my hand. With big questioning eyes she searched my face for any noticeable reproach. Finding none, she poured out to me the secrets of her life. "Didi, I cook daily. But one day I dared to defy my father, seeking permission to be allowed to attend school instead. He burnt my hand," she said, her voice cracking. In her next statement though, there was an element of pride, "Rahul, (2), my younger brother, has been brought up by me. Mum was expecting another baby, so I took care of the entire family, earning enough by way of seeking alms." All of a sudden her eyes were pools of sadness. "Didi, it's, it's.....," she sputtered tearfully, unable to go any further. After a long pause, she added, "Among the numerous jobs I'm expected to handle, one is to clean my dad's head of lice. He thrashes me up if I don't do a neat job of it."

Suddenly her eyes lit up. She was looking out of the window as the bus had halted at a signal outside a temple. With a look of reverence on her face, she folded her hands and made me do likewise. "Please, bow down to God, didi," she reprimanded me. Friends, I've always believed in God but that moment held special significance as just then I was experiencing divinity in the form of the child next to me.

"Other children claim my mum is mentally challenged. It's not so. She simply keeps muttering to herself." After a pause she switched on to another topic and added matter of factly, "I just heard you say to a child at the backseat that you too are feeling hungry. Do not worry. I have ten rupees. That should suffice for the two of us." Unable to fathom why I refused, she simply said, "But I always take care of Rahul, my parents and even my younger sister. So why can't I feed you as well?" The next moment she appeared sick and in extreme pain. Her body felt warm as she clung to me. She was running temperature. "Didi, I can barely sit. I've had these boils on my bottom for a long time now ....." The more she revealed of herself, the more I could feel the tension within her subsiding. Eventually, she dozed off, her grip on me loosening.

Upon reaching Aksa, she let me check the multiple wounds over her body, though reluctantly. The worst one on the bottom required immediate medical attention. As I cleaned up the wound after giving her a bath, she winced in pain. Pus and blood oozed out of the 2-3 inches big lump, yet she bore the pain noiselessly each time I changed the dressing. Though in pain, she felt enveloped in a happy glow. "Oh, I knew it, I was sure that you'd relieve me of my pain. I had said so to dad, who had otherwise been unwilling to let me come to Aksa," she said with misty eyes. I wanted to thank Chhaya Sutar, one of our dedicated staff members, for having taken the trouble to wash Tina's heap of soiled clothes, but my 8-year-old beat me to it. She ran up to Chhaya, threw her arms around her neck and planted a kiss on her cheek. Then turning to me, she announced, "I've taken a decision. I'm going to buy each of you a candy from the ten rupees that I had saved for this picnic. So that you shouldn't run out of stock from the number of candies that my limited amount can buy, please count me out." It was now our turn to be enveloped in her boundless spirit of affection. We considered it our privilege to be in her company. She was one rare child who had taken upon herself to live for others at such a tender age, even though her own life was in turmoil.

By evening she had reconciled to the idea of allowing us to take her to the doctor. Within an hour she was back with Jyoti Narkar, her Sunbeam teacher. For a long time she sat deep in thought. Finally, she spoke up, "I'm sorry didi. I don't think I can keep my promise of giving candies to each of you. Jyoti didi has spent so much on my medication. I just have to offer my entire savings to her." After this declaration, she walked up to Jyoti and handed over the ten rupee note to her saying that it was all hers. Jyoti, who has been recently transferred to the Charni Road Centre, felt a lump in her throat. She had been awarded the world's greatest honour – a child's complete trust in her. When she finally found her voice, it was to mutter a hurried thank you to Tina and an assurance that she would buy a candy for each of us. The effect of Tina's act of love was electrifying. She had made it sound so simple. Unspoken, but understood, was the fact that she was too overwhelmed with someone caring enough to relieve her pain, and she wished to repay that kindness by parting with her savings.

Satisfied with herself, she walked up to her bed and drifted off to sleep - or so it seemed - till she suddenly sat up to reveal more about herself. "Do you know I have stopped begging? Kokila's mum allows me to weave flowers with her and pays me for the same. And do you know, Oh but how would you know unless I tell you? Well, when dad beats me or burns me, it's my Rahul, my brother Rahul, who comes to my rescue. Now he walks on his own. When he grows up I'll bring him to school. I've myself resolved to attend school. Every child's parent is going to pay 50 % towards uniforms and other school items. Even I don't want anything in charity. One day a man scolded me for begging and advised that I should earn my living and not beg. I'm doing so now." Glancing all over the room to make sure that no one was around, she said, "Let me tell you a secret. I've saved almost a hundred rupees by selling flowers and have managed to keep it hidden from dad, who would otherwise spend it on drinking. But I made the mistake of sharing my secret with my friend Kanchan Kharwa. Do you think my piggy bank will still be there under the tree where I had left it deep down in the mud? I'm not so sure. What matters most is that the lump has vanished and I'm relieved of the pain." She said all this in one breath and then lay down on the bed. As she slept, her face looked serene; her heart content with what the present moment had to offer her.

Tina's gift to me, the insights she had provided me with that day, set me thinking, 'Giving of myself selflessly should not be difficult. If an 8-year-old living on the pavements can do so consistently, why can't I?' The thought that - 'The situation is so bad that Sunbeam is not making any significant difference in their lives' - no longer comes in to weaken my will to do the best I can for our children. One of the most powerful aids that Tina has gifted me with is how to renew my energies by drawing them from the inexhaustible source of pure and luminous love and goodness lying all around and within oneself. I have personally experienced the consequences of the power that Tina consistently demonstrates in the face of pain, neglect and exploitation of all sorts. In her company one experiences multiple emotions. But gratitude stands above the rest. Gratitude at the opportunity to have a glimpse into the way in which she copes with the emotional and psychological wounds (besides the physical ones) that life has inflicted upon her at such a tender age.

When asked to relate one of the happiest moments she'd be taking back home from Aksa, she said, "Didi, I enjoyed blowing the balloons. I also felt happy participating in the game of lighting candles. Unfortunately, I could light only 7 candles with one matchstick, hence lost the game." Unknown to her, she had won. Her statement sounded so symbolic. It rang so true with a much deeper meaning. In the hearts and minds of the 7 staff members present at Aksa, she had managed to light the candle of a new definition of love and of the impact it could have on those over whom it poured.

Tina was one of the countless children dwelling on the streets. How was one to experience the boundless, selfless love that was simply waiting for an opportunity to get showered upon all that it came in touch with? Not a day goes by at Sunbeam when we are not blessed with such experiences. It's been years since I experienced Tina's fighting spirit, but the memory of it lingers as a vividly imprinted image. It's amazing how her tiny acts of magic could transform our lives in unexpected ways.

Tina's way of making a difference to every life she touches

At the Aksa camp (in 2003), she was recuperating from her illness and I was surprised that for once, my sweet child,

Tina Satadia, was making a fuss over having a cup of milk. But she put her foot down and did not let me have my way. "Sometimes your vision gets blurred. You claim that because I'm taking heavy doses of medicines, milk is a must for me. I'm already 9. Why isn't it a must for the 3 years olds to have milk? In this group of 75 children of my age, you missed out on the 2 who are nursery kids and only 3 years old. They are used to having milk at home. But busy as you seem to be with other things, you've been giving them tea with the rest of the lot. It's not that I don't want to have milk, but their need is greater than mine," so saying she went and fed them.

Tina had been a mother to her younger siblings since years. Now, I had seen that the mother's heart in her listened to and responded with love, for others as well. But that was not all. I had underestimated the extent of her love that encompassed one and all, regardless of their age.

Almost a year after the above incident, she met me at the office. "Didi, I've not been attending school since my father's demise. Now I've an additional responsibility - taking care of my mentally challenged mother; besides that of my younger brother and sister. Without dad around, I'm not so sure if I'll be able to protect her well enough on the streets, especially at nights." I was feeling really sorry for her. Just then, with motherly affection, she began scolding me, "Didi, since the past few days I've been noticing that instead of the homemade food that you used to carry for lunch, you're having junk food from the restaurant yonder. I hope you learn to value your body. You work so hard, you need good food. Anyway, I cook for the family. Today, I'll cook an extra portion of the brinjal and chapatis for you. I cook on the streets by placing together 3 bricks, and use pieces of wood to light a fire. I'll be back by lunch time." I had an inspiring teacher in Tina.

Sure enough, she returned at 1 p.m. with steaming hot food prepared by her. That moment is unforgettable; all of us at the office were deeply moved. Here was a child stepping outside herself, every moment of her life, to make a difference to someone else's life.

Before I could place the first morsel into my mouth, Hira, Tina's mother rushed in and desperately tried to stop me from eating. Impulsively, she thrust a Rs.50/- note into my hand and said, "Please order a full meal for yourself. This kind of food is not meant for you. Tina doesn't understand because she is a child." I pacified her explaining that Tina was as much my daughter as hers, and it was my privilege to be fed by her at least for one day.

"Didi, I remember that Shanta and you had stayed with me and my children at the Cama hospital day and night. I don't have riches to offer you, but please don't refuse my humble contribution. I may never again be able to offer you anything." Tears stung my eyes - Was this the same mentally challenged woman who had harassed the life out of me during my few nights stay with her, just 6 months ago?

Why, it seemed just like yesterday, when night after night, as I lay in the hospital, on the mat spread out on the floor next to her bed, the nurses had come and screamed at me, "Aye, you lazy person. Can't you understand it's feeding time? Wake up. Social workers like you just talk grand; when it comes to action, you dare to sleep." Every couple of hours, I had to go through the ordeal of coaxing Tina's mother to hand over to me, her 6 month old baby - a skeleton of a child - who was almost on her death bed due to dysentery and malnutrition. I knew too well the grave odds against the baby's survival. As I would sit feeding her from the bowl the nurse would have left behind, or would clean up the mess on the bed every hour or so, the mother would simply stare at me angrily for having disturbed her sleep.

Overcome with weariness, on and often I'd myself doze off, only to wake up to witness the lady about to feed her child with a spoonful of skin ointment! The bottle of drinking medicines would be empty, and she would proudly explain to me that instead of waking me up, she had already applied it all over the child's body!

One night I woke up with a start - she had decided she didn't want two children next to her, and so, threw one straight to me. The next night, I could not put up with the pain as I felt her pulling at my hair, but when I opened my eyes, I found her standing right above my head with her feet firmly on my hair. "I'm hungry, very hungry. Give me something to eat. And, why are you not getting me treated? I'm in pain, in unbearable pain." - The doctors claimed that she was fit.

The next night, I could hear a scratching sound, and the most sickening sight met my eyes. With the sharp edge of the piece of tin that she used, she was scratching away at a big, ugly, gaping wound just above her ankle, the blood and pus oozing away. She hurriedly pulled down her saree to cover the wound, and wailed, "Will you still stay with me or leave me now that you know of my illness?" With me, she was not as comfortable as with Shanta Koli (who was then the Supervisor at the street children centre, where Tina studied) - Shanta, who stayed with her from 9 a.m. to 9 p.m.; Shanta, who daily bathed and fed her children and nursed her wounds. At times, other staff joined her as Hira and all her children were ill or down with Tuberculosis or with skin diseases, and each had to be taken to different departments for check ups and treatment. Reluctantly, Hira let Shanta and myself nurse the multiple wounds all over her body. This was the turning point in her life. She could sense not pity, but affection and compassion. (That stayed with her forever, long after she was discharged from the hospital though mentally she is not so stable even now. Today, in January 2009, with her husband no more, the burden of the entire family is borne by Tina, (15), the eldest child.)

Physically and emotionally, the daily strain was too much for me. But there was no choice. The medical authorities at the Cama hospital had given us a private room, and admitted the entire family - the mother and the 3 children, together, on the condition that someone from our organisation stay with them round the clock. They claimed that twice before when they had admitted her, Hira had run away from the hospital midway during the treatment and that they could not take the risk all over again. My staff were all young girls in their early 20's or even younger, and their parents would not hear of them working late evenings, let alone nights. Even though Shanta had offered to stay 24 hours, I did not want to stretch her to breaking point. Help came in the form of a volunteer.

"Khurshid, who is Mridula Shah? She has been trying to get in touch with you since the past few days. Upon hearing that you stay at the hospitals at nights, come home only for a wash and rush to the office / centres, she said that this should not continue or else you would spoil your health. So, she has offered to relieve you tonight by coming to the hospital." - My mother's voice and the words that it carried was music to my ears. Yes, I needed rest desperately, needed to catch up on sleep.

Mridulaben was an extremely caring woman of 70, who had been volunteering with us for over 4 years now. She had been of the most accommodating nature, willing to offer whatever service was required of her. Till date, she had played multiple roles - she taught Maths, joined the children on excursions or spent time with our children by sharing interesting stories with them. She even took them to her home at Napean Sea Road, and along with her daughter-in-law, cooked and fed 15 to 20 kids at a time. Of late, because her knees had been giving her too much trouble, she had requested to be assigned an education center where she could be spared the ordeal of climbing steps.

Now, the same lady was telling my mum that it wouldn't be inconvenient for her to sleep on the floor! Of course, my conscience never let me accept her suggestion. Perhaps, I just needed to know that I was not alone. That there were people like Mridulaben who'd always be around to offer their dedicated services to Sunbeam.

How Tina sees a silver lining in the clouds

"Albeit not very happily but in a grudging manner, they sanctioned my 4 days leave. After initial resistance, they came around because I stood my ground. I believe you take leave twice a year. I am not so fortunate. It's been over 2 years since I went on a long vacation. Yet, our lives are similar at least so far as our working hours are concerned. I too work late hours."

Friends, you might well think that this was a colleague talking to me. But no – this was 12-year-old Tina Satadia unburdening her grievances to a patient listener. She is one of the few unfortunate street children whose circumstances in life made it impossible for her to attend Sunbeam education classes. A few years ago she lost her father and her struggle for survival intensified because she had to play the role of a mother to her younger siblings, Rahul and Bharati, as well as to her own mentally-challenged mother. Of course, her relatives have been supportive – but only up to a limit.

Now in April 2005 at Aksa, her face wore a glow of happiness and triumph as she shared in detail how she had managed to convince all the relatives in her family that she deserved a breather – from her daily 12 hour routine of endless duties. "For once I'm relaxing, and do not have to worry about household chores. I know my joy is short-lived but I'm going to make the most of it while it lasts. Didi, I do not want you to form a wrong opinion of my relatives. It's not as if they're exploiting me. While I prepare the chapattis, my uncle cooks the vegetables. Although filling up water for cooking and washing is my responsibility, my aunt washes most of the clothes. My uncle and aunt also ensure that neither my mother nor my siblings and I ever go hungry."

Tina's wisdom defies her tender age. She has tremendous fortitude. She is neither overwhelmed by adversity nor does she pretend to put up a brave front. She quietly accepts her misfortune and continues with the daily business of getting on with her life.

The 4 days spent at the yearly camp at Aksa were a welcome break for her – and like every other child, she thoroughly enjoyed herself. She harbours no feelings of resentment, despite being aware that the delightful time that she had must come to an end, as she cannot frequently indulge in such revelry, which for her would amount to luxury. Her life has to continue in the same monotonous manner, offering little relief of rest and aid that would enable her to relax and experience the contentment of a carefree childhood.

Despite the anguish and desolation that she undergoes each day, she knows that Sunbeam is one place where she (and others like her) will always be welcomed with loving care and open arms.

Prakash's Struggle for Survival on the Streets

One of the many important lessons that children taught me way back in the year 1997 was that if I were to make a place for myself in their hearts, I had to drop the teacher's mask. That was when our bond grew stronger. If I have discovered anything about unconditional love, about life - I have learned it in the company of children.

Behind their bright smiles are the hidden harsh realities of their lives. These children with their ever-smiling faces have taught me that there is little correlation between the circumstances of their lives and their happiness. Children, as I have experienced them at Sunbeam, choose to find the positive in virtually every situation. Hence, they are blessed with happiness.

To cite an example, let me share with you a touching incident that took place in 2002 but has stayed with me till date.

At the Chandanwadi Municipal school, our children used to be given 3 kgs of rice per month as an incentive for the parents to ensure their regular attendance. While for the children at the other centers this is something to look forward to, it's different for the families dwelling on the streets of Mumbai. While on the topic, Kiran explained to us that they had no space to store anything. Moreover, the municipality confiscated even their meager belongings because they were not supposed to live on the pavements. Hence, they were left with no option but to sell off the stuff, only to buy it from the same shopkeeper in installments at double the price.

All of us hearing Kiran were too overwhelmed to respond when to our surprise Prakash Kharwa, (8), our 3rd standard student, tried to lighten the atmosphere in the classroom by sharing with us how he had managed to find a way out of the situation. "Didi," he whispered into my ears, "I am an expert at climbing trees. That's the advantage I have over others." He was grinning from ear to ear leaving us guessing as to what connection this had with the rice story. Sensing our confusion, he added, "I have outwitted the municipality people who would not know of my hidden treasures on tree tops. Daily before dawn, I climb up and remove the day's quota so that we are not deprived of what we have rightfully earned from the Municipal school." To this, Jyoti Satadia, (6), chirped, "Ah, but your parcels of rice may not be hidden from the crows for long. They will be pecking at them soon and having a hearty meal." The others burst out laughing.

Sunbeam meant the world to our kids dwelling on the streets. (Unfortunately, we had to close down that education center for want of space in the Hindi Medium Chandanwadi school and for many other reasons beyond our control.) And their health and happiness was what really mattered to us. So the above incident set me thinking. Without a roof over their heads, a 9 - 5 organised life at Sunbeam / formal school would not have much of an impact on their otherwise traumatic existence on the streets. A night shelter for these children is one of my few dreams that have not been fulfilled.

Insights into what it takes to Make or Mar a Child's Future

It was August '99. Vicky (name changed), who headed a small grass root level NGO like ours, that worked in the field of Education of underprivileged children, claimed that given his qualifications and vast experience in the field of development, he had much to offer me at Sunbeam. I believed that he'd be able to provide me with invaluable inputs on Sunbeam matters, which is why I acceded to his request of allowing him to conduct our next monthly meeting with the parents of the child beneficiaries. The prospect of his visit had seemed quite promising to me. At that point in time, Sunbeam's outreach was limited to approximately 60 - 70 children. It was much later (i.e. on December 10, 1999), that the organisation was christened "Sunbeam" and got registered as a Public Charitable Trust.

But contrary to my belief, this is how the meeting went. Let me quote 2 of the many instances that are still etched in my memory:

"How can you all be so ignorant as to not be aware of the presence of the Golden Temple so close to your native place? You mean to say you haven't visited it even once?" Vicky's tone had an accusing note to it as he addressed the parents of our beneficiaries and mocked at them, claiming that he had never come across people who were so ignorant about the important places in India. One of the parents responded with, "Day and night, we are busy making two ends meet. We're migrant labourers, here in Mumbai to etch out a living. Yes, we are indeed ignorant about the wonders of the world; we aren't even sure of our next meal, given that on days when construction work comes to a standstill, we go without wages. We hope that our children will have a better life if they continue to be with Sunbeam long-term." I felt humbled.

"Can any one of you tell me about a single valuable or lasting change that Sunbeam has brought about in your children?" Vicky now asked them in a haughty tone. Yellamma Mulwad's mother was quick to respond. She mentioned how a week ago, she and her husband, Ramanna, had decided that since Yellamma was now over 12, as per the customs of their society, she should discontinue with her studies. In protest against her right to education being curbed by them, their child had not touched food for 3 consecutive days, until finally, she and her husband had reconciled to her choice in life and had permitted Yellamma to continue with Sunbeam. Her mother added with an element of pride in her voice, "Unlike me, my daughter had the courage of her convictions. She could stand up for her right to education. As a child, I hadn't ever dared to defy my parents. In our society, girls are not allowed the privileges that the boys are because...."

Vicky interrupted, "Education? Well, let me check it out for myself how bright your child is before we decide whether Sunbeam has managed to bring about any positive change in her, whatsoever." So saying, he turned to Yellamma, made her sit next to him and handed her a book and a pencil, after scrawling a few maths problems for her to solve. She stared at the book mutely, as he put a large cross over each of the sums that she couldn't solve correctly. A wave of cold fear passed through me. My child's eyes turned piercingly to mine, as though questioning me on my silence. I lowered my gaze in helplessness and shame, at the insensitive manner in which my child was being treated.

She looked about the room as though seeking escape, and then turned her pleading gaze towards Ganesh, her younger brother studying in the 2nd standard. Ganesh, solved the problems accurately within no time. This made Vicky pass some more sarcastic remarks aimed at Yellamma. Two clear teardrops stood in my child's eyes. My heart was bleeding with guilt. Treating her with respect and dignity would have been acknowledging the lasting change that Sunbeam had already brought about in her. But that was not to be so.

Eventually, she got up and walked away with her parents, telling me softly, "I now understand that education is not meant for children like me. I'd rather remain at home and help mom with household chores." So saying, she left, never to return to Sunbeam. She did come every afternoon – but only to hand over to Ganesh, the lunch she had prepared for him.

Immediately after the meeting, I made a resolution: Vicky could never be one of the core group members handling Sunbeam, neither now nor ever in the future.

What made the problem more profound was that in his case, I was up against a very wrong mindset. Only if I could let him know of the damage he had done to the child's self-esteem, by having viewed her through the narrow domain of his own limited perception, perhaps it might prevent him from repeating a similar error in the future. So, a fortnight after that fateful meeting, I met up with him and poured out my anguish and hurt. Uncontrollable tears were coursing down my face as I related to him how much harm his harsh speech had done to the self image of our emotionally fragile child beneficiary. Incredulous, he made a vehement protest, "I will not accept that I was, in any way, by my words or actions, insensitive towards any of the Sunbeam beneficiaries!" Then, on a softer note, he added, "O Khurshid, I've always seen you as a person completely in control of yourself. Today, I realise how vulnerable you are. I'm really sorry if I have hurt your sentiments."

"Can meaningful dialogue be carried out in isolation from the realities of one's life? Our children's world - full of complexities, uncertainties and challenges - calls for a greater understanding and a meaningful partnership that has to go beyond academics. The secret of understanding our beneficiaries is to be able to identify with their problems," thus I continued to reason with him - but in vain. I guess people see what they want to. Vicky's perspective, unfortunately, differed from mine. Because he was so focussed on measuring a child's success only by the yardstick of academic performance, he overlooked the real empowerment in the child's life that had already come about – a child standing up for her right to education within a month of joining Sunbeam. In that sense, hadn't Sunbeam succeeded in achieving its goal?

How I wished I could turn back the clock and do it all differently – speak up for my children. What had happened to my child was a deliberate act of cruelty, in which I had played an equal role. How could I have absolved myself of all responsibility?

Friends, I had lost faith in my ability to deliver justice. Yellamma's leaving the organisation had made me resolve, as a starting point in my fight for children's rights, that I'd swiftly restore that lost faith in myself - by being a mother who'd never again fail any of her children, a mother who'd stand by them, come what may. What I'm trying to say, and the reason why I found it difficult to forgive myself, is that a leader without a will to administer justice – a leader who looked the other way when her child's self-esteem was being ripped apart - was not worthy of leading Sunbeam.

After that fateful day, I embarked on a journey of self-discovery and self-improvement. I prayed to God for one more opportunity, He provided me with endless ones. Each time, I went by the voice of my conscience, and have never had to regret any of my decisions at Sunbeam. Admittedly, the past 10 years have not been so easy, but nothing ever again weakened my resolution. I've stuck to my values, kept my word to God.

Sadly, I couldn't do much for Yellamma except be in touch with her by inviting her to our children's yearly overnight camps at Aksa and then trying to see if I could lessen her hurt and once again build on her self-esteem.

Then in January 2006, I struck upon a plan. Harsha, our teacher at Sunbeam, was getting married and would be away for a couple of months. Though it was necessary that her secondary section batches of students be handled by another B.Ed trained teacher, the 1st and 2nd standard batches could be assigned to Yellamma for a period of two months! Taking her on as a temporary teacher could serve as a platform from which I could begin to give back her lost self-confidence. Atoning for my wrong act was my way of creating a different world for Yellamma; a world where she'd view herself as a teacher – a contributing member of the society, and would take back with her happy memories of Sunbeam when she would get married and settle in the village, a few months later.

It was not just the act of appointing her as a teacher that was important, but the manner in which it was done with utmost sensitivity - assuring that though she had never gone beyond primary schooling, she was accepted by the permanent team of staff members as an equal - an invaluable member of the Sunbeam family. (I had ensured that another temporary teacher assist Yellamma, just in case she couldn't manage handling the 40 little 5 to 7 year olds, all by herself, even if for a short period of 2 to 3 months.)

"Yellamma, you'll have to be utmost careful in your speech with the children under your care, so as not to hurt their sentiments," I told her, only to regret it because by saying so, I had ended up hurting her. "Didi, I've been a student of Sunbeam in the distant past, and understand how it feels to be treated with insensitivity." Her voice trailed away, leaving me full of remorse.

Today, as I pen her case story, this is how I can describe my child, Yellamma; a soft-spoken girl of few words, she exudes warmth, loves being with our children, and is the happiest in their company.

One day, in 2006, realising that I could be possibly right in my assumption that the child may have never forgotten that ill-fated day and the events that made her leave Sunbeam, I mustered enough courage to broach the topic and apologise to her, "Yellamma, I'm sorry for what happened at Sunbeam 7 years ago to cause you to leave the organisation. Please forgive me if you can." She seemed visibly moved by my sincere apology. With angelic tenderness in her voice, she responded by a counter-question, "Didi, why are you seeking my forgiveness? It was bhaiya (she was referring to Vicky) who said everything. You did not utter a word." "That's precisely why I'm seeking your forgiveness – for having remained silent in the face of injustice being meted out to you." Holding my hand in hers, she quietly said the words I had been waiting to hear, "Didi, I forgive you." With her answer, I felt a weight lift from my heart, dissolved forever in her generosity.

If her story is being told, albeit rather belatedly, even after this chapter of her life, in which I tried to make amends, it is out of the expectation to share my learning in life, to provide a better understanding into that which can make or mar a child's future.

My singular error had ruined a child's future. That knowledge, torturous as has been its coming, stands as a meaningful outcome of the terrible mistake I made. The other consequences of that event I'm less sure of. That is, I still do not know to what extent my silence in that meeting had affected the morale of the parents of our beneficiaries who too had been treated with indignity in my presence.

I can, nonetheless, say with honesty that I couldn't spare or forgive myself for being a silent spectator in the face of victimization of our beneficiaries.

Yet, what I can say with conviction is that from that day onwards till date, I've left no stone unturned to ensure that our 1000+ child beneficiaries be given due respect at Sunbeam. There have been, during those innumerable good and not so good encounters over the years, opportunities to make Sunbeam a home full of nurturing family members, for our children. And, I've emerged from all these experiences a better human being.

Time to time I take a reality check on the ethics benchmark that I had set for myself. I use my role at Sunbeam as an effective tool to practice what I so often promote as the work ethics / values of the organisation.

One morning Yellamma called me up to inform me about a few happenings at Sunbeam and also on how very sensitively, she had handled one of her 2nd standard students who had stolen her purse containing her full month's salary! Let me share with you that episode of Yellamma's life where she played the role of a mature teacher or else her own case story would remain incomplete: "Didi, you must have got to know that a child from my class stole my purse. But she is too young to understand that it was wrong on her part to do so. With that money she had gone to buy some toffees for herself. That's when the shopkeeper noticed that she had lots of money that couldn't possibly belong to her. So he took her to the school peon who made her return the purse to me. Didi, it's natural that she was scared, and so she denied having stolen my purse. I told her that I understood her feelings and that I loved her dearly even now. The next day, of her own accord, she returned my bangles and the ring that I had kept in my purse. I've acknowledged her honesty. She has not been made to feel small by me in any way, and continues to be a Sunbeam student who'd never again repeat her error. Khurshid didi, please do not disconnect the line. Ganesh, my brother, has something important to share with you," so saying, she passed on the line to him. "Didi, Yellamma's marriage has been finalised for May'06. I'll be sending you an invitation card. Please do attend her wedding at the village. It's only 14 hours by train from Mumbai."

Yellamma took back not only happy memories of Sunbeam with her wherever she went but was planning to do similar work in the village – that of motivating children to become literate! I consider myself fortunate to have had her teach me invaluable lessons in life.

Today, in January 2009, she is a mother of a 1 ½ years old baby girl, Komal. She has adjusted well with her in-laws and comes to visit me each time that she is in Mumbai.

The Beginning of Community Work

Friends, this child's case study is of a time when I had no experience, whatsoever, of handling a project. I simply used to spend time with the parents of our child beneficiaries after my office hours, trying to understand their lives better. Our outreach was limited to the 15 to 20 children at the construction site adjacent to the CRY office where I worked full time. I hadn't, yet, managed to build a rapport with the building contractor in order to sensitise him towards his labourers. Those were the days when I myself learnt along the way.

Chinnamma was returning to her construction site one evening, with 6 month old Kavita, her youngest child, tucked under her arm when her foot slipped; and though she managed to resist the fall in time, her baby slipped from her hand. The child fell headlong down the bridge and lay in a pool of blood. She brought Kavita in an unconscious state to me at the CRY office. "Didi, people gathered around the baby as she lay bleeding from her head injury, but not a single person extended a helping hand," she addressed me.

Taking charge, I rushed her to a nearby hospital. Fortunately, prior to our reaching the hospital, Kavita regained consciousness and I saw hope. The doctor stitched the wound on her head and sent her back home with her mother, instructing us to return on the 6th day for the removal of the stitches.

Four days later, when I passed by the construction site, I saw Chinnamma waving frantically at me. She, excitedly, dragged me to her shanty and pointing out to her baby, made a statement that made me shiver. "Look at this. I've already done the job of cutting off Kavita's stitches. Why wait for a doctor when I have a blade at home? Why take a half day off and let go of wages?"

I recoiled at the very thought of the unexpected act on the part of the mother. But after hearing what she had to say next; her miseries, concerns, betrayals and the fear of the consequences of taking the day off unfolded before me.

"In this week, I had already taken a half day when we went to the hospital to have Kavita's head wound stitched. The very idea of asking for another half day off fills me with dread. What if I'm thrown out of the job? Why don't you just mind your own business and leave us alone? I take one day at a time. If Kavita has to die, I've to accept it and carry on for the sake of my other two children and my husband, whose survival depends on my daily wages." In silence, I faced a barrage of words from a disturbed mother. It was hard for her not to be resentful. I could only manage trying to perceive the world through her eyes.

I told her that I'd have a word with the labour contractor and that I'd also take care of the follow-up visits at the hospital, if need be. Feeling reassured, she agreed to take Kavita to the hospital. I realised that my support to her and her children was helping forge a link with the other womenfolk in the community.

"Didi, my parents have taught me how to treat my husband with respect. So what if he blows away his wages on alcohol? Isn't it my duty, as a wife, to fulfil all his needs? So what if he abuses me or beats me? As a husband, he has a right to treat me the way he likes. I've always gone by my parents' advice and taken all kinds of abuse silently." All the way to the hospital, Chinnamma spoke and I listened.

Playing the role of a community worker, I understood how Chinnamma's parents, through her upbringing, had managed to weave into her life, the belief that her husband was superior to her. But from her words I could gather that nothing could have been further from the truth. That it wasn't faith in her parents' words that continued to bind her to her alcoholic and abusive husband, but the fear of the consequences were she to go against his wishes.

"In our society, in most of the families, it's a life of double-standards for men and women. This is the first time I'm ever sharing my fears and disappointments so openly with someone." With her voice laden with fear, she added, "I don't think I'll ever want to follow in my friend's footsteps. She dared to defy her husband by just working one shift, when she was expecting. She made the mistake of refusing to work overtime. As a woman, I understand and appreciate the stand she took, because being a labourer at the construction site is a difficult job and she was due any moment. Unfortunately, she had to suffer the consequences of her defiance. She was thrown out of her house. Today, she lives on her own. Didi, you've no idea what that means. It's better to put up with one man's abuse than let everyone in the vicinity take advantage of you."

In the past few months that I had known her, Chinnamma had always been calm and composed, betraying none of the turmoil she was experiencing. Today, she was simply crying out on a willing shoulder.

A week later, Kavita had recovered. Chinnamma's life went on as usual. We were on an excursion trip at a park, all of our child beneficiaries were thoroughly enjoying themselves when Srinu, Chinnamma's son, took me by surprise with an unexpected request, "Didi, I don't want to play. May I be allowed to sleep throughout the picnic time in the bus? The rest of you can carry on without me."

Srinu's request sounded strange, even a bit scary. Was all well with him? I had to find out the reason for the odd request. Somehow, I forced the words out, "Are you all right, Srinu?"

"Didi, yesterday night, dad came home drunk. I heard mum beg of him to spare her just this one time, that henceforth she'd ensure that dinner would be ready in time and that it would always include one dish of mutton. What hurt me most was that none of the onlookers (our neighbours) were distraught. They stood surveying the scene, without feeling concerned for my mum. So, I decided to take quick action. Dad was drunk and was trying to stab mum, who had somehow managed to save herself till then but she needed help. Therefore, I rushed to the main gate of our construction site and called out for the security guard, who immediately responded to my call and soon brought the situation under control."

Srinu glanced up at me, and I noticed his swollen and red eyes. He lowered his head, obviously fighting back tears. "I still haven't been able to gather my strength and absorb the shock of what took place last night. Long after the security guard and the neighbours left, long after everyone lay asleep, I sat shivering but stood vigil over my mum. I don't want any harm to come to her."

Hearing out 5 year old Srinu's trauma, I understood that I couldn't work with children in isolation. Their family members too needed special attention and counselling. With that was born the decision of taking on our first part-time community worker at Sunbeam. Today, we have an entire team of child counsellors and community workers spread over our different centers, covering hundreds of families.

Bhurji's smart appeal

There were a few Sunbeam children, who'd suddenly run into our CRY office after a long stay in their village. Being available to them also involved visiting the construction sites they had shifted to. One such day was when Bhurji, (10), along with Sujata, (8), gave us a surprise visit at CRY, some time in mid 2000. "Didi, there is so much to be done. Lot's of work for you, most of which is already completed because I took the initiative. Now, all that is left for you to do is to start another center with immediate effect."

Before taking me to the site where her parents worked, she expressed a desire to visit our NFE (Non-Formal Education) centre at Arthur Road. Picking up a piece of chalk, she wrote her name on the blackboard, "Didi, have a look at what I've written on the board." "It's your name," I replied casually. Obviously, I had been insensitive and had hurt her feelings. "Is that all you have to say?" she demanded and then, almost in tears, whispered words that till date continue to ring in my ears, "Even after a year of being away from school, I still remember the Hindi alphabet. And I want to learn much more. Doesn't that give me a right to education?"

As we walked upto the bus stop pointed out by her, she told me that no. 2 or 20 would take us to her home. At every bus stop beyond Lower Parel, she peeped out of the window confused, looking out for a familiar sight. She had lost track of where we were heading. A co-passenger volunteered to help us by calling out the names of a few forthcoming bus stops. When she mentioned 'Shivaji Park bus stop', Bhurji, who was too preoccupied in her own thoughts, did not hear it completely, and responded by glaring at a man at the bus-stand and then at her co-passenger, blurting out in an irritated tone, "I don't know who this Shivaji is. I am seeing him for the first time. Now don't disturb me or else I'll miss my bus-stop." Oh, it was so hilarious! While all the passengers in the bus sympathised at my dilemma, they were enjoying the company of the innocent child. Finally, at my insistence, she got off with me at the next bus-stop. I had no clue where she trotted for the next 45 minutes, assuring me every now and then, that we were nearing our destination. With the cab strike still on, I had no option but to follow her. Suddenly, her face lit up and, beaming with joy, she said, "Here we are, finally at my home." With no major construction site visible, I turned to her for further details. Pointing out to a 25 storey tower at a distance, she chirped, "I can see the same building from where I stay, just as we can see it now. So, I have done my bit of searching; now, it's up to you to find my home." This was really too much for me to take. My patience had worn out by then, but I didn't have the heart to show it. Luckily, we were able to find our way because she mentioned the Dadar flower market which was close to her construction site.

What took place at the site amazed me. She called out to her friends and within minutes I was surrounded by 40 eager faces looking expectantly at me. She had managed to convince all of them of the need for education and of its availability at the site itself! She had also managed to take a promise from all the community workers to contribute to their children's fees! To top it all, Sunbeam needed no introduction to the labour contractor, to whom she had spoken a week before; he simply told me that he had kept a room for us and was ready to provide any further assistance required, because in the past 5 years, none of the children had ever had a chance to education and therefore, he'd consider himself fortunate to be of any help to us! I turned to meet Bhurji's gaze as she waited for my commitment on beginning a centre at her site.

Why, it seemed just like yesterday when she had begun to learn the first alphabet. The past year may, very well, have not been! A full year that she was away in her village, taking care of her 3 siblings and her ailing father, but full of hope for a better future. All that was left was a handful of misty memories. The little child, who had to be coaxed by her friends to attend school, had now become a self-starter - a leader, who had done all the ground work for me to start a 4th Sunbeam centre that would continue at least for another 5 years, by which time all the children would be motivated enough to continue with formal education even without Sunbeam's support.

"If you didn't know your way back home, how did you manage to reach CRY office?" I queried. "Actually I am not at all familiar with Bombay city, but had never forgotten the words 'Arthur Road Naka' - so I found my way to your office after walking upto Lower Parel and then boarding a bus to Arthur Road Naka." This child had walked all the way upto Lower Parel from Dadar, only because her faith in herself was unshakable!

I had often caught myself thinking, "What if I am not so lucky to have adequate number of committed individuals join Sunbeam at the meagre salaries we can afford to give? What if donations do not match the growth of our organisation?" or "What if I am unable to raise a strong volunteer force to assist us in our cause?" and so on. Bhurji put an end to the endless volley of "what ifs" that had till then been extending its way into the unforseeable future.

This 10 year old girl has made me take on the responsibility to change the block in my thinking pattern – I no longer worry about staff, funds or volunteers. It is impossible for me to not go out to raise funds for her, and will be equally impossible for anybody's heart not to melt in face of such conviction, courage and trust placed by a child. One of the most important lessons we can learn in life can be imbibed from children like Bhurji. Every day, in a hundred ways, they demonstrate the courage and conviction that they can change their destiny, if they choose to, with a little financial assistance from us.

Medical Science comes to the Aid of Ramu

In 1997, our outreach was limited to 18 children and 1 part time teacher. Way back then, I played the role of the community worker and the counselor to the beneficiaries and their parents, after my working hours at CRY. At that point in time, Sunbeam was not fortunate enough to have the facility of a mobile medical van, with its team of doctors, to come to the construction site for regular check-ups. Hence, I shouldered healthcare work as well.

To my consternation, 8 year old Ramu, one of our very regular students, was absent from the Sunbeam activities class since over a week, and I decided to pay him a visit at the nearby construction site, where his parents were employed. Ramu was a new entrant at Sunbeam. He hailed from Andhra Pradesh and he and his family knew just one language – Telugu.

What met my eyes, was a painful sight. A big gaping wound, close to his ankle, left me anxious. 7-year-old Anita, his friend and neighbour and the only person who could understand Hindi, was our translator. I was informed that a week ago, Ramu had hurt himself, and that a nail prick had caused the wound. It had festered because it had been left unattended.

The minute I suggested medical treatment for him, his mother looked at me reproachfully. Anita translated what she had to say to me - "There is absolutely no need because I have easy, practical remedies, whereby my child can get treatment at home itself." Time dragged on. Neither gentle cajoling nor serious counseling seemed to work with his parents. They sat stiffly with the same response – "Our child requires no medication."

Their mind was far more at ease with the rigid customs that they believed in, than with medical science. The next evening, when I paid them one more visit, what I saw shocked me to immobility. The mother had burnt her own hair and had placed a handful of it right into her child's deep, open wound. She said that this would bring about the desired healing! I cringed at the very thought of it. Had I known that this was the remedy they had decided upon, I'd have stopped them before they actually went about administering it. I felt a suffocating despair at their ignorance of the gravity of the situation and of being responsible for increasing their child's suffering.

"Can we not take him to the hospital just once, so that his wound can be attended to?" "No," they said in a resolute tone. I was anxious all of that night. The mother's stubbornness at not willing to avail of medical aid, and moreover, her ignorance at the consequences that her child would have to face due to any further delay in getting the wound treated, made me feel I'd have to act fast before it was too late. Since she had denied me the permission to take her child to the hospital, I was left with no option but to put my plan into action during her absence. Hence, I visited Ramu at his home while both his parents were at work.

Because of our language barrier, we were incapable of directly communicating with each other. Many of my child's feelings and thoughts were still a mystery. But I did know one thing – he trusted me enough to want to accompany me to the hospital for the required treatment.

"How can you be so careless as to let the wound fester to this extent? Only when we start operating on his foot, will we know how bad the wound is. There is a possibility that despite all our effort at trying to save his foot, we might just have to amputate it ankle downwards." - The surgeon's voice kept ringing in my ears long after he had uttered those words. Tearfully, I mumbled, "It's OK, doctor. Do whatever you can, to save his life." "His parents' signature on this form is required, to state that they have no objection to what we have just discussed," he said in a grave voice. "If you can make do with my signature, then, as his guardian, I'm willing to sign the documents. I'm his guardian."

It was a chance I had to take. I could not fear the risk of his parents' displeasure and anger that would be inevitable, were the doctors to amputate his limb. Panicky thoughts raced through my mind; in the worst scenario, I'd be responsible for the child having to live without a limb. Ramu's parents would be the first ones to hold me responsible for the same and I wouldn't know how to face them. Little would any of them realise that had medical intervention been delayed any further, it could have cost them their child's life. And what about Ramu himself? He might never be able to forgive me for granting him the life of a handicap. Yet, I chose to sign the papers. This decision of mine stemmed from a promise I had made to myself, right at the time when I had taken charge of the beneficiaries, months ago.

In the hospital lobby I paced nervously, my eyes darting from the clock to the operation theater door, waiting for it to open and to hear what the surgeon had to say. Finally, after what seemed like eternity, the door opened and the doctor walked up to me smiling, to give me the good tidings. "The operation has been successful. His wound was deep but we've managed to save his leg." At the surgeon's words, relief spread through me. I heard him out as he added, "I'd advise you to let him be in the hospital at least for a week. But since you insist that his parents will not hear of it, can you promise me that you will ensure that no infection sets in? Can you arrange for someone to bring him to the hospital to have his dressings changed every alternate day?" I assured him that I'd do so. A short while later, Ramu regained consciousness. Then, feebly waving at me, he smiled in recognition.

Even today, 11 years after the event, as I pen these lines, I can vividly remember Sashikant, a CRY colleague, picking up Ramu from his home each morning and carrying him in his arms to take him to the hospital, by cab, for post-operation treatment.

It had been a fortnight since the child had been operated upon, and I went to pay him a visit. Gently, his mother squeezed my shoulder, with tears of gratitude running down her cheeks. For a long moment, she was too choked to say a word. Then, she turned to Anita and told her to convey to me her heartfelt thanks for saving her son's foot through my timely action.

The ordeal had changed 4 individuals - Our child felt loved and well taken care of. As a result, he could be seen prancing about as before! His parents now had a greater understanding and appreciation of medical science. And, I experienced once again the healing power of God that had guided the surgeon's hands to save our child's limb.

After all these years, Sunbeam can take pride in having succeeded in its efforts at Community Development. The parents are now empowered enough to take the responsibility of their children's health. These communities avail of the medical facilities available at the Government clinics / hospitals.

Influencing prejudiced mindsets – the major struggle

Friends, this time I'm going to write about Jagdevi, my child who, at the age of 5, was expected to complete all household chores if she was to be granted permission to attend school!

In 1997, each time that Jagdevi came to our office, she was conscious of herself being shabbily dressed - would the CRY employees accept her presence at their office, in the not-so-good clothes that she was dressed in? She was a construction labourer's child. Yet, hers wasn't the kind of poverty that our children dwelling on the pavements of Mumbai had known; she at least had food, clothing and shelter. I could sense her shame through her repeated statement, "Didi, I always feel embarrassed to be in your office in these clothes."

"Of course, you may have not just one but two of the empty mineral water bottles," one of my colleagues at CRY responded cheerily one day to Jagdevi's request. It had been a simple request from a child, one that had been complied to immediately. Hence, I didn't even give it a second thought, let alone imagining that there was any connection between the water bottles and her absence from the Sunbeam classes. It was natural for children to stay away from the study classes once or twice a week. Hence, Jagdevi's absence merely for a day shouldn't have had me worried. But my instinct told me that something was wrong with my studious pupil.

"At your classes, you all pamper children too much. I want my Jagdevi to grow tough and strong. So what if she has fractured her hand? It's under plaster and is sure to heal in time," responded her mother in an impatient tone when I inquired about her!

Once her mother was out of sight, I asked Jagdevi on how she happened to fracture her limb. In a sad tone, she responded with, "Didi, I've to fulfil a condition put up by my mother if I'm to be able to attend study classes and the formal school thereafter. She expects me to fill up the two huge water drums i.e. enough water for our family of 6 to bathe, wash, cook, etc. Our room, in the building under construction, is on the 2nd floor, and the only two taps from which the entire labour force and their family members receive water are located on the ground floor. As you know, I've always had a very weak constitution, and it's beyond me to carry a bucket of water up the steps that are slippery because of the construction work in progress. So, I carry water in the two 1 ½ litre mineral water bottles, one bottle in each hand. That's the most I can carry at a time. The day before yesterday, I had already made 5 to 7 trips from the ground floor to the second floor, when I was exhausted, and in danger of falling off the steps. But in order to avoid my mother's wrath, I decided to carry on with my work without a break. Suddenly, I collapsed. Didi, instead of rolling down the steps, I fell sideways, from the 2nd floor and landed with a thud on the ground floor. As the building is still under construction, the staircase didn't have any banisters. When I came around, my hand hurt terribly, my head weighed a tonne and I felt I'd never be able to stand again. But mum immediately rushed me to the hospital and got my hand plastered. I'm feeling much better today."

It must have indeed been tedious, exhausting work for a 5 year old. I couldn't believe that her mother, of all the people, had forced it up on her. Upon being requested to share what compelled her to make her child work in this manner, she said, "It all leads to incredible guilt that I feel at times, and yet only if I were able to explain to you my situation in life. The fact, that at her in-laws' place, my child will have to slog day and night, is sufficient reason for me to believe that I'm doing the right thing in teaching her the household chores from now itself."

When I told her that like other children attending our classes, Jagdevi too had great potential, she expressed her fear of me making her child chase a dream that might lead nowhere. "What are the chances of her father allowing her to study beyond 6th or 7th standard?" A sceptical mother asked. "Very slim," she answered her own question. Then, without missing a beat, she added, "In a community where a boy's education carries more weight than a girl's, Jagdevi's irregular attendance at school and her lackluster academic performance is not at all a matter of concern to me, especially, given her bleak future prospects."

"Learning early on how to put up with injustice, is essential for my child to become a successful adult who will quietly and meekly bear all kinds of exploitations that will befall her, once she gets married. She could end up getting an alcoholic husband (of her father's choice). Moreover, what is the guarantee of her being fortunate enough to have in-laws who wouldn't torture her physically and emotionally?" Thus, she went on to paint the most discouraging picture of her child's future. She wouldn't dare to dream of a better one because she didn't have the emotional strength, she claimed, to see it not come true.

I had often wondered if the hard life that these womenfolk had endured, had made them into mothers who wanted their daughters to be like themselves and to bow in submission to injustice. Now, I understood that their anxiety about the future of their girl child was the main factor affecting their current behaviour towards them! The world the womenfolk of this community inhabited seemed natural to them. But I wanted to drive home the unfairness of it. The struggle to change mindsets had never been tougher. Part of my work was to convince Jagdevi's mother and the rest of the ladies in the community that they needed to make other choices. Neither did they themselves have to endure abuse in silence nor was it correct on their part to expect their children to do so, because nothing can make a child feel worse about herself than the conviction that she didn't deserve to be treated with dignity or to be loved.

Eventually, she agreed to her daughter continuing her education. But she also added that once her fractured limb healed, she'd make sure that her child attended to the household chores, as before, for the rest of the day.

A week later, Jagdevi was back at Sunbeam. It took quite some time for her to be able to catch up with the other students. But when she finished reading her lesson with as much fluency as the rest of them, her classmates broke into applause. Jagdevi herself was shedding tears of joy and success. I looked around the room, my own vision blurred.

Sadly, Jagdevi's case happens to be among the few where Sunbeam failed to impact the child's life in any significant way, because we couldn't change the mindset of the adults in her family. She had to quit school as well as Sunbeam at the age of 12. Her parents used guilt as a tool, to make her take up a labourer's job at the construction site where they themselves were employed, and justified their action by claiming that it wasn't out of any selfish motive that they made her work. "The income that we earn between the two of us is sufficient to take care of our monthly expenses. But how will we manage to save the substantial sum of dowry that her to-be husband will demand?

Isn't it her responsibility to earn enough to pay at least part of that dowry, so as to lessen our burden?" Her mother went on in this vein for a long time.

Since 1997 till date, it's been a very long journey. Yet, today, 12 years down the line, it goes without saying, that Sunbeam has achieved its goal of changing the mindsets of the adults in the families of our child beneficiaries. The parents of our 1000+ children have been very supportive - regularly attending the community meetings (the parents' – teachers' meeting) held at our education centers. Proud of their children's academic progress, they even willingly contribute part of the expenditure towards their children's education!

Thanks to the tireless efforts of our staff – the community workers, teachers as well as the counsellors – today almost 50 % of our beneficiaries are girls, that too up to SSC, and if all goes as anticipated, we are sure they will continue with further studies as well!

Sagar's Unfulfilled Dream of Finding a sense of Belonging at Sunbeam

In November'04, at the overnight camps at Aksa, as I sat jotting down the wonderful feedback on Sunbeam from the secondary section children, I noticed a child who lay on a couch in the staff quarters close-by. He was about 7-years-old. As he wept into his pillow, I was left wondering what he felt and what he'd been through.

I reached out to him, enveloped him in an embrace and held his shivering body till he calmed down. He was burning with temperature. "Is there anything I can do for you?" I asked gently. He violently pushed me away and once again started crying. "Didi, I'm feeling very lonely. I want to go home," he whispered. "All of us are there for you, my dear child. Once your fever subsides, you'll feel better," I whispered back. "Please call Anil and Sunny Kharwa. Tell them to be at my bedside. I'm so scared to be alone. Please call them," he implored.

I hoped that there was still a small window from which the ability to trust a grown-up could enter his little mind. How I wished that the teacher who was in charge of healthcare and medical cases at the camp would have seen her role as beyond giving a crocin tablet, to that of giving moral support and her loving company that the child was in need of just then.

Anil and Sunny were summoned. For a long time as I sat writing, I saw them silently sit next to the figure of their sleeping friend, Sagar Vagela, who was unwell. Now, Sagar's breathing was even. On waking up an hour later, he walked straight up to me. He looked at me for a moment, may be deciding if he should trust me. Then, most unexpectedly, he pulled his chair close to mine and sat relating the story of his life. He narrated in detail how his early sheltered and happy life had reached the point of lonely existence - he now lived on the streets. Friends, let me share the same with you as it came in whispers and with lots of breaks. Each time he would slowly raise his head, and would look at me intently to make sure that I was giving him my undivided attention.

"Didi, I stay on the streets of Kabutar lane close to the Sunbeam education center at Gol Deval. My father is no more. My mum is my only companion," he whispered. "No didi, he is lying. His mother too is no more. Why don't you ask him why she died?" Sagar looked defiantly at Sunny who had made this statement. "It's OK. Everyone dies one day or the other. She must have been ill," I said quietly to put his mind at ease. "She used to drink a lot," Sagar said, his voice full of embarrassment. "Why don't you also share with her about those strange men in her life?" This was going too far so I silenced Anil, who had uttered those words. One look at Sagar's face was enough for me to understand the pain he was going through at his private life becoming public.

In a subdued voice, my child continued, "Didi, I'm an orphan. My maternal granny is the only family I have left. She is willing to do anything for me. Still, every night I cry myself to sleep because I miss mummy." Lowering his voice further, he added after a pause, "Do you know something? My mum's soul is still wandering about. I don't think she is at peace even after her death. She often appears in my dreams. I know that her soul is still roaming." "No, my child, her soul is at peace. I'm sure of that." This statement of mine was to make him feel better but it had just the opposite effect on him. He grew hysterical and demanded of me, "How can you make such a statement? How can my mother's soul be at peace when she knows I'm so lonely on the streets?" I found myself choking.

"Didi, would you like to know how we survive on the streets? Mother (granny) purchases used, empty oil tins @ Rs.15/- per tin. She then cleans them up with kerosene. The next morning she goes all the way to Dongri to sell them @ Rs.25/- per tin. There are days when she is able to sell as many as 20 boxes and on other days not a single one." Then he wailed, "Here, at the Aksa camp, I'm not happy because I'm unwell. Early in the mornings it's quite cold and I keep shivering and feel sleepy when the didis expect me to join the other kids for jogging and exercise at the beach. Moreover, my mother must be lonely without me." Once again there was a long silence. As he looked at me waiting for an answer, I assured him that I'd instruct the Sunbeam staff that all those children who were unwell or down with fever need not join the group for early morning sessions. Feeling relieved, he went back to sharing more about his personal life. "Didi, on the streets we are often robbed of our meager earnings of the day. Mummy (granny) keeps the money in a small bundle of clothes that she uses as a pillow but on days when she is very tired after the day's work, she can't even make out when someone steals away the bundle right from under her head. If we don't take care of all those tin boxes, then they too get stolen. So mummy ties them all up in a row and makes me sleep on those boxes at night, ensuring their safety. Since the boxes are very cold, she spreads a saree on them to make them warm enough for me to lie on. Didi, the thick blanket, that Sayeshta didi had given me some time back, has been stolen. Believe me, I didn't sell it off." I was feeling sorry for my child and thought that that's about all that he had to share, so I didn't say anything. He seemed distracted. On my part, I felt sad that there was no way I could protect him from any harm on the streets.

"I can't recollect the face of my father. I lost him when I was 2. About a year ago mum died. Her ageing mother decided to take over my responsibility. This enraged her son i.e. my maternal uncle, who threw her out of his house. Now she lives on the streets with me though uncle and his family live in a proper home. On the streets of Kabutar lane, the municipal officials do not let us cook. Daily I have to make do with rice and dal from the hotel. Mummy is aware that I crave for homemade food. So she keeps saving a bit from the daily earnings. Every Sunday, she purchases 2 kgs of vegetables, grains & oil - enough to feed a large family. Then we trot to uncle's place. He doesn't mind our presence provided mummy cooks for the entire family. Aunt can't stand my presence though. We put up with her taunts every Sunday. Didi, I think I'm a burden on mummy and don't know what to do with myself." Sagar, was simply looking for someone to listen to him and accept him as he was. So I let him cry.

"Sagar it's OK. You may come and talk to me whenever you feel like it. But tell me something. Aren't you happy at Sunbeam? I hope you are." Now he looked at me but I knew he wasn't seeing me. "It's expected. What better treatment can a child like me expect from our didis?" he said in a flat, defeated tone and shrugged his shoulders as if it didn't matter. "It hurts but only for a little while," he added.

"We're bad children who deserve no better treatment." Now it was Anil who was speaking. "Didi doesn't beat us up so much when we are up to some mischief. She does so when we can't pick up the alphabet. We have no brains and can't seem to meet up with our didi's expectations. We're so dumb," he said, his voice trailing away with disgust at himself. "I believe we deserve all the beating we receive at Alka didi's (name changed) hands." Sunny nodded in agreement to this statement of Sagar's. Then he added his own bit, "Just two letter words. That's as far as I could reach in the past month."

I looked away from him. I could not bear to hear any more. Now it was me who was crying. His voice started to drift off. I couldn't concentrate on what he was saying anymore. I was totally disillusioned. Still numb with shock, I accepted with resignation that Sunbeam had failed in its mission – as far as this batch of students was concerned. The same isolation and indignity that filled their lives on the streets, had followed them at Sunbeam.

Sagar couldn't have shared his sorrow in more detail. He had wanted me to know about the coping skills he had developed-to compensate for growing up on the streets without parents, and at Sunbeam without love and acceptance for what he was.

That was not the end of my experience with Sagar and his friends. The most painful truth I had to accept was his next appeal to me – to call Alka didi to Aksa to give him company! I tried to calm him but he ran away from me, inconsolable. He claimed he felt secure only in two people's company - his mother and Alka didi. I was speechless. When he saw my puzzled expression, he clarified, "You may not raise your hand on me, but then the sad fact is that you do not seem to be having any time for good-for-nothings like us. But Alka didi lives just for us. She knows each of us by our names. Nobody else even knows who I am." Sagar's reaction was one of the most profound and deeply emotional one I had ever witnessed. Here was a child so lonely, that he wanted to cling on to the only didi from whom he believed he got his identity – even if it meant undergoing ill-treatment at her hands.

My thoughts kept shifting from the positive feedback that the majority of the 6th to 9th std. had given to this batch of students, who were still searching for an identity for themselves. Mixed feelings of anger at the staff concerned and shame at myself, for not having been able to mould that staff member to fit into our culture, enveloped me.

For once, while the 80+ children at the camp and their respective didis were busy with the events at Aksa, I felt removed from it and went for a quiet walk in the woods. In the dark, I could hear footsteps and I turned to find the 3 kids following me- "Please call up Alka didi from your cellphone and let me hear her voice." Unfortunately, the person who picked the phone informed me that she wasn't at home.

The days to follow were happy ones for most of them at the camp. Wrapped in their joys that they were, nobody even noticed the 5 children tug along with Meenakshi didi (Meenakshi Mishra – one of the teachers) on their way back home. They left the camp half-way through because they felt secure on the streets rather than face the isolation amongst us.

At Sunbeam we have watched dreams of hundreds of children being fulfilled. Our organisation's very existence is to help kids emerge from their difficult childhood and become self-reliant, responsible, caring adults, having experienced unconditional love and acceptance during their childhood. From my end, therefore, I make every attempt to sensitise our staff to the special needs of our beneficiaries so as to ensure that every child gets ample opportunities to experience Sunbeam as a nurturing, secure home away from their homes. Sadly, some of our staff members who can't mould themselves into the organisation's culture despite our efforts at orienting and re-orienting them, leave us with no option but to request them to move away from Sunbeam.

5 year old Mahesh's plea to the adult world

A long-gone evening at the Shiva Home (name changed) would never fade from my memory. This charitable institution housed terminally ill children and their family members – those who lived in the villages but were temporarily in Mumbai for medical treatment for their cancer affected children.

During my visit to the home along with a volunteer who taught academics to the children, I was informed by one parent that some children were responding well to the medical treatment, others weren't. Some of these children went to the hospital for treatment during the day and returned to the Shiva Home in the evenings.

Mahesh, (5), caught my special attention for resembling our Sunbeam beneficiaries in being lively and playful. He was also the youngest amongst the lot. He had leukemia and a life expectancy of anything between 3 weeks to 3 years. He had already been through a grueling month of chemotherapy and the rest of the necessary treatment. But my child was too young to understand what was happening to him, or to sense the despair that his parents felt. I was told that there were times when he felt too ill to take food and would get confined to bed for long spells.

He came and sat next to me and asked, "Do you love me, didi?" "Yes." The answer had come straight from my heart. To my shock, he responded by giving a sudden twist to my wrist with all the might of a 5 year old, and was successful in dislocating it, leaving me dazed and in excruciating pain! Others in the room were equally stunned.

Mahesh seemed to be captivated by the result of his action. At the same time, he appeared to be driven by a restlessness that did not seem to have quelled. "You are in pain, aren't you?" "No," I replied. He appeared unconvinced. That a child who had met me for the first time had so much anger against me and wanted to hurt me, was very bewildering.

Within seconds, he sped across the room and started rummaging Jagtap's schoolbag. He gingerly took out the compass from the geometry box, claiming that his need for the same was more than Jagtap's. My attention was soon drawn to another child, who was engrossed in painting. I watched on as he splashed colours and his painting took the form of a school in a village environment. Suddenly, I was hit by someone. For a moment I wondered what had happened. It was Mahesh once again. He had pierced the sharp end of the compass right into my hand. The pain was unbearable.

"This time, are you in pain, too much pain?" he asked, pausing to study my reaction. "Yes, it's paining a lot," I replied honestly. "Good, it makes me feel a bit better to hear you say so." Then, pausing, he gave a sad smile, and with deep feeling, continued, "I'm sorry. My intention wasn't to hurt you in any way. But you needed to experience the pain I undergo on a regular basis whenever they bring me to Mumbai. That's how I feel when needles prick my body. Can you please convey my message to all adults to stop causing pain to us children?"

It was one of the most profound communication experiences I've ever had. As he saw the blood trickle down my wrist, he froze and turned pale. Then, in a very stern voice told me not to cry and added that he'd see to it that I'd soon be feeling well. So saying, he popped out a Colgate toothpaste tube from his pocket and applied the paste on my wound! It didn't take me long to comprehend that Mahesh was enacting the scenes of his own medical treatment at the hospital, where ointment or dettol must be being applied to his wounds after the injections or blood tests.

Amid the silence that filled the entire room, the voice of a concerned parent could be heard asking, "Didi, are you OK?" "I'm managing. Just leave us alone," I responded quietly.

I was moved that Mahesh believed he had finally met an adult whom he could trust enough to express his hurt by actually hurting her, and yet not have fears of any repercussions save that of a deep understanding from her of the pain he underwent in life. He had communicated this message to me so powerfully by all his actions in the past half-an-hour! It appeared that his anger that had built up in the past few months, had transformed into determination today. His anger was directed at the adults whom he believed were responsible for his pain. And his determination to bring the same to their notice via me, an adult again, by causing me similar pain!

Gradually, the reality of his pain-filled life began to hit me. He had given me an opportunity to see beneath the surface (of his smiling face), beyond the obvious and the evident. No doubt, he was a terminally ill child. But wasn't he also a child in need of a special kind of support at all levels - psychological and emotional? He searched my face for any anger and relieved at finding none, he came and sat on my lap, and within minutes he was fast asleep!

Mahesh's simple ways of expressing his confusion and anger at the discomfort he underwent at the doctor's hands, had unlocked something inside me. The experience had touched me to the core. I realised I was the only 'didi' he had treated this way. Trust is the key to all relationships. The high level of trust that the child had placed in me had made communication between us effortless and instantaneous.

With Mahesh still fast asleep on my lap, I now turned my attention to the larger group of children. Those who were 8 and above seemed to understand that their lifespan was short, and appeared shattered. They lived day-to-day with no clear purpose in mind.

"I'm sure each of you are going to pass your exam papers with flying colours," said the volunteer cheerily at the end of her study session with them. A few children gave her expressionless looks. One child sank deep into her seat, as though trying to make herself invisible and then sobbed uncontrollably. Sheila, (9), asked me in a voice loaded with cynicism, "Have you too come to teach us academics so that when we go back to our village in a month or two, we can keep pace with the school syllabus?" The boy sitting next to her managed a brave grin.

With a grave face, a 12-year-old girl sitting behind him looked up to me, introduced herself as Aruna, and said simply, "Didi, you wanted to hear us sing. You're the one who gave Mahesh the space that he needed so I'd like to sing a song to you - in my mother tongue, if you don't mind. For all I know, I may not even survive to go back to my village this time. Or, in all probability, I may not be feeling well enough to sing when you decide to visit us next." I studied her expressive face, surrounded by a mass of unruly hair. There was love and softness in her eyes as she added that she'd always remember me with fondness. Now I could understand why the teacher's encouraging words were not having the desired impact. Because her words were getting drowned by the frightened voices within their minds: 'Chances are we're not going to survive through the yearly exams period.'

Until that moment, not even I had appreciated how vulnerable the children seated before me were. As a visitor I was taken aback by the uncertainty of their lives, and the trauma that they underwent due to the awareness of their illness and its possible consequences.

Aruna sang in her flawlessly angelic voice and held everyone in the room spellbound. I didn't understand her language but others translated it for me, saying that it was an appeal to the Lord to let the bird out of the cage and allow it to fly into His arms.

No academic success could compensate for the lack of emotional and spiritual support in their lives. My convictions about the same grew deeper and stronger after this evening.

Mahesh woke up and gave me a lovely smile. "Didi, will you visit us again? Every week? Or even more often?" The urgent plea in my child's voice broke my heart. His request was straight and simple. But as I replayed the last 2 hours in my mind, I had to admit to myself that it was a commitment I couldn't make. The almost instant trust that Mahesh and the other children had placed in me had seemed a genuine miracle. But a miracle that brought along immense responsibility and commitment of time, and an emotional and lasting friendship that they were expecting of me. And I couldn't promise them that.

If I had promised to visit Mahesh again – it would have involved a painful sacrificial process – especially when he would have then got emotionally attached to me to want me, to be next to him all the time. And I would have been able to accede to that kind of a request only at the cost of my work and time at Sunbeam. Besides, knowing myself, and considering how much I felt drawn to these children, I wouldn't have been able to restrict my visits to once a week and at the specific time that the rules at the Shiva Home would have demanded of me as a volunteer. Moreover, I couldn't risk getting emotionally involved with these children - their life was ebbing away and I may not have the spiritual strength required to be able to take the stress that would go with it, especially each time that I'd helplessly watch a child succumb to his / her illness.

Nothing destroys trust faster than breaking a promise. So, I didn't promise Mahesh another visit. I explained to him that I too hailed from a village, was on a short visit to Mumbai, and would be returning home in a day or two. I also explained to him, in as simple a language as possible, that those adults who were pricking him with needles truly loved him and that they were making every attempt at helping him become stronger and lead a healthy life. But I did promise him, as per his request, to pass on his message to the world: that adults need to handle children with utmost sensitivity. He seemed to understand, and gave me a warm and tight hug as he bid me farewell with a broad smile on his face.

Friends, I've kept my promise to Mahesh by not only sharing his story with all of you who are reading this book, but by sensitising the Sunbeam staff members to treat all our child beneficiaries, including the two of them detected with acute leukemia, with utmost love and dignity that they deserve. One of our children ultimately succumbed to her illness a few years ago (i.e. in January'06) after immense suffering for two long months that she spent at the hospital, but where she found Sunbeam didis a constant presence, reassuring her that she was not alone in her struggle. The other child seemed to be on a roller-coaster ride – on the road to recovery one moment and then a relapse put him back into the hospital. After a long period of suffering, he too succumbed to the illness. In both cases my only consolation is that our staff had been there for them to make their journey easier.

When I had met him in 2000, Mahesh may have been not over 5 years. Sometimes I think of him and wonder whether he survived his illness or succumbed to it. But in my heart, he'll always live on as the child who had loved and accepted me wholeheartedly and made me a more caring human being.

Here are some of my questions to nursery / primary section children and their unique and spontaneous responses:

- *"Biswajeet, what is it that you don't like about me?"*

  "You have no dress sense."

- *"And you, Rajan, my dear fellow, what is it about me that you like?"*

  "You are as full of faults as I am (by your own admission), and that's really comforting. It makes me feel better about myself despite my limitations. My own class teacher is too perfect. I don't think I can ever be like her. Instead, it's so easy to be like you."

- *"Rakesh, do you have to say something to me?"*

  "Yesterday night you appeared in my dream."

- *"O that's wonderful. Did I give you some gifts?"*

  "No, even in the dream, you seemed to scare the wits out of me - by appearing in the doorway the moment Sayeshta didi threatened me of complaining to you if I didn't stop playing mischief in the class." The little devil gave me a tight hug and said, "Oh you are such a demon!"

- *"Nanda, why are you holding the pencil this way? I think that's the reason your handwriting is not up to the mark today."*

  "Since the past 5 minutes I've been making unsuccessful attempts at writing. I was simply trying to imitate you by holding the pencil the silly way you do, because I want to be like you in every respect."

- *"Kanchan, what can I offer you to make you happy? An ice-cream, toys or an outing?"*

  "Your residence number. Then I'll know that you're just a call away, and I can be sure that I am not alone on the streets."

- *"What is your dream in life, Tina?"*

  "Do you see the wedding hall yonder? Every night I am at the gate, and they hand over the leftovers to me. The fish and meat is sufficient for my entire family. But I wish that one day someone would invite me to a party. When I hear the band and watch the children of the invitees dance, I too feel like joining them."

When I recount the intangible achievements of Sunbeam, I'm at peace. No doubt, the academic progress of our children is of utmost importance to me, given that Education is our main focus area. Yet, rather than insisting that the yardstick to measure Sunbeam's success be just academic progress, I have begun to appreciate and understand the deeper impact we have had on innocent minds and hearts of our 1000+ beneficiaries.

Friends, as you must have gathered from the above case stories of children; we have been blessed with implicit trust and affection from them. Years may pass before anybody will be able to witness the absolute power of the unconditional love and support that they receive in equal measure from the Sunbeam staff during their interaction with us. Almost everything that the kids experience at Sunbeam will form happy memories that would later resurface, taking the same form of beautiful unconditional love and support. The only difference would be that this time the gift would be passed from them to others - the gift that they have been blessed with at Sunbeam, the gift of total acceptance for what they are.

4

Learning from the Children

Introduction

Maths, Language skills, History, Science and Geography – subjects, the knowledge of which is considered vital if one is to become literate – that is what Sunbeam wishes to give its beneficiaries by an entry into the mainstream of education. But that is not all – a strong foundation based on sound values and principles is even more important to enable every child of ours to grow up into cultured, caring and compassionate human beings.

However, life being hardly a bed of roses for the underprivileged, opportunities get taken away quicker than they come, the features learnt beyond the four walls of a classroom, though cannot. This chapter is devoted to the narration of the lives of a few of those who had embarked on their journey to a bright future with us, but who could not persist. Yet, each of their lives is enriched with values – many of which they imbibed during the short duration that they spent with us.

The reasons for having to quit Sunbeam were varied – parents shifting residence to far-off suburbs, unavoidable hardships of life, or the loss of one / both parents to death or to circumstances. Yet, every one of these children are presently leading dignified lives – none of them have gone astray, or given in to antisocial practices. Deeply ingrained morals and ethics have led them to pursue honest jobs – Shiva works as a courier boy; Maruti, as a salesman; Durgadas desires to drive an auto-rickshaw. The lessons in zeal and courage they received at Sunbeam have prevented them from surrendering to the unfairness of life, however depressing matters might seem.

There's Sunita, who is educated till Secondary, but who vouches to school her off-springs in future; Padma, who succeeded convincingly in preventing herself from becoming a child-bride; Shiva, who still wishes to obtain a degree via correspondence studies; Naresh, who doesn't hesitate to share possessions with fellow-students, even after having lost a great deal to life. These children uphold truthfulness and honesty (as witnessed in the case of Nikita). At the end of the day they are human. And at times, they do tend to get frustrated with life, and vent out the desperation on other similarly unfortunate people. But, proper guidance and an appropriate channel to voice their feelings can transform the unintentional insensitivity to consideration.

Sunita – a School Dropout not out of Choice

In 2001, Sunita Patel, (9), got to know of Sunbeam, but had to take the tough decision of staying away from school, in order to supplement her mother's income. Babita, (7), her younger sister, became a part of Sunbeam classes, thanks to Sunita.

It seemed that Sunita, by herself, did not have the slightest chance of winning life's battle. But as the months and years unfolded, my vulnerable child suddenly appeared to have overcome quite a few obstacles. Luck did not play any part in her victory; it was her sheer will-power.

Looking at her smiling face, that always reflected joy and peace, one could never feel sorry for her. One day, sometime in June 2002, she surprised me by her resolution of earning and learning at the same time. She got herself directly enrolled into the 4th standard with Sunbeam intervention and attended classes once a week till she could convince her mum of the need to attend school regularly.

At 5.30 a.m. she would wake up and go to the Byculla wholesale market to buy flowers or berries for her mum to sell. After helping her mom prepare a mid-day meal, she'd be off to school. Evening saw her back on the Charni Road station bridge selling seasonal fruits, flowers or berries. Thereafter, from 8 p.m. onwards, she coached other children attending Sunbeam classes and then before going to bed, finished her household chores.

What had moved me so deeply about this fragile child was her capacity to defeat me in my belief that she needed protection and support to make her dreams come true.

In June 2003, once again it was different. It was a very heart-breaking end to her past 2 years' struggle for continuing her education. One day, as always, she was the one asked (by her mother) to make sacrifices, to defer her dream of carrying on with her education.

Regretfully, her mother advised her that it was time she quit school and started supplementing her income by once again selling flowers or berries on the railway bridge; this time from morning till night, with no respite. Sunita took her counsel to heart. No amount of coaxing or reasoning with her mother - that we were willing to give her (i.e. the mother) a permanent job, as a household help, that would fetch a decent income for the family - made her rethink. Her casual attitude towards her own children's education and future was appalling.

At first, I could not bring myself to venture to that railway bridge. Sunita's frail and vulnerable form – the mournful look on her face - broke my heart. The same bridge held too many memories of our journey together during the past 2 years, that had made her reach up to the secondary section in the formal school.

Her parents' separation is something she had not fully understood as also her mother's total indifference to her academic career. Any child in her shoes would have felt challenged. Sunita had endured more than she could. It wrenched my soul to see my girl hold up with such grace and strength. I could imagine her trauma at having to give up on education, especially after all the effort she had put in to gain admission into a private school on merit. Sunita faced that setback, with the same bravado she had when facing the school authorities, two years ago.

The parents' role, in development work with children, is crucial. In Sunita's case (as in a few others'), we failed to change the course of her future. But, a majority of the parents do cooperate with us. To them, nothing is more important for their children than the chance to education. They also believe that, given the right direction, their children will some day, carve out a niche for themselves. Such aspirations stand as a beacon over their living conditions. These devoted parents want to give their children advantages, however small, that their own parents never dreamt of giving them. Hence, over 90 % of our child beneficiaries are, today, availing of formal education provided by Sunbeam, as you would have read in the Academic Progress Report that forms a part of this book.

After living all their lives under the Charni Road station bridge, fortunately, they were amongst the few families of street dwellers who were allotted permanent premises at Mankhurd - by the Government authorities. In order to sustain themselves, up until 2006, the mother and daughter continued to come all the way to Charni Road to carry on with their work of selling flowers or berries.

However, in 2008, through another child beneficiary, we got to know that Sunita got married at the age of 15. Unfortunately, we've lost touch with her and are not aware of her whereabouts or wellbeing.

Padma, (12), Playing the Role of a Surrogate Mother to her Siblings

In 1999, with her mother away in the village for yet another delivery, Padma had, unquestioningly, taken upon herself the role of a mother to Laxmi, her younger sibling; and was missing out on the carefree joys of childhood. Three more of her siblings had succumbed to illnesses. Her father was a labourer at a construction site close to CRY. Her food – plain rice, twice a day, with a handful of chillies – had a direct bearing on her health. All the time she looked exhausted. One day, I gently inquired of her as to why she was not to be seen since the past few days, and she revealed that she was sort of bed-ridden. She added that for almost a week, she had been running temperature. Amidst sobs, she said that the day before, her father had given her an ultimatum - of getting herself cured or else of facing the consequences of being sent to the village permanently. Initially, I took her to a private doctor. A few days later, when the fever didn't subside, I took her to a hospital where the doctors concerned didn't see the need to admit her, though her temperature was fluctuating between 100* - 104* since almost a week.

The cramped, unhygienic and unsafe 5 ft x 7 ft room at the construction site, where I left the sick child, comprised of a world of horror. Unhygienic, because of the filth around, with no electricity and with water dripping constantly through the roof, the damp room was their kitchen-cum-bedroom. Moreover, it was an extremely unsafe place for Padma because other children had shared with me, the encounters that they had had with the older boys staying at the construction site, at whose hands they had suffered physical abuse. I watched on helplessly as Padma, burning with temperature, crouched in the only dry ground space available. "Padma, is your room always so damp? Where do your younger sibling Laxmi, and your dad sleep?" I inquired. Thinking that she was being blamed, she blurted out, "Didi, I know I am the eldest child. Everyday I allow Laxmi to sleep in the dry space. Didi, I do not have a blanket. Today, even after covering myself with this cloth, I'm shivering. So, I thought it wouldn't be too bad on my part to request my younger sister to take my place just for tonight." Then she covered her face - Was it anger at being misunderstood, or an attempt to conceal a child's pain?

The next morning, I got her admitted into Harkishandas hospital, where she was diagnosed with Malaria. It took another week to bring her temperature under control. I shudder to think what would have been her fate had not timely medical treatment been administered to her.

On the first day in the hospital, Padma's father had begun opening up, bit by bit. The man, who, in the past, must have watched on helplessly each time a child of his died, was left speechless as he witnessed the love and care his daughter received from the hospital staff, and as didis from the CRY office took turns in staying with her at the hospital. It reduced him to tears, and for the first time, he, who had always looked upon my presence (rather, that of our project) with either indifference or mistrust, now, amongst sobs, shared his feelings with me. He managed to confide how rotten he was feeling for not being able to do much for his daughter; for being cruel towards her, by expecting her to do all the household chores in spite of the fever, and that he did not know how to repay our kindness. Then, he walked up to Padma and enquired, with genuine love and affection, as to what he could bring along when he next came to visit her at the hospital. (He was even willing to stay at her bedside, but the hospital rules did not permit a male member in the children's ward.) I felt I was witnessing a major turning point in their relationship. The man kept his word and, every alternate day, was at her bedside with the promised fruits and biscuits.

One of our CRY colleagues came forward to foot the hospital bill. Padma was discharged from the hospital 10 days later. It was not just medical relief that helped her. What speeded up her recovery, and was indirectly responsible for giving a new lease to her life, was the love, care, compassion and affection of all CRY staff members but more so, of her father. For the next 2 weeks she attended our study classes. Thereafter, she and her younger sister took turns to stay back home to take care of their 3-month-old baby sister, since her mother was back in Mumbai and at work, as a labourer, at the construction site.

The circumstances in her life did not enable her to study further and join the mainstream. She could never attend a formal school, yet Padma's is a case that tells a story of success at a unique level – that of woman-empowerment.

As she moved ahead in her own life, Sunbeam lost touch with her over the years. Time brings about vast changes in people, and takes each one of us to diverse paths along the journey of life. Memories were all that had been left of her, as hope of meeting her again got diminished by the day.

It was, therefore, a grand surprise when she turned up at the Sunbeam education center at Ambedkar School in Worli, one lucky day in 2007. And an extremely pleasant surprise at that! For my frail little girl had grown into a dainty, healthy and lovely woman. Her innocent face clicked immediately in memory – she needed no introduction.

She revealed that she had been married for 2 years and was leading a happy life. Immensely gratifying was the fact that she had convinced her parents not to get her wedded before she turned 18 years of age, even if she had not been studying. "I've witnessed the innumerable problems that my mother had faced as a consequence of an early marriage, and I wasn't keen on history getting re-made with me. 13 years is not an age to get married at, 18 is," the 21-year-old's words are a source of pride and gratification at succeeding in bringing home the most vital message for girl-children.

One factor that helped get her point across to her parents was the role that she played at her maternal home – almost that of a home-maker: tending to the younger children and helping with the daily chores. Not that they wanted to exploit that opportunity, but somehow it deterred them from giving her away in marriage at the earliest.

She considers herself fortunate to have a kind and caring husband, one who gives due importance to all her needs. A supervisor at a construction site, he doesn't demand that she work to supplement his income. He feels his earnings suffice for both of them, even after sending a part of it to his parents who stay in the village.

Another encouraging result of Padma's short association with Sunbeam is her decision of delaying having children until she is mature enough to be a parent. "Didi, years ago, you had explained to me that even if one has to get married at an early age, one should not hurry into starting a family. There is an appropriate age, and only when one is confident and able enough to shoulder the responsibility of a baby, should one go ahead with having one. That's the reason we did not plan a family for 2 years," she said.

Those lessons learnt beyond the boundaries of the classroom have struck a chord so deep that she is determined not to have more than 2 children, to value equally a girl-child, and most importantly, to give them the lasting gift of a sound education, a right that life had denied her.

Beneficiaries can Count on Sunbeam for Justice

Once, a 9-year-old beneficiary shared with Shanta Koli (our Counselling and Community Development Manager) her trauma of having been molested at the hands of one of our male staff member. For the sake of the rest of our beneficiaries, I prayed that this be the only sad case which would never repeat itself, and I sincerely hoped that this incident wouldn't diminish the faith that our beneficiaries and their parents had placed in us. Moreover, I consistently prayed that I be able to handle the matter utmost sensitively.

If our child had kept it to herself for 2 long months and now was able to talk about it, it was because a similar incident (less graver though) had occurred. During the interval of her weekly sports session with another NGO, a passer-by had tried to molest her. She had managed to escape unharmed. The man was caught and mercilessly beaten up and later taken into police custody by the NGO in-charge. Yet, from the way our child reacted – she didn't seem to calm down at all - Shanta, who is an extremely caring mother, friend and mentor to our children - someone who the kids find easy to confide in - got the child to open up. To Shanta's horror, the child disclosed to her the real tale of trauma that had occurred at Sunbeam itself - trauma that she had not yet gotten over.

It was crucial that I take the right steps to rectify the situation or the damage to the child's psychology would be irreversible. So, we decided to lodge a police complaint against the concerned staff member. The child's parents needed to know that the Sunbeam management would stand by them in bringing justice to their child. After giving her verdict to the police during her second visit to the police station, the child did calm down. Her tears dried up. On our way home, I found her face expressionless except for the tiny hint of a smile at the corner of her lips - a glint of gratitude perhaps, or sheer relief at having ultimately been given an opportunity to unburden her pain so that she did not have to live with it just by herself. Moreover, medical reports confirmed that it had been a case of molestation and not of rape.

Though she felt too embarrassed to come to the Sunbeam classes after the above tragedy, she didn't discontinue with her formal schooling. She continues to study on her own and has politely declined our offer of sponsoring the cost of her private tuition, claiming that she could manage without support at least up to the 8th std. Her parents' faith in our organisation is intact, and they continue to send their son to Sunbeam classes.

The Story of a School Drop out - in his own Words

"Didi, Shiva is not eligible to be a part of our project," shrieked Birju, a migrant labourer's child. "He has a permanent house in Bombay. Doesn't that place him in the category of the privileged?" demanded Durga, another child living in a makeshift tin-shed at a construction site. This was in December '97. I decided to pay him a visit at his house to find out for myself whether we could enroll him at Sunbeam, and whether his economic status would make him eligible for the same. His house of bricks and concrete turned out to be the 2½ ft x 8 ft space beneath the steps of a building, close to our education center. That was the house that the other kids were talking about, a house that accommodated his mother and the belongings of the family. Shiva, his two elder brothers and dad slept out in the open.

Shiva Pathak was a school drop out who had undergone bypass surgery in 1996 (due to malfunctioning of valves) at the Sion hospital (also known as Lokmanya Tilak hospital). His parents claimed that his medical expenses, to the tune of Rs.1,00,000/-, had been sponsored by a host of individuals / trusts who had come forward to support them in their hour of need. They consisted of Mr. C.M. Gandhy, Trustee of a philanthropic organization; Mr. Navratan Kothari, a diamond merchant; one of the Tata Trusts, and their own distant relatives. Thereafter,

Shiva had given up on himself. When he was nearly 10 years old he got to know of Sunbeam (known as the CRY neighbourhood project in those days). He had visited our Arthur Road center 2 months back. His health was still fragile, but not as bad as to make him stay at home anymore. So I was determined to get him back to a normal childhood and had succeeded in doing so.

Disturbed to note that Shiva had stopped attending our classes since a week, I went to his house to find out for myself what had held him back once again. "In Bombay, every inch of space fetches money, and the owner of the building premises - bent upon making us homeless - very nearly succeeded in the plot he had brewed. Last Tuesday, Shiva was brutally beaten up by the police for the alleged robbery of a costly golden crown adorning the statue of the divine mother." Pointing out to a nearby temple, Shiva's mother continued in the same dry tone, "This kind of an entry in the police records was apparently sufficient to force us to vacate our premises and to scare Shiva enough not to dare to pass by the temple ever again. Unfortunately, it happens to be the route that leads to your project center. But with God's grace the culprit has been caught. Imagine the culprit being the temple priest, of all the people! Being an influential person, no action was taken against him." Shiva's mother's voice was wary, forlorn. She looked up for the first time during her painful recital. For a moment, my suggestion - that since the issue had resolved itself, it was now safe for Shiva to once again start attending our class - was met with disapproval. She claimed she couldn't risk another attack on her child. Her eyes were defiant. With the passing of time, the look of despair gave way to a flicker of hope. She grasped my hand and looked deep into my eyes to make sure that I wasn't making light of her trouble. Then, she dropped her head on my lap and sobbed.

Once his mother was convinced, Shiva was back at Sunbeam, and, in June '98, was enrolled into the 5th standard.

His parents were proud of him. It was as if they had come through a long, dark tunnel. They have not emerged from it yet - but are reasonably positive that, at last, they would see light beyond the tunnel. They have travelled the route from the state of complete helplessness to that of a better childhood for Shiva. His mother's eyes were again brimming over with tears, but this time around they were tears of joy.

Friends, after penning the above story for my book on children's case stories, rather my learning experiences with them, I found myself stuck. This was an incomplete case study. I wanted to update it but didn't know how to go about it. That's because after a few years of being with us, along with his family, Shiva had moved to the suburbs of Mumbai. Hence, I had lost touch with him, except when he called me up once a year to inform me of his promotion to the next class till he reached the 10th standard. In 2006, it had been over 2 years that I hadn't heard from him and I surmised that he must have failed his SSC exams, which was why he must have been feeling too embarrassed to call me and share the news.

On 8th June '06, my cell rang. It was Shiva on the line - "Didi, how are you? I haven't spoken to you for a while. I was thinking of you and so called up. After failing in my SSC exams, I've been working at some place or the other. I'm on night duty at my current place of work." He couldn't have called me up at a more appropriate time. "Shiva, I'm in the process of writing a book on children and yours happens to be one of the case stories. Would you be comfortable with the idea of your case study getting published? In any case, I plan to change your name prior to its publication. Besides, if you can drop in at my place whenever time permits, I'd be happy to get more details from you, especially on the kind of job you do. Are you well? Are you happy at your current job? Have you thought about your future?" "Didi, Sunday nights I get to sleep well because it's my weekly off. Hence, let's meet up at your place on Monday afternoon."

On 12th June '06, my child took me by surprise as he entered my home. He was almost 6 feet tall now. He was still his usual shy self though. Yet, there was a vast difference in the child standing before me and the one with whom I used to interact in the past. Now, my 18-year-old was a confident, independent adult. After lunch, in a businesslike tone, he requested that we get down to work – updating his case story. He had to reach home by 6 p.m. so that he could catch up on sleep for a few hours before going to work, where duty hours were 11 p.m. to 7 a.m.

As I read out the details of his childhood days to him, he suggested a few changes. This is what he had to say. "Didi, would you like to mention the date when the bypass surgery took place? It was on 19th March '97. And you've mentioned the size of our house as 2½ ft x 8 ft, but you seem to have overlooked the fact that we lived under the staircase. Therefore, in reality the space was about 2½ ft x 6 ft. The rest of it was a steep slope under which we could keep our few belongings, but were not able to sit or lie down. And, by the way, in the alleged robbery incident, you have mentioned that the stolen crown was one that used to adorn the divine mother's statue. There you have got it wrong. It was Lord Dattatreya's temple."

After I jotted down the necessary changes, he started giving me an update of his life beyond Sunbeam.

"Didi, I was studying in the 7th standard, when the harassment from the residents of our building reached the limit. They cut off our water supply. Dad's salary, over the years, had risen from Rs.1,600/- to Rs. 2,564/- p.m. He worked as a security guard for 12 hours a day. My eldest brother, Sunil, who works as an electrician, currently earns a salary of Rs.3,300/- p.m. and overtime of Rs.700/- p.m. which was earlier lesser. Over the years, between the two of them, they had been able to save some money. So, in 2001, dad took the courageous step of purchasing a small house of 250 sq.ft. for Rs.95,000/-, at

Vithalwadi near Kalyan. Initially, he made a payment only of Rs. 45,000/-, and the balance he paid off in easy installments.

A sweetmeat company absorbed me as a worker where I worked for 3 - 4 months during the monsoons. I worked 12 - 16 hours a day, and spent the nights too over there. I was promised a salary of Rs. 2,000/- per month, with food and accommodation. But every month, I received only Rs.900/-. And, I worked under extreme heat, right inside the room where the sweetmeats were being prepared." Here, Shiva laughed. Not out of anger at his bosses who exploited him, but out of embarrassment. Then he continued, "My next job was at a small unit that made Chaklis. (Chakli is a fried food item made of wheat flour.) Here, I was expected to handle two kinds of jobs. One was that of working in the bhatti i.e. the place where the chaklis were being prepared; hence, once again I had to work under scorching conditions. The other assignment was to hunt for wood, collect and bring back a huge load of it by 4 p.m. I used to scout the area on a cycle, and that made it easier for me to finish the work in time. The people working at this unit were staying next door, so they used to come and knock on my door at 6 a.m. to wake me up. I'd get dressed and leave by 6.30. They dropped me back home late night, sometimes as late as 11 p.m. This was Mondays to Saturdays. I was never expected to work on Sundays. Moreover, if I'd be unwell or take a few days off, they never cut my pay."

Friends, throughout as he shared his story, he had a smile on his face, and his eyes lit up every now and then as though they were not sad memories but those that gave him the satisfaction of knowing that he could earn, even if it was very little. Then, getting a trifle annoyed with me, he asked, "Didi, why are you planning to change my name in the story? I'm quite comfortable with my story being published in my own name."

After a long pause and upon receiving my answer that it would be as he wished, he carried on with his tale, "Currently,

Pradeep, my brother (elder to me by 3 years) and I, are employed with a courier company, since August '05. We started off at Rs. 2,600/- p.m. each, and now our salaries have been raised to Rs. 2,900/- p.m. I'm assigned the job of manually entering the incoming mail. We have approximate 50 - 60 employees doing the night shift. I work overtime on Sundays, and get paid @ Rs.125/- for 8 hours per Sunday and @ Rs.10/- per hour beyond 8 hours."

"Shiva, are you happy with what life has to offer you?" He met my gaze with a look of contentment as he answered, "Didi, I give away my salary to my mother, but the overtime money that I earn – an approximate of Rs.165/- per Sunday - I keep as pocket money, and it's more than enough for me."

"Shiva, what's your dream in life?" Here his instant response was, "In my free time, I've started learning data entry on the computers. Because in the company where I currently serve, those working on the computers get paid in the range of Rs. 4,500/- to Rs. 6,000/-, depending on their seniority in the company."

Shiva had then joined the computer course which he could not pursue beyond 10-12 days, because the faculty required him to complete a module in MS-CIT before they could enroll him for the data entry program. Presently, Shiva is 20 years of age, and still works with 'On Dot Couriers' (Goregaon). Having been employed with them for 4 years now, he draws a salary of Rs. 4,000/- per month, the same being Rs. 4,500/- per month for his elder brother. The overtime has also been raised to Rs.1,000/ -a-month.

However, Shiva gives all of his salary and overtime earned to his mother now, and requests her for the cash for his personal needs whenever required. Both his brothers have been married, and all of them stay together in their Kalyan home.

About his work, he says, "My work involves sorting the varied kinds of documents that arrive from metros such as Delhi, Bangalore, and from all over India in general, you know didi – the kind of documents that must be getting delivered to your house by courier boys."

The end of November'08 saw him hospitalized with a serious bout of malaria. Despite the infirmity, the matter weighing more importantly on his mind was the heavy expenditure (Rs. 50,000-55,000) that his family had to incur as a consequence.

Though he is happy with his current job, he does not plan to work in the same capacity forever, because the night shift is fast taking a toll on his health. He desires to study further and have a suitable career, and he plans to start this from the academic session beginning in 2009.

He spent 4 years of his academic life with Sunbeam. "Shiva, do you believe you gained anything from Sunbeam in the few years that you were with us?" I asked. "Didi, had Sunbeam not entered my life 8 years ago, soon after my bypass surgery, I may not have continued with my studies. If I'd have remained illiterate I'd not have landed up with this job, earn for myself and lead an independent life that I do now."

Maruti's Priorities in Life

At Sunbeam, our children always face challenges with a smile. Maruti Kamble is one of our ex-students who has set his own goals, and done his best at everything he set out to do.

This dates back to October '04. When urged to share with our students, his own experiences in life, the then 16-year-old boy looked around hesitantly, shy to speak in front of an audience. So, after taking his permission, I related his story to them, just the way he had narrated it to me.

"In 1999-2000, when in the 5th standard, I had the privilege to attend education classes at Sunbeam. My father used to be on daily wages at the Kamala Mills construction site, where he served as a labourer. Unexpectedly, our entire family shifted to another construction site, this time far into the suburbs. The didis at Sunbeam put us in touch with another Non Government Organisation in the vicinity, so that our education would carry on uninterrupted. While my younger siblings Suvarna, Bhau and Archana could make it to the tuition classes, I was not so fortunate.

Dad doesn't earn enough and mum's health does not permit her to work at the construction site. So, I was left with no option but to take up the job of a part-time labourer at the site, where I worked after morning school. Thereafter, I secured a job as a liftman and served there for about a year. All throughout, I, somehow, managed to continue with my studies. I've made sure to keep in touch with the Sunbeam didis over the phone, and join all of you each year at the yearly overnight camps, where I volunteer by helping the didis in handling the younger children.

This year I'm in SSC. I'm weak in almost all the subjects. Currently, I'm employed as a marketing person for a factory that manufactures pens. Keeping the bare minimal profit margins, the pen costs Rs.30/- to them. Then, when I get orders from the clients to get their names embossed on the pen, it costs another Rs. 5/- per pen. Hence, the cost to the company is Rs. 35/- per pen. And we salesmen are allowed to quote the price at Rs. 50/- per pen. This gives us an earning of Rs. 15/- per pen.

I continue to make two ends meet. This time, the job allows flexi timings, leaving me free to attend school regularly. But I'm sorry; I can't take up Sunbeam's offer of enrolling me into private coaching classes to see me through SSC. My priority is my family's survival."

We are grateful to Maruti for allowing us to share his story with our hundreds of students, to make them understand how fortunate they were at receiving the opportunity to education and full support from their parents.

That evening, as Maruti approached me, I could tell from his face that he was excited - as if he had some good news to share. He quietly placed a gift-wrapped parcel into my hands and wished me a Happy Diwali. It contained a pen with my name embossed on it. Little did my child know that by sharing his story with our other beneficiaries, he had already given Sunbeam the best gift of the season.

Five per cent of our students drop out of Sunbeam almost each year for various unavoidable reasons. 70 - 80 % continue with their education, at least, up to SSC. Later on they take on a vocation of their choice. Similarly, in Maruti's case, since years, there has been no one in his family to take over the parenting chores from him, so that he can be a child or accept quality education that Sunbeam has to offer. Although he could not appear for his SSC exams, his case may still be considered a success story: He has given of himself to higher ideals – to his family's survival and well-being.

Maruti's tenure with Sunbeam was limited to just a year (1999 – 2000). Our teachers did not have the privilege of providing long-term education opportunities to him, ones that would have taught him to make a comfortable living through a bright career for himself. But, they did succeed in teaching him something far more valuable and lasting – how to live, while continuing to make a difference to another's life.

Friends, I had penned the above case story as an attachment to our Sunbeam monthly report in end 2004. Thereafter, I had added it to this book in 2006. After going through the draft of this book, a friend suggested that wherever possible, I could consider giving the full names of the people involved, as that would add to the authenticity of the case-stories, and that I should also be using full names of children, if available, except where I had chosen to use a cover name in order to protect a child's identity. Having been with me on my journey with our beneficiaries for over 9 years now, Shanta and Mohini are the staff members whom I turned to, for providing me with the required data on children who were mentioned in the book. Within an hour they dictated to me the children's full names, except where the case studies belonged to a period prior to themselves having joined Sunbeam i.e. the 1997 to 1999 period. Shanta got in touch with Maruti via Anjana, a distant relative of his. Maruti was touched at the idea of his didi writing about his life. He readily complied to meet me at my home the very next day (i.e. 16th July '06) as it happened to be a Sunday.

"Didi, I no longer sell pens. It's nearly 2 years since I met you at the Aksa camp which is about when I gave up working for that company to join a pharmaceutical concern. This company was at S.V. Road at Malad, where I worked as a delivery boy for about 5 months, 12 hours a day, at a salary of Rs.1,700/- p.m. Thereafter, for a year, I did a very different kind of a job. My role now involved installing terminals at the PCOs (public telephone booths) all over Mumbai to activate the Reliance phone service, for a remuneration of Rs.2,000/- p.m., for 8 hours of duty. Besides, the customers were quite generous with their tips. Moreover, I did a side-business to earn some more income. I'd purchase PCO coin boxes from the distributors @ Rs.1,900/- per box, and market them to the customers with a profit margin of a few hundred rupees per box."

Meals were ready, and I told Maruti to join me for lunch. I added that he should bear with me if he found the food too bland as compared to the spicy meals that he and our other beneficiaries are used to having. He graciously responded with, "Didi, the food served at the canteen of the Atharva college (where I'm now employed as a peon since the past few months) is also somewhat bland, just as the meals prepared at your home. So, don't worry. On days when I'm unable to carry my tiffin from home, I do have meals at the college canteen. I'm quite content at my current job at the Atharva college located at Charkop Naka, Malad West, very close to my residence."

Before he could take my leave, I asked him if there was anything specific Sunbeam could do for him. "Can Sunbeam sponsor some vocational training for me, for instance, a course in mobile repairing?" was his prompt answer. I've given him the contact number of our Manager in charge of Vocational Training. My child left my home, content in the knowledge that he could always count on Sunbeam's support.

Maruti continued to look for opportunities through which he could earn a decent livelihood, and could make a difference to the lives of his dear ones. During early 2008, when he approached me once again, looking for a change in job, he was welcomed back warmly into the Sunbeam family – as an Office Assistant. He performed various kinds of duties from 9.30 a.m. to 5.30 p.m., handling most of the outdoor chores – the bank work, delivery of important documents to and from the education centers, as well as handing over parcels in appropriate hands – for a remuneration of Rs.3,500/- per month. However, this task could not hold his interest for long, causing him to be irregular at times. 3 months later, he took leave from this job ruefully.

Reminiscing fondly about his tenure as a Sunbeam employee, he says, "I used to enjoy part of the outdoor work, like going to the bank. It used to take me 3 hours of traveling to and from work each day (Malad is 1½ hours from Charni Road office by train). I do regret quitting Sunbeam."

However, his warmest memory of Sunbeam is the day he had joined the organization as a student. "Amongst the many values I learnt at Sunbeam, the most important one is the significance of hard work. It was one of the best periods of my life. I would love to be a part of Sunbeam once again some day," he says respectfully. He keeps in touch with me regularly and I wish him good luck for all that life has in store for him.

He, then, started working as a salesman for a CD shop, for a salary similar to the one offered to him at Sunbeam, the only difference being that he had to work 12 hours-a-day to be entitled to the same. He took it all as a part of the process of growing up though – life teaches the hard way sometimes. He was content because he saved commuting time due to the shop being located in Malad.

Currently, his father is unemployed due to lack of suitable jobs in the construction field. The responsibility of the entire household rests with 20-year-old Maruti, the eldest of the 4 children. He presently works in two shifts. As a peon at Atharva college, from 8 a.m. to 6 p.m., for a salary of Rs. 3,000/- per month. And at the CD shop from 7 p.m. to 11 p.m. He is paid on the scale of Rs. 40/- per day on week days; and Rs. 140/- per day on Sundays and holidays, when he works at the shop from 10.30 in the morning to 11 p.m. as the college remains closed on such days.

Of his current occupation, he says he is more at ease at the shop. He enjoys the work, and according to him, it helps him to get more business experience about the "line", which would help him start up a small venture of his own in the future.

His younger brother studies in the junior college, and a younger sister is a student of the 8th Std. Sunbeam assists in bearing the education costs of both these children.

As for his career ambitions, he muses, "At present, I have no educational aspirations as such. I know I can't study because I've no time for it at the moment. For me, earning and acquiring a CD business of my own is of utmost importance as of now. Nevertheless, I'm keen on my siblings completing their education. I shall see my dreams and ambitions come true through them." Our boy has turned into a responsible adult, whose selfless desires touch the heart and inadvertently moisten the eyes.

Importance of Value Education in a Child's Life

Mahesh Kamble, who had recently joined Sunbeam as a community worker, was in charge of hygiene at the 4-day yearly camp at Aksa – a camp for 100 children from the 5th standard. One afternoon, he approached me seeking my assistance. Some of the children whose turn it was to clean up the hall that afternoon after meals, unlike other children, shirked their duty and had fled. He wished that I counsel them and imbibe in them a sense of responsibility, while he got busy cleaning up the place himself.

Friends, I've already discussed at length (in the earlier pages), my views on how I'd like a child with limitations such as learning disabilities, etc. to be treated. Now I move on to an equally important aspect of a child's life – on how he needs to be moulded. Being firm is also being loving – for the child's own well-being.

Moulding a child to be an ideal student is by no means an easy affair, and certainly not limited to the academics. Though it begins with formal education, it does not end there. Until a child has learnt the basic values in life, he has a great deal of ground to cover. To my mind, it is as important, or even more, for children to be morally educated as having academic knowledge. In their formative years, education is a must but if we overlook teaching values and ethics to them, somewhere we'd be failing as friends and didis to our children.

Acceding to Mahesh's request, I approached the batch of students who were in charge of hygiene for that afternoon. They were playing on the swings. Instead of lecturing them, that might have had a minimal impact on their behaviour, I tried to look at it a little differently. "Mahesh bhaiya is looking for you all. Why don't you go and lend him a helping hand?" I said in a light tone. In an off-handish tone, Radha (name changed), one of the students replied, "Mahesh bhaiya has almost finished doing the work all by himself. So, now there's no need whatsoever for us to be there." "In that case, don't you think you need to go and say sorry to him for having disobeyed him and made him do work for which you were responsible?" I asked seriously. My suggestion was met with an unexpected rude reaction. "Well, then why should I just say sorry to him? If you say so, I'd better still, go and touch his feet. Will that satisfy you?" Initially my child's tone was a trifle incredulous and in the latter part of her response, downright rude.

In a firm tone I made myself clear, "You have two options. Either let Mahesh bhaiya know that you're willing to do your share of work or, no more camps for you." My ultimatum seemed to have the desired effect on her. She nodded, a little crestfallen though for not being excused. Aarti (name changed), her didi at the education center where Radha studied, had always been extremely lenient with her batch of students, who never received even a gentle rebuke from her for any lapses on their part. Aarti mistook firmness for harshness and therefore her children couldn't tell right from wrong.

I explained to Aarti and the other staff at Radha's center, who thought on the same lines as Aarti did, as to where they had slipped. Children needed education that would build fundamental traits of character – such as respect for elders, sense of responsibility, good manners, etc. Just as a potter shapes clay, it is in the teachers' hands to mould their children so that they grow up to be independent, contented, happy, spiritual, contributing adults in society.

Nikita Upholding Sunbeam Values

One has a tendency to believe that underprivileged children lack in values. But Sunbeam children have, time and again, proved that it's a myth.

11-year-old Nikita Patil who had lost her father, now stayed with her maternal uncle along with her mother. She used to study in the 6th std. at our Chandanwadi center. Our child didn't think twice before picking up a cell phone that she spotted in the sands of the Chowpatty beach, where she was playing - not so that she may take away what belonged to another, but rather, out of honesty. She intended to return the phone to its rightful owner. And she instantly put her intention into action. She informed a policeman at the beach who called out to the passers-by to find out if it belonged to any of them. Getting no response, he too gave up - leaving Nikita with no choice but to return home with the mobile.

Her mother advised her to hand it over to her Sunbeam didi. This is what Chandraprabha, her class teacher, had to say of her, "Didi, I'm so proud that I'm a part of Sunbeam. My role is very demanding and at times I'm not sure whether I can handle the kids. But after Nikita's gesture, I believe that no challenge is insurmountable." She assured Nikita that now that the phone had been handed over to her, she'd do the needful.

Our office staff managed to trace the owner of the phone from the Airtel authorities, who provided them with his name and address. Upon receiving his lost cell phone, Mr. Pandiraj Garappa Naidu, residing at Dhobi Talao, called up. What overwhelmed him was the fact that it was a child, that too from the underprivileged society, who had found the phone and had thought of returning it.

Mr. Naidu, personally, called me up at the office to let me know how grateful he was. He added that he was proud to know that Sunbeam was doing such commendable work, because Nikita's act of integrity spoke of the values we imbibed in our children. Before he disconnected the line, he made it a point to request me to thank Nikita on his behalf.

Sunbeam Reunites Bhura with his Family

One day in end March'03, Shanta (who was then the Supervisor at the street children center) walked into our office with 3 extremely quiet boys. "Didi, poverty led them to run away from their hometown. But now they are tired of living on the streets of Mumbai and want to return to their families."

My first impulse was to tell Shanta that we had never handled such runaway cases. That it would be extremely difficult to trace their families and hometown. Besides, at Sunbeam we had never as yet taken street children living on their own in Mumbai. Our 130+ pavement dwellers in themselves had always been such a big challenge even though they did have family support and therefore, some amount of protection on the streets where they dwelled.

Hence, the innocent and naughty faces smiling back at me, with complete faith that they had reached the right place and would soon be on their way back home, left me wondering. Given that Sunbeam's outreach was limited to just daycare centers and for child beneficiaries who had parents or guardians to take on their responsibility during the nights, at an organisational level, there wasn't much we could do for these children. Yet, Sunbeam could at least put these children in touch with the right kind of NGOs in Mumbai – those which had night shelters or those which catered to the needs of children who had runaway from their villages. These NGOs would then see to it that they were eventually reunited with their families.

I immediately called up organisations whose focus area was to nurture and send back the children where they belonged. I also contacted some NGOs who have 24-hour service for children in distress, and others who have night shelters - but with no positive outcome. They either expressed inability to be of help in any way or they recommended me to yet another NGO where I was informed that the staff concerned was on a week's holiday and that I could get in touch with them later.

During the day, Bhura (11), Raju (9) and Pappu (7) had survived on the streets of Mumbai (since the past month or so) by begging, and the nights were spent on the platform no.1 of the Charni Road station. The very first day that they landed in Mumbai, these children had been robbed of their few belongings that they had brought along with them. To add to their misery, they had no roof over their head and never knew where their next meal was to come from, and wanted to be back home.

"Didi, we came from Mansor to Mumbai. We want to go back but at the Mumbai Central station, the ticket-checker won't let us travel without tickets. Can you help?" The travel agent whom we contacted, was at a loss to understand where exactly their destination was and named at least 8 - 10 similar sounding stations in Madhya Pradesh, but nothing close to Mansor. I had almost given up when the agent asked me if I could gather any specific information on their hometown. The children mentioned Fatehgar in Madhya Pradesh. The travel agent was losing his patience. Just then, I suddenly remembered that the eldest child could read the clock precisely and had a sharp memory. He revealed that his grandfather used to live in Indore, where he had visited him as a child. Now it was the agent talking directly to the child and he did the impossible – got the facts out of the child. "Madam, I am booking the tickets both for the children and the staff accompanying them – from Mumbai to Ratlam, and from there on, by a connecting train to Mandasur." I wasn't sure whether it was the right destination but he insisted that the child had said that if he boarded the train at 9 a.m. from Indore it would reach Mansor sharp at 3.30 p.m. So we booked the 1st available confirmed tickets to Ratlam.

After spending 4 days in the company of loving and caring didis of Sunbeam both at the office and at our Chandanwadi center, to my horror, they had very nearly changed their minds and didn't want to return home! It was an extremely diffficult task for me to make them understand that it was in their best interest that we wanted them to live with their family. This was not because of rejection or lack of love on our part but because they'd be safer in their home-town than to be all by themselves on the streets of Mumbai.

On the 5th day, they were on their way back home. Each of them was returning with memories of days filled with fun, movies, center visits and lots of unconditional love. The youngest seemed to be eager to be back home. Raju, (9), the most mischievous among the lot, seemed a little pensive. But it was the eldest one - Bhura - who could not come to terms with the idea of leaving Sunbeam, where he had felt valued and secure as compared to with their parents, where all 3 of them were expected to beg for a living.

"The 3 of us together earn about Rs. 30/- per day. On lucky days the amount goes up to even Rs. 60 - Rs.70." "And what do you spend the money on?" I asked gently. "Bus fare costs Rs.10 per day (since we have to daily travel from Fatehgarh to Mansor to seek alms, for there'd be no one to turn to in Fatehgar, that is merely an impoverished little village), 1 kg of wheat flour, a few onions, may be rice, and 100 gms dal." What do you do with the balance money that you earn on the lucky days?" "I buy a coconut, walk up to the village temple and offer it to Lord Hanuman. Still if some money is left I purchase chana flour and prepare sevai at home or go for a movie." "Do you have a school in your village?" "Yes, we used to go there. Now, they have stopped the midday meals, and during the monsoons, the roof of the classrooms leak. After such a long break that we have taken this time, I doubt that they'd take any of us back. Yet, we promise you we'll be back in school half-day and shall beg only for the rest half of the day."

"Why did you insist on a photograph with us? Is it so that you can remember us? I too am going to treasure our snap together. Didi, I don't think I'll ever forget Shanta didi or you. I've decided to keep my commitment to you - of not running away from the village ever again. I'll even keep calling you up from an STD booth closeby. Years down the line, when I come to Mumbai, I'll no longer be the child you've met, but a grown-up man. What if you fail to recognise me? That's when I'll produce our photograph to prove my identity." Bhura said these words with deep feeling and with respect.

On our way out of the Sunbeam office, Bhura kept on touching the walls of the building and said, "I'm saying bye to the only place in Mumbai that I'll never want to forget." The unspoken words were clearly visible in Bhura's and Raju's eyes, "Do we have to go back? Is there no way you can keep us with you?" Mamta, our accountant, entered the office with a beautiful frame from a gift shop nearby. Bhura rejected the kind gesture. I found his behaviour confusing but only until he whispered into my ears, "Didi, there is no point in wasting Rs.175/- on the frame. In the village a photoframe will cost me merely Rs. 20/-."

Simply sending them back home didn't seem to be the right thing to do. If only I could ensure their basic necessities in life - their education and wellbeing - would it mean that Sunbeam had actually succeeded in bringing about a change in their lives. But my problem was that I wasn't sure that Mandasur (the place the kids were heading to, as per the travel agent's decision) was the same as Mansor, that they were talking of as their hometown. Or were we on a wild goose chase? Even if Mandasur did turn out to be the destination, I didn't know a single soul in that place who would want to help children in distress.

At the Mumbai Central station, just as I was thinking on these lines, a gentleman next to me said, "Come, let me help you read the train booking chart where your tickets are still on RAC – (reservation against cancellation). I'm a C.A. by profession and am on my way to Indore. I know extremely influential and caring people in Mandasur. Rest assured that Fatehgarh is a village just a few kilometers away from the station. So the children are travelling to where they should be. Here, take down the names and numbers of the Manager and the Head Clerk at the Central Bank in Mandasur. Give my reference and they will do the needful, both in tracing the children's family and also enrolling them into school, sponsoring the cost of books, uniforms and other education-related costs." Then this kind gentleman, Mr. Shankar Somani, guided our office staff to the connecting train to take to Mandasur in time to meet the concerned people at the Central Bank. Because, on Saturdays, the bank would be closed in the afternoon. All the while, Bhura's eyes were fixed on a 15-year-old boy who had entered the train to beg - a child with both his hands missing. The train was just about to leave. Holding on to Shanta and me, with tears brimming in his eyes, he said, "Didi, if someone were to cut off my limbs, I wouldn't even be able to make a call to you to let you know of my plight."

That Saturday morning, I called up the Manager of the Central Bank at Mandasur. He gave me the good news that our staff members and children had reached, and were standing right before him. He added that he was more than willing to do whatever was required, to see that the children received support towards education.

Within an hour of the conversation, I received a call from Sanjay, our Office Assistant, who had escorted the children back home. "Didi, the mother's joy knew no bounds on having her children back. The father who has left the village in search of them has not returned as yet. But everyone is hopeful of seeing him back in the village. The Central Bank Manager is a genuinely kind and caring person. But didi, what I called you for is not only that. The Sarpanch of the village (the village head) has called a meeting of the village-folk, who are rejoicing at the reunion of the children with their mother after almost 2½ months of futile search on their part. The Sarpanch personally wants to thank you for all that Sunbeam has done for their children." So saying, Sanjay passed on the line to the Sarpanch who expressed his heartfelt gratitude for the children's safe journey back home.

Who says that there is no kindness left in a world full of strife and pain or that there is no hope for a better future for our children, with so many individuals wanting to walk that extra mile?

Jyoti's Nursery Kids Keep her in High Spirits

Commitment is too mild a word for what our staff brings to our work place. Their passionate involvement finds expression in selfless, dedicated support to our cause that stretches beyond the normal working hours. It stems from a feeling that God has given them all an opportunity to bring about light and laughter in the lives of those children and thereby, in their own lives as well. It is this strong belief that gives them the emotional strength to carry on despite all odds.

Some time in 2002, this is how our discussion at the orientation workshop, for the new recruits, went about. Each one came up with positive experiences while Jyoti Narkar, teacher at the Worli center, was the last to speak up. "I believe that at our center, we haven't managed to bring the children's academic levels up to the expected standard. It makes me feel so low." I asked her to relate any one heartening episode at the Worli center that had taken place in the recent past. Immediately her eyes lit up and she responded with a touching and hilarious story!

"It was past 8 p.m. when we had finished with our community meeting. As I got up to leave for home, disappointed at not having received much of a response from the parents, the scene that met my eyes made every setback I had faced at our Non-Formal Education center worth the effort. 18 children – age group 3 – 5, stood in a neat row with slates in their hands, the first one tugging at my dress and another holding my hand, ready to march off to the garden where their daily classes are conducted in the natural surroundings under the trees. The little ones didn't realize that it was 8 p.m. and not 9 a.m. All that had registered to them was that their didi had come to fetch them!"

Even while relating the message, her depression began to lift. She suddenly became aware that what the 3-year-olds had given her that day was a moment of insight into the kind of place she had made for herself in their innocent hearts, a gift far greater than any kind of appreciation from me, for giving of herself completely to Sunbeam and its cause.

Each time, I apply the same policy to myself as well. At times when things don't seem to work, and self-doubt assails me, all I have to do is pause at the door of one of the education centers and allow the sweet, angelic voices to wash over me.

Our field staff members continue to tell me their experiences with children, and like sunshine, their words nourish my soul, displaying their strong convictions that each of us at Sunbeam share, touching my heart and mind, spurring me to action.

Children's Defence Mechanisms to Cover up their Vulnerability

"One day, on our way to the sports ground, Kiran Kharwa broke the queue and ran off. But it didn't appear out of the ordinary, considering that he was a child who never paid heed to what I had to say," Shubhangi Shelke, teacher at the Chandanwadi center, responded softly to our request of sharing with us any of her experiences with children. Strangely, there didn't seem to be any frustration in her voice. Instead, joy and achievement were written all over her face. Her statement, to follow, made it all clear – "Didi, I was too stunned to believe my eyes. Kiran had noticed a visually impaired person testing the ground with a white cane, with cars whizzing past him by inches. Concerned, he hurried towards him and offered to hold his arm. He not only aided him in crossing over, but also took him all the way up to the railway platform, before running back and joining our group."

'The seeds sown in a distant past bear fruit in a future we can never envision' – The thought struck me like lightening as

I heard her out. In a flash, before my mind's eye appeared the scene of a few years ago – a complete contrast to Shubhangi's narration. It was an unsettling experience revealed to me by Jyoti Narkar, another teacher:- One day, under her supervision, the same group of children was being led to the formal school when they encountered a mentally-challenged woman, sitting in one corner of the road in tattered clothes. Before Jyoti knew what was happening, she found a child pick up a stone and hit the woman. The others followed suit. Then, all of them carried on with their journey to school as though nothing had happened!

I couldn't believe that children could be capable of such extreme cruelty towards a fellow human being. How could they be so insensitive? Suddenly, I put a check on such thoughts and chided myself for my own extremely judgmental attitude towards my little ones. Even though their act did not have to be condoned completely, I didn't have to react too soon. Hence, even just in thoughts, if not in words, I was making the error of playing the role of a typical teacher – a teacher who could not resist the urge to launch into a long sermon with the children, who were sure to resent the same thoroughly. I had to get attuned to their emotional state; hear out their side, instead of sermonizing them and as a result shutting down any meaningful communication between us.

I told Shruti (name changed to protect identity), (8), who had been the first to stone the sad soul oblivious to the happenings around her, to feel free to share with me the reason that could have possibly led her to cause pain to another fellow human being. She seemed to be far away, immersed in her own thoughts. Her face masked any emotions she felt. She looked at me thoughtfully for quite some time. Finally, she broke down and cried. In bits and pieces she related her own story of pain. The teacher was not around, and the child claimed that it made it easier for her to talk because she had already received a proper scolding for her insensitive behaviour.

Just then, my child was in no frame of mind to understand the gravity of her error. So I simply let her talk and unburden herself. I could understand her reasoning as she tried to justify her action. She could never express her feelings either at home or at school, and today her suppressed anger had found a violent expression.

Simply being heard made her feel better. My silence and acceptance of her, telling her that I could understand her feelings and that she had me and the didis to turn to, had a calming effect on her mind. "Didi, do you think I did something very wrong in hitting that woman?" "I believe, it was very nasty of me to have done so. I won't ever repeat it," she said as an afterthought, as she prepared to leave. All I had done for her was to give her the space to sort out her conflicting emotions and find her own answers. Empathic listening on my part sealed our bond.

Perhaps my expectations of my staff was too high. Perhaps. Anyway, I explained to the teachers that sometimes our criticism could be disproportionate to children's wrong actions stemming from the pain that they were themselves undergoing. No doubt, we had to reform but we must handle such cases sensitively.

After 2 years of this incident – 2 years of Sunbeam's presence in the lives of these vulnerable children (i.e. in 2003) – hearing Shubhangi relate an extremely positive story of a child from the streets, whose life we hadn't yet managed to change in any radical way, was a sure sign of Sunbeam's impact. Consistently, showering these kids with unconditional love, we have indeed brought about a transformation in their lives. They were growing up in an environment of love. And the didis at Sunbeam with their unconditional support, put a check on these children's feelings of bitterness before they grew out of proportion or took the form of any kind of violence. Shruti, after spending 2 to 3 years at Sunbeam, one day enthusiastically declared, "I want to become a Sunbeam didi when I grow up, and I'll teach many, many children."

Naresh's Father Continues to Live Via Naresh

The day he entered our lives (some time in 2001), he captured our hearts. He had a high sense of self-esteem and self-confidence that the majority of his friends living a similar existence on the pavements of Mumbai lacked. He was chirpy, kind and loving. He overwhelmed us by his little acts of kindness to his friends in need despite him not being any more fortunate than them. Six-year-old Naresh was simply adorable. From him the Sunbeam didis and I received lessons in unconditional love, caring and sharing.

I vividly remember my yearly overnight trips with my children at Aksa and at Karjat. More often than not, during the year, I visited them at their study centres or the slums / streets where they resided. But that couldn't compare to being with them on these camps - staying up late, talking, remembering, laughing.....

During the Aksa trip in May 2002, one afternoon, to my confusion, a few of the children got up from their dining table and announced that they had decided to skip lunch. While one said he didn't feel hungry, another quipped that she wasn't feeling too well. A few more joined them saying that they too would play in the garden rather than have lunch! I checked out on the dishes to see if there was something that they possibly wanted to avoid eating.

Naresh Kharwa, (9), who was both a mischievous prankster and a warm-hearted good samaritan, solved the mystery, "Didi, according to our teacher's timetable, today it is Papu's turn to serve food along with the few others who are on the list. For your information, he is a sweeper's son and some children consider being served by him to be below their dignity, an act that would pollute them. This is what their parents have ingrained into their heads." "And, what about you, Naresh?" I asked. "Papu is my friend and I'll happily partake of the food he serves."

We had a long chat with the group. Some children gave in, having understood that all of us were one, regardless of the caste we belonged to, whereas a few remained stubborn. "Evening tea and snacks, as well as today's dinner, will be served by Papu along with the others chalked out in the list," I declared, much to their dismay. But that did not make them change their minds, and they skipped lunch.

That evening, while the rest were playing at the beach, I called aside those few. "You insist that I daily sit with you all and have lunch. Very often, you have even offered me food from your own plates, fed me with your own hands, and I've always felt privileged to be your friend. Do you really consider me as your friend?" "But of course, didi," they all answered in unison. "Well, I never knew that the caste of a person is a matter of concern to you. Frankly speaking, I too belong to the same caste as Papu. Will you still allow me to join your lunch group? Do you all really believe your lives have become polluted by my touch?" Two of them looked away and the others sat crying. "Come, let's have tea with you," said one pulling at my hand. "But then why discriminate between Papu and me?" "He too can join us," they answered meekly. (Temporarily, I had managed to help them do away with the conditioning that they had grown up with, within their own homes. I had made a mental note that in the next monthly meeting with their parents, this topic would form a part of the agenda.)

Handing over a pair of his own clothes to Papu, Naresh addressed him as an elder brother would, "Papu, why give others a chance to criticize you? Here, I've have an extra pair that you may change into, after a bath. And here's a soap to scrub the pair you've been wearing since the past 2 days." After Papu left, I thanked Naresh profusely for his generosity. "But why thank me, didi?" he asked with a puzzled frown. "Dad always taught me to share. He used to tell mum to always cook more than for the 3 of us so that no hungry soul could leave our door empty-handed. I'm simply living the way he'd have wanted me to, had he been around."

Naresh had lost his father a few years ago, but he always remembered him with fondness and pride. This was one such occasion. Naresh lives on the streets of Bhuleshwar, and his mother weaves and sells flowers for a living. Today, that episode of 7 years ago is still fresh in my memory. My child's face reappears before my mind's eye and I can clearly see him frown once again, his question echoing over and over again, "But why thank me, didi?"

A child's mind is open to the many influences that he is exposed to. The impressions made by his father on Naresh's mind have remained there. The good thoughts and values he had cultivated in his child have stayed with him long after he is gone, though I believe, his father is not gone, he lives on in Naresh.

The Deepest Desire of a Child's Heart

The day he entered our lives (some time in 2001), his high sense of self-esteem and self-confidence captured our hearts. As you must have read in his earlier case story, the chirpy, loving boy overwhelmed us by his little acts of kindness to his friends in need, despite himself not being more fortunate than them. 7-year-old Naresh was simply adorable.

His transition from a life of illiteracy to that of joining the educational mainstream was smooth and easy due to his positive attitude towards life. He attended the Chandanwadi BMC school for 5 years – up to the 5th std. – during afternoons, when Sunbeam didis were allowed to teach there. His mornings were spent weaving and selling 'gajras'.

Just when Naresh had started to paint the canvas of his life with hopes and dreams, the school authorities barred the services of Sunbeam teachers. With the BMC staff now teaching them, the children missed the rapport, warmth, and patience of Sunbeam didis, and started remaining away. Gradually, they accrued enough reasons to discontinue studies and go back to the streets, where they felt at ease. Naresh was one of them – for him, learning once again became dull and pointless.

Having lost his father at an early age, Naresh now had his mother admitted to the TB hospital at Sewree, Mumbai. Her condition was critical. Standing at the crossroads of life, all by himself, fearing to face the stark reality of the life that lay ahead, the 13-year-old was missing Sunbeam's presence.

Fortunately, our plans of re-starting the center for the pavement dwellers of Chandanwadi / Bhuleshwar had begun taking form around the same time. When Naresh and the other students visited our Charni Road office, we offered to make a new beginning to the learning process, which had unfortunately stalled mid-way. All of them promised to give it one more try – Naresh promised to cover the portions up till the 7th std. level through Sunbeam coaching. It was the period of Diwali festivities, and the entire group accepted joyously, our invitation for the Aksa Resort overnight camp from 14th to the 16th of November '07.

Naresh had become very desolate; he didn't seem very enthusiastic about participating in the games and other events that were held for the students' entertainment. To help him forget his sorry state, even if for a brief period, the concerned didis tried to persuade him. But what he said shattered their spirits. "Didi, I don't doubt my competence, rather I am sure of winning and also of receiving a 'trophy'. But I do not want to join in because there is no one back home whom I may go to and share the news of my victories with."

Supposing himself to be a burden on his uncle, he wished to begin fending for himself. He recalled how his parents had been instrumental in supporting numerous migrants from his village into Mumbai. His mother had even adopted a street-urchin, who, estimating the mother's terminal illness, had left them when he turned 19 years of age. The eloping of his sister added to his miseries. Yet, a few days with Sunbeam staff at the camp brought him back to the education classes, and he showed remarkable improvement in studies. Admirably, instead of the Chandanwadi center, he preferred to join the Worli one, notwithstanding the daily travel all the way from Bhuleshwar, to study with the other Higher Secondary students his age. Naresh had neither lost interest in studies, nor the old charm of coming up with quick-fire answers – whether they were correct or not, didn't bother him much. It was heartening to see our child as his own confident self once again.

It was the first Sunday of December '07. Amidst all the enjoyment at a water resort at Virar, we received the expected yet devastating news of the passing away of Naresh's mother. Mohini didi's visit to her and her assurances of taking care of Naresh (via Sunbeam) might have helped her depart peacefully. Though grieved, Naresh was in control of himself, as we had taken enough care to mentally prepare him to face the impending tragedy.

At his pavement residence, it was yet another day to weave flowers, to earn their livelihood... nobody seemed to give much credence to what had occurred, no one tried to comfort the bereaved child. The funeral was a mechanically executed formality. Our hearts ached at our child's plight.

Naresh went on to live with his friend Kishan and his mother on the pavements. He could avail of food from a restaurant outside Gol Deval, for which coupons had been provided to him by Sunbeam. Though he felt hungry lots of times in between meals, he refused coupons for snacks and breakfast, saying that he could earn that much by selling 'gajras'. Worried about the coupons getting stolen, he kept them with a fellow-student, Pooja.

Naresh never lost the importance of the values instilled at Sunbeam. When offered Rs. 500/- for clothes and slippers, he graciously accepted just Rs. 200/-, so that the rest could be utilized for another child. He returned after the funeral. Timely support made him more responsible – he never failed to inquire if a particular day was a holiday, or to inform of his absence in advance.

He presently stays with his aunt, though his married sister also stays in Mumbai. Despite little family support, the boy does not give in to temptations.

During Diwali of 2008, he called me up. He had injured an eye while bursting firecrackers, and had lost vision in that eye. After 2 days' local treatment, he was advised to get hospitalized. When he visited me with a friend, he was given a sum of Rs. 1000 for his medical expenses. By evening though, he had not been admitted. Upon inquiring, it came to light that weaving flowers, and completing the orders for the day, so as not to miss out on wages, was more important to the family than eye-cure!

And yet, a few days later, when I called him to follow up on how he was getting along, I was told that the doctor had prescribed wearing spectacles, as his vision was getting normal by the day. He said, "Didi, I spent Rs. 200/- for medicines. I have my hospital case-papers, but I have misplaced the bills. Also, this month I could not manage to earn, and hence, had to spend Rs. 20/- daily for my meals. This amount too came from the one Sunbeam had given me towards medical expenses. I am left with just Rs. 500/- now, which I wish to return to Sunbeam."

Such is the self-respect in the child who has no one to turn to in this vast city. Rather than take assistance all the time, he prefers to earn for his own self.

He tried joining the Worli center, but found it difficult to mix with the group. Nevertheless, he wishes to complete his studies by joining night school, and to build a secure future for himself.

His heart-wrenching desire...

The heart of a child longs for the warmth that only a mother can give. His craving took me unawares once. "Khurshid didi, is there any possibility for you to adopt me?" he asked. I was left in a dilemma, which he immediately pulled me out of. "It was just a fleeting thought. Someone just gave me this idea," he said. Though the void in his life cannot be filled, we at Sunbeam shall ensure that he is made to feel accepted and is able to lead a dignified life.

Ambitions Amidst Struggles

The life of Durgadas up until now has been quite a journey – fairly remarkable in a way. He is one of the very few with whom Sunbeam had begun to shine. Highs and lows, successes and failures, distress and joy ….. the 20-year-old has seen them all. Not disregarding his humble childhood, he is confident enough of having his story been told in his own name. And so, here follows an unusual story, bringing out the marvelous facets of human nature – courage and perseverance.

Sadly, Durgadas' family could never meet his basic needs of emotional support and having a sense of belonging. He never got to share either his joys or sorrows with his own parents. Sunbeam filled in that gap for him, and also made every attempt to make the elders in his family see the crucial role they were supposed to play in his life – but in vain.

In 1997, as a child of 8, Durgadas had joined Sunbeam with the first batch of children. An introvert from the beginning, he had a stammer, and hence preferred to stay aloof and quiet. I wish I had taken him to a speech therapist. Within a few months, at his parents' insistence, he had given up studies. Next, I found him serving at a roadside tea stall - washing dishes from early morning till late at night, and a year later, he had switched over to serving tea to the customers. With a heavy heart I had had to let go of my child. Once, every few months, he used to visit the construction site where his parents worked to hand over his earnings to them. His younger siblings attended our classes.

At Sunbeam, we always ensured that the dignity of human life was never crushed. But Durgadas faced humiliation at his workplace every day. And one day in 2002, he was suspended from his job, where he had been earning Rs.1,000/- per month. His crime: he had offered a cup of tea to two of his friends, and had not paid for it.

His parents allowed him to spend a night with them on the condition that he would return to work and would continue to hand over the entire salary to them. In desperation, he took to stealing. He stole a few iron rods from the construction site, with the intention of selling them and passing on the proceeds to his parents. In the event, he got caught. The building contractor gave the family an ultimatum - either they throw their child out of their lives or they themselves look out for work elsewhere. It was a question of survival, and without giving it a second thought, my child was made homeless. That's when he came to our office seeking support. For the first time in the 5 years that I had known him, I saw him break down. He was aware of the disastrous consequences of his presence at the construction site. I explained to him to set aside his self-respect and once again join the same place of work, where the owner was willing to take him back if he apologised.

On each of my subsequent visits to his workplace, I felt guilty at my inability to change his destiny. But the last visit changed it all. It made it easier to forgive myself because my child never, even for a moment, had felt let down by me. It was some time before Diwali (2002) that he eagerly shared his plans of how he was going to spend a part of his salary which he had saved as he had not passed on the entire amount to his mother. "Didi, nowadays I work full-time. But, when I used to study at Sunbeam, I had been made to feel ashamed quite often because of my handicap and you've no idea how rude the children at the education centre can be. I want to spare you the anguish of having to face embarrassment for any limitation of yours. The other day when I had been there, I overheard some children remark on your torn purse. So, I've decided to buy one for you." Gently I explained to him that it had been lack of time and not of money, that had held me from buying a new purse for myself.

Sunbeam could not gift him the opportunity to formal education, not even a happy, normal childhood. But, all this, now, faded into insignificance. He understands that given the lack of cooperation from his parents, the didis at Sunbeam may never be able to change the situation in his life drastically, and that yet, they are his well-wishers, whose intentions he will never doubt.

A couple of years later, Durgadas quit the job at that tea-stall, and took up a similar role at another one, for the simple (and significant in his eyes) reason that the pay was marginally greater – Rs.1200/- per month. He worked here for around 8 months, at the end of which he followed in his father's footsteps, and got employed as a labourer at a construction site. He justified the shift thus, "I was 16-years-old then, and hence, old enough to take up the strenuous work."

Presently, he stays in the Kamala Mills grounds with his parents and younger brother, Narsha. He has been working as a labourer at the site for 4 years now, for a daily wage of Rs.120 for almost 10 hours of work (8.30 a.m. to 6 p.m.). At times, due to little or no work at the Mills, he is sent to work at sites in Tardeo, Santacruz or other such addresses within Mumbai. Narsha, too, works as a labourer; whereas their father is employed as a mason for 15-20 days in a month, with double the salary earned respectively by the boys. With their mother too supplementing the income as a labourer, together the family manages to earn Rs.14,000/- - Rs.15,000/- a month.

However, the earnings still leave them tight financially, due to the loans that their father has to repay. In order to meet the expenses towards jewellery and dowry for their sister's wedding, Durga's father had had to incur a debt of one lakh rupees in 2007, which he had borrowed from their village friends and acquaintances at a monthly interest of 3%. Accordingly, Rs. 3,000/- from their salary goes towards the interest every month. The brothers have been working in double-shifts (from 8.30 a.m. till midnight) for months, and would soon be able to pay off the entire sum that they've thus saved.

His sense of duty propels him further, "Even later I shall continue working long hours as I wish to save enough cash to buy 2 auto rickshaws – for myself and Narsha – which we could drive in our native village (Zairabad), after we settle there. Our regular income would spare my parents the toil of hard labour. It's my duty to take care of them," he says wistfully.

"Are there instances when you feel angry at or dejected with life?" To this he replies, "On certain occasions, due to monetary constraints, I have had to request the monthly ration from the grocer on credit, and I felt utterly let down by life when he refused to accept my plea." At even a small age, he has come face-to-face with the harsh realities of living.

Fortunately, his father has given up his earlier habit of alcoholism. I wondered aloud that his parents must be very proud of their child, and asked whether they had any un-fulfilled expectations of him. "Their only demand that I find extremely unreasonable these days is that I get married as I've turned 20 years of age. Conversely, I want to give this thought another couple of years' time, by when I would have bought the auto and become well conversant with my chosen line of work," he replies confidently.

Forget the reticent, irresolute boy; in 2009 Durgadas stands tall and independent. Experiences he had with the supportive and affectionate Sunbeam staff have altered his way of looking at life, and its shortcomings. He is sure the values and principles he learned in his early days with us would hold him in good stead for always.

5

Our Beneficiaries' Humble Achievements Through The Decade

Introduction

Joys, sorrows, anxieties, re-assurances, setbacks – the past decade saw them all. The intervention brought about a considerable success – the effects of which are highlighted in the achievements of our students. As the case-stories unfold in the upcoming chapter, the sheer grit, perseverance, and spirit of the younger generation of the so-called less privileged society comes forth.

It gives immense pleasure and pride as I share with you Ramesh's and Salman's desire as well as talent and determination for qualifying as an Engineer; Sangeeta's remarkable success at the H.S.C. exams and her life as a student of the B.F.A. course; Ganesh's wonderful success at Board exams, as also being a Sunbeam staff member. BCA, BFA, B.Com, Diplomas – these students are astonishing, as they gain entry into prestigious contemporary courses. Girls like Anjali exhibit a strong will to transform gender biases.

Not all of the students currently with us can make it big in life though. This is a fact we realize. We haven't managed to bring forth engineers as yet, but, as they have begun to move from school to college, it can be said with conviction that 5-6 years hence, a few of them will be professionals, while many others will have taken up suitable careers of their choice.

On the other hand, there may be many who might not be able to finish studies and acquire degrees. Nevertheless, the Sunbeam experience, we hope, shall aid them see through difficulties and make the most of circumstances. As in the case of Israfil, who, though with us for a short while, is a manager in his own!

Their modest successes give us that much-needed push, the sense of achievement, of direction, the feel that efforts have been worth the while, and, most importantly, the will to continue serving.

Mizba's Growing Sense of Self-esteem

In the past few years, there have been large numbers of children who, at the time of admission to Sunbeam, were not up to the desired academic levels for various reasons. Some were school dropouts, and others either never had an opportunity to attend school, or even if they had, they still lagged behind their counterparts. For such children, Sunbeam conducts special coaching classes, which are termed 'bridge courses', to bridge the gap between illiteracy and education. Today, thanks to our dedicated teachers at Sunbeam, it has become possible for the majority of these students to be at par with their classmates in their formal schools. What better example can I give to prove my point than Mizba's, who is one amongst the hundreds of children who've travelled the path that she did, in the past year or two.

Mizba Sayyed is a 9th std. kid at our Bandra education center. She is full of life, bubbling with happy anticipation of a good future for herself. Out of the many positive stories that the children have shared with me over the years, Mizba's is one of the few that has stayed with me – rather, has gotten engraved in my memory.

Mizba knows that she has scaled just the bare minimum, but is confident of reaching greater heights. She believes that Sunbeam should take under its fold, more of bridge course students rather than the general batches. Not all of our children may feel so deeply, or wish so hard, that others too get an opportunity to join Sunbeam. But Mizba does. In her very own words, let me explain why:

Once, when she was in the 5th std. and we asked the children what influences had motivated them towards success, Mizba's spontaneous response was, "Lalita didi!" Then in a voice full of love and gratitude, she added, "When I had joined Sunbeam a year and a half ago, I always felt like a misfit; where everyone else was up to the desired level in academics. Lalita didi changed that with her unconditional acceptance of me. I realised that in the village school I had reached the 4th standard just for namesake when I could not even read the alphabet, so I decided to take some corrective steps before it became too late for any academic success, and hence joined Sunbeam. Lalita didi taught me from scratch. Within a year she upgraded me up to the 5th standard level. This year I was enrolled at the formal school directly into 5th standard – that too on merit! Today, I don't feel embarrassed at school because I'm able to read as fluently as the others in the class. For this I thank didi. She had always believed in me and encouraged me."

She continued, "This year Lalita didi teaches me at Sunbeam. When I failed in two of the subjects in the mid-term exams, I thought she'd be far from satisfied at my poor results. But she claims I have done wonderfully well, given that within a year I've managed to upgrade myself to the 5th std. level. I promise that by year end, I'll be at par with the other students, and pass all the subjects." Then, still holding my hand, Mizba turned to Bharati, our community worker at the Bandra center, "I feel loved, valued and wanted at Sunbeam because Bharati didi comes to my house, if, for any reason, I am unable to attend the Sunbeam classes."

With their unconditional support, Lalita and Bharati had made their mark on Mizba's young mind. It was a bond that would last forever.

When we stood up after the open session, and children ran for the events planned out for the day, Mizba whispered into my ears, "Didi, bridge course children too deserve an entry into Sunbeam. Please, please, promise me that even in future such children will not be denied admission to Sunbeam." Upon being assured that it would be so, she clapped in delight, and hugged me before catching up with the other kids.

The above mentioned story was drafted by me in November 2004. Today, in January 2009 it's been almost 4½ years since Mizba and I made some promises to each other. Mizba scored 49% in her 9th std. mid-term exams conducted at Sunbeam. The chart of the academic progress report of Oct'08 printed in this book, speaks of keeping our commitment to our beneficiaries who join the bridge courses and then move on to the general batches. They are well prepared for the yearly exams as per the syllabus in the formal schools that they now attend regularly (besides Sunbeam classes before or after formal school hours). The dreams of our 1000+ children are taking wings, and all of us at Sunbeam are proud to be travelling with them on their onward journey.

Mizba's father has studied up to SSC, and is employed as a driver of a company truck. He earns Rs. 4,000/- monthly, for putting in 12 hours of work each day, including Sundays. Despite their humble circumstances and community-biases, her parents are extremely cooperative – they want her to complete her education before she ties the knot.

Mizba is still quite young to understand and appreciate fully, the significance of various career avenues and professional degree programs, and has not yet made up her mind as to her academic aims. Nevertheless, the altruistic child is keen on continuing to study, so much so that even after shifting residence from their Navpada home, she manages a 25 minute walk, from her house to the Abhinav classes every day!

A part of the general batches now, Mizba still feels strongly for the bridge course children, and wishes Sunbeam to continue taking such children under its fold. She is a source of inspiration to all of us.

Their Hut Went up in Smoke, but Shoaib and Shahrukh did not Miss a Single day at School

Shoaib and Shahrukh Sheikh live in one of the hutments that run adjacent to the water pipeline in Bandra East. Both the children are hardworking and regular in class. Last year, a major fire broke out and engulfed 25 huts in their area, including the one where Shoaib and Shahrukh lived. What touched us most was their mother's account of the tragedy. Before their hut went up in smoke, the children rushed to retrieve their study books and school uniforms. Most of their belongings and provisions were destroyed, leaving them with little material to even cook for themselves.

Despite the tragedy, Shoaib and Shahrukh did not miss a single day at the formal school as well as Sunbeam. Their mother made sure that they were well prepared for the exams.

If there was any incident that highlighted the value that the parents and children have begun to place on education, it's this one. Earlier, half our task involved sensitising the community about the importance of education. Now, in most cases, they themselves are proponents of the same.

(The above incident had occurred in the year 2005. Today, both Shoaib and Shahrukh are studying in the 8th std. and regularly attend Sunbeam classes besides the formal school. They are bright, studious students.)

Sanjay's Mother Now Works so that her Child May Study

Sanjay Gupta, studying in the 4th standard at one of our education centers, was not playing truant when he left his study classes midway every afternoon. He had to rush to work! He happened to be one of the few children from amongst our 1000+ child beneficiaries who had to work 5 - 8 hours a day, either to supplement their family income or to earn their livelihood.

Daily, from 4 p.m. to 10 p.m. he worked with a clothes vendor who displayed his wares on the road. At times, he found it strenuous to stand for long hours and took rest when customers were not around. He was paid Rs. 600/- p.m. Monsoons brought along its own set of problems, and he quit that job. When a few months later, the economic condition of his family worsened, he had no choice but to resume work, his employer was kind enough to take him back.

Sanjay's father and eldest brother sell peanuts to make a living. They move about with their handcart from place to place. During police raids, they incur losses as their material is confiscated, and they end up paying a heavy penalty.

Before disengaging Sanjay from his job, Sunbeam saw to it that the loss of his income was compensated by way of providing his mother with an alternative source of income. We offered her a sewing machine. Today, she does beading work on clothes, but it fetches her very negligible income. She plans to take up garment stitching on order, till such time that she becomes a full-fledged tailor.

Thanks to our community workers, today Sanjay is back at our classes and attends the regular hours i.e. 2 p.m. - 5 p.m. batch. It's 3 years now since he left his job and is studying in the 7th std. Once again, he is enjoying a carefree childhood which is the right of every child. No longer does he have to worry about earning for his family.

Pratik's Struggle for Survival

As you enter a classroom and watch our children busy at their studies, don't get taken in by their outward appearance. They've learnt to cover up their wounds and appear cheerful. For all you know, some of them may still have harrowing memories lurking behind their grins.

On November 22, 2005, during my visit to the Worli center, a shy, fair, chubby, cute looking kid who introduced himself as Pratik Nagodkar, carefully picked his way amongst the children seated in neat rows, headed towards me - his hands grabbing what turned out to be his prized possession. It was a golden ship encased in a transparent plastic frame. "Didi, this is a gift that I received from God who appeared to me in the guise of a lady." Everyone's ears pricked up and I told him I was eager to hear more. "Come children, let's close our books for a while and sit in a circle to hear what Pratik has to say." Turning to the volunteer who was teaching English, I requested her to allow us to end the class 15 minutes before time. Finding me and his classmates interested in listening to him, he started reminiscing about the days when his life was different - full of struggles and not half as easy and secure as it currently was.

"Three years ago, when I was 10, my parents, younger sister and I were made to vacate our premises (in a chawl building) by my uncle, who claimed that we had no share in our ancestral property. Suddenly we found ourselves on the streets, from where we shifted to a hutment colony and ended up occupying a small shanty, where we were expected to pay a rent of Rs. 500/- p.m." His eyes had a faraway look when he added in a matter of fact tone, "Dad was devastated and went under depression. Given his ill health, he quit working. My younger sister's infirmity compelled mum to leave her job at the canteen. I pondered what to do next, how to make ends meet. I'd have to act fast, be self-reliant and also take care of house rent, besides the other expenses at home. So I struck upon a simple plan."

My cell-phone rang and Pratik stopped talking. I told the caller (in Hindi, so that Pratik could follow) that I was in the midst of an important meeting and would call back in an hour's time. Thereafter, I put my cell on silent mode. My child got the message that he mattered and that the time I was spending with him was meant for him alone.

"Didi, I took a route (where newspapers had to be delivered) to earn money but could barely scratch a living. So, I also started selling magazines like Femina, Woman's Era, Designer, India Today and the like. My need was for a minimum profit of Rs.50/- to Rs.70/- per day." There was a long pause. "Pratik, did you manage to earn enough?" He hadn't heard my question so he responded with, "You and the others know me by my real name. But, on the streets and on the road signals where I did my business, I was known as Pinto by some and as Deep by others."

The chirpy, charming lad carried on with his tale, and I encouraged him with a nod of my head or by simply inquiring more about the phase. "Things didn't work out as I had anticipated. I did try to stick to dignified means and earn through hard labour, but couldn't. That left me with no choice but to be upfront and ask for more money than the actual cost of the newspaper. I'd tell a customer to give me an additional Rs.5/- so that I could buy a vada pav as I'd feel famished by 10 a.m. Oftentimes, customers would get angry with me and tell me that I was a 'chalu' (crooked) guy. I'd immediately answer them by acknowledging that what they said was true, but that my need for food was also genuine."

"Pratik, did people give you money to eat?" I could guess what was coming as I looked into his eyes that arrested mine, eyes that were now full of anger. "No, they didn't. Honesty didn't work. This left me with no choice but to resort to unfair means of telling a customer in a hurry that I did not have the necessary change to give him the entire balance amount. Moreover, I started cashing in on the feelings and emotions of those who were rich." "And how did you do that Pratik?" My question was met with a shrug and a statement uttered in a matter of fact tone, "At the cost of physical pain to my self. I stopped wearing footwear. In the scorching heat, as I continued to tread the tar roads, to sell newspapers or magazines at the signals, I'd have to run to keep myself from being in too much pain. I had blisters on both feet. I also sold magazines in the buses – though not during the peak hours. The bus conductor allowed me if I gave him a few extra rupees. The traffic police, on their part, allowed me to sell magazines on the road signals, provided I purchased special tea for them."

In a voice devoid of emotion, my child mentioned the sore points, stating that he had to be practical if he wanted to survive. If he had felt victimized, he didn't mention it. I looked around at his classmates. Many eyes had welled with tears. For a long while no one said anything. Then much against their will, a majority of the children had to leave in order to go home for lunch and from thereon, to their formal schools. However, eight of them stayed back saying that they'd have their lunch in the class. I could sense that they were with Pratik as he was re-living the pain he had undergone all by himself.

Our boy chattered on, hopping from one traumatic incident to another without taking time to draw a breath. "Sometimes I asked people for a lift and they obliged. This was to save myself the trouble of having to walk long distances. But didi, one guy gave me the jitters. He did give me a lift but wouldn't let me get off at my destination. We passed Worli and then even by Haji Ali. Finally, we reached Peddar Road. He threatened me not to make noise or else I'd regret it. I realised I had got myself into trouble and had to act fast. At the next signal, I looked around for help and luckily spotted the friendly policeman – the one whose bill for special tea I used to foot! He came to my rescue as I banged on the car window and screamed to be let out. This brief encounter with the not-so-good a moneyed man left me scared and deterred me from asking for any more lifts. It was not worth the risk." Then, in a sad tone, he added, "Didi, on the other hand, sometimes the well to do people who're genuinely caring individuals, were taken in for a ride by other children who sold magazines on the roads. One evening, four of them took a lift and robbed the lady of the huge amount of cash in her bag lying in the backseat. Fortunately, I was not with them or else I too would have been rounded up by the police along with them the next morning."

There was a long pause. This time when he went on with his tale, a look of mischief and then a grin, spread across his face. "Didi, I pretended to be a handicapped boy and entered the trains with my feet bent. This plan worked. Taking pity upon my condition, the travellers would buy the newspapers from me. O didi, you should have seen the expression on their faces as they later saw me stand straight and run out of the train. A look of disbelief followed by anger at feeling cheated would spread across their faces and I'd derive great fun from it!" I could hear laughter from some of his classmates and muffled gasps from others. As for Pratik, he was now grinning from ear to ear at the reactions that his tale had evoked.

Suddenly, a recent recruit's voice rang out clear as she reprimanded him for what she believed to be all kinds of wrong actions on his part. Friends, from my view point, Pratik was not to be looked upon as someone who needed to be rehabilitated! He was actually a moral compass for his classmates. He met their gaze and our staff's questioning eyes steadily. Then turning to me, he mumbled, "I never felt happy doing what I did – cheating customers by not returning their change, or acting lame. But I had no choice, I wasn't able to make up for the shortfall in my monthly income otherwise." Within seconds, the wave of anger ebbed and his classmates' faces shone with admiration for him! My child had expressed his emotions and feelings in a way that had humbled me.

What completed Pratik's rare qualities, was that his determination to survive and his resolution to be optimistic under all circumstances was backed by a wittiness and a sense of humour that sustained him through the most trying times. He didn't seem to have any prerequisites for happiness. When things didn't work out, it didn't make him less happy. It was as though he was living an adventure.

Now, as he sat joyfully sharing my lunch, I said, "O but you've still to tell me about the incident when God visited you in the guise of a lady." He didn't disappoint me. Before leaving for his formal school, he shared yet one more of the touching incidents in his life, once again literally leaving me in tears. "Didi, one day I really became lame. Believe me, that day I was not pretending. As I walked barefoot, I stepped on the burning stub of a cigarette unknowingly. It hurt terribly as it pierced an already deep, hurting blister. As I limped up to a car at a signal, the lady at the wheel gave me a note of Rs.50/- for treating my foot, a parcel of snacks that she'd just bought from Big Bazaar, and this beautiful gift of a ship. From that day onwards my life changed - dad got a job as a security guard. Mum got employed in a canteen and I got enrolled into Babasaheb Ambedkar school. Thereafter, through my classmates, I got to know of Sunbeam, and here I am. Today, it's the first time I've brought this gift here so that I could show it to my new teacher at the Ambedkar school. All along I had kept it safely at my maternal uncle's home out of fear of it being stolen from my hut. But after speaking to you, I'm confident that it will never be stolen. Bye, didi," So saying, he got up to leave.

But he retraced his steps from the classroom door, and sat facing me. This time, he looked lonely and depressed. I held his hand and he said, "Didi, our hutment is soon to be demolished, so my future once again seems to be uncertain." Before I could assure him that our Sunbeam didis would look into the matter, and meet up with his parents to see what could be done, he had darted out of the class.

My child's sharing had brought me face-to-face with the stark reality of the cruel and cynical exploitation of his innocence and helplessness. Also, of the joys of a carefree childhood that had been denied to him. Fortunately, Pratik happens to be a child who has survived with minimal emotional damage or setback to his self-esteem, despite his struggle for survival and the unavoidable pain that went with it up until a year ago.

One of the special ways to show we care is to simply listen to children when they want to be heard. And that's all that I had done. Did my listening to Pratik's story change his life in any way? Of course not. Did the majority of his classmates who lived a sheltered life learn anything? Perhaps. The only thing that I can say for certain is that by the end of his sharing I had learnt something; I felt blessed and honoured that my child had shared with me a part of his life that he had kept to himself for so long, And had given Sunbeam an opportunity to make his future secure.

Today, in 2009, it's been more than a year now that his father has left them after marrying someone else. His mother makes chapattis in a canteen, for a living. Though her hands ache by the end of the day, and her income isn't enough (especially since Pratik and his sister, Netra, have a tendency of falling seriously ill at least once every year), she seldom complains, and never pressurizes her son to work and earn.

Pratik is the same spirited boy, attending classes regularly. He is in the 9th std now:- morning sees him at the

Vidyarthi Classes where Sunbeam has enrolled him, after which, at 9.30 a.m., he has his breakfast before leaving for the Conversational English coaching at Sunbeam center. A quick lunch later, he heads for his formal school in the afternoon.

Bright and sweet child that he is, he rather upsets his English teacher inevitably at times, which actually later turns out to be quite comical. For instance, having made up his mind to impress her with the knowledge he'd gleaned in the classroom that day, he once wrote her a letter, saying, "From now onwards, I shall inform neither you, nor the other didi, when I am not able to attend classes." He actually meant to apologise, ensuring that he would inform either her or some other staff of his absence henceforth!

Upon another occasion, he misunderstood the term 'irregular', and wrote to her – 'Didi, I promise to be irregular from now onwards,' - when he really meant to be more consistent at the classes! Though we were in splits later, initially the teacher took a while to observe that she was not being made fun of, rather it was a genuine attempt by an innovative mind.

Aware of his inclination for pranks and mischief, to make him understand the importance of discipline, I once suggested, "Pratik, would you like to teach English to the 7th std students?" To this, he agreed and, behold, the next day, was dressed immaculately in a fine shirt, and with a file in his hand, he pronounced, "Today, I am the Sir!" This is what he shared of his experience, to everyone's amusement – "I was extremely happy to be able to teach, though I found it quite difficult with the few mischievous ones. I was caught in a Mitul-didi (his English teacher at Sunbeam) like dilemma – just as we make noise when she explains, these students showed indiscipline at times, and I knew then what she must be experiencing each day with us! Nevertheless, I learnt that though weak in the subject, all the children are very fond of learning the language."

Sunbeam feels privileged to have children like Pratik walk with us and for giving us the opportunity to give them a secure future.

Intentions Conquer All

Ramesh is an 8th std student of Kherwadi Hindi medium BMC school. His father had to sell off his farmland in Narayanpeth, Karnataka and, they migrated to Mumbai. His parents started working as construction labourers the day they landed in the city and from that day onwards, the family has been shifting from one construction site to another like gypsies. This constant shifting took an unprecedented toll on Ramesh, Mahadev, Suresh and Sunita who had started making attempts to educate themselves through BMC schools and Sunbeam classes. But we are more than happy for Ramesh and Mahadev that they overcame all the obstacles and kept in line with their education timetable till date.

Recently, the family shifted accommodation once again – from Andheri to Vakola in Santacruz. The distance between Santacruz and Bandra has not deterred Ramesh from traveling and attending school and Sunbeam classes. He wakes up at 6 a.m., freshens up, prepares tea and dips bread in it, completing his breakfast. He reaches school at 8 a.m., has one cup of milk provided by the BMC authorities during the 10 a.m. break. He attends the school from 8.30 a.m. to 12.30 p.m., rushes to the Sunbeam center, relishes the lunch provided by Sunbeam, and then attends regular classes till the end of the day. Finally, Ramesh reaches his home in Santacruz by 6.30 p.m.

He finds his parents still at work, trying to put together Rs.180/- for their combined hard labour. He searches for vegetables – but the basket is empty. Ramesh is angry as he will now have to walk a long way to buy vegetables from the main market where they are cheaper so as to save a couple of rupees from his parents' hard earned money. After his long, tiresome walk and the hectic day at school, Ramesh immediately starts cooking. His weary parents flash a bright smile when they see that the food is ready, prepared by their dear son. Their tired minds and muscles heave a sigh of blessing as they forget the tough day they had had and the one that is yet to follow. Most of the days, he also fills water for the family at 4 a.m. from the municipal taps, as he wants to save his mother the tiresome task. Such is the worthy contribution of Ramesh in keeping his family together. During his free time, he enjoys drawing and watching T.V., as also keeping up with homework.

Ramesh is a very mature boy considering his age. Sunbeam had announced an incentive for those students who would achieve 100% attendance in a month. Out of the 35 students, only 4 were able to achieve the target. And Ramesh was one of them. He would enjoy one extra picnic and would also be entitled to a cricket bat and ball. Ramesh was full of smiles but also quick to express a better option. Instead of the bat and ball, he'd prefer a school bag because the one he already had was in a bad condition. Moreover, he did not want to add an extra burden on to his parents. Sunbeam decided to give him both – and apart from these, he would also get warm clothing, since he leaves his home early in the mornings even during the winter months.

He has a deep desire to learn, and to make it big in life. "I haven't decided as yet, but I wish to be an engineer," is what the strong-willed boy answers when asked about his aim in life. He is keen to join the automobile sector as he pins his hopes on Sunbeam and its staff who has encouraged him for his every small act that he did individually and collectively and appreciated his regular attendance despite having to travel long distances every day. But he is frank enough to admit that there are temptations to discontinue studies and start working in a garage as an apprentice since he has many friends who work in a similar profession. He, however, will stand firm on the promises that he has committed to his Sunbeam didis who are his constant companions, philosophers and guides.

"What's that which pulls you to Sunbeam despite such odds, Ramesh?" I inquired curiously.

"I've been with Sunbeam since I can remember. Sunbeam meri pehchaan hai. (Sunbeam is my identity.) It is my dream to get highly educated and qualified, and Sunbeam is assisting me realize it. All the didis help me a lot. I've friends here, which I have nowhere else."

Sangeeta, the Representative of Change

Sangeeta's family comes from a small village called Yaadgir in Karnataka. For her father, Hanumanta, the city of Mumbai always held a charm and attraction and he had often visited the place before his marriage. He had even tried his hands at a couple of odd jobs but always returned back to his native place. Even then, deep down in his heart, he had a compelling desire to settle down in the city where he had hoped to make it big. After his marriage, he struck a deal with his grandparents: they were willing to give him their house in Mumbai if he would part with his share of ancestral land in the village so that they could live in peace and tranquility.

Once in Mumbai, the family moved into Room no.318, Phool Gulli, Behram Nagar, Bandra (East). Not all who migrate to this city can scale great heights and the same applied to Sangeeta's family as well. When the city plays havoc, the best of plans fail. And that is what happened to Hanumanta. Initially, he felt rejected by the place where he had hoped to build his destiny. But he did not succumb to misfortune. Today, he works as a manager in a small restaurant close to V.T. station. The hours are long but he rarely protests. Even though there is a conspicuous mismatch between what he had hoped for and what has come to pass, he is at peace with himself. With integrity and hard work, he has managed to look after his family quite well.

His daughter Sangeeta is proud of him. She has been a student of Sunbeam since she was in the 7th std. (2002-03). After securing a **first division** in the SSC Board exams, she joined Chetna College, from where she passed her 12th std. Board exams in 2008, amazing everyone with her remarkable 71%. To our extreme joy and pride, she is currently pursuing the B.F.A. (Bachelor's in Finance and Accountancy), which is a 3 years degree course.

Sangeeta is the youngest in her family of 6 comprising her parents, 2 brothers and a sister. Unlike most in their vicinity, they are a family of aspirers and achievers in their own way. While the elder brother works for a private company, the younger one is looking forward to re-joining studies after his short tryst with odd jobs. Her sister is a graduate, and is taking a course in Computers to upgrade her skills.

An early riser, Sangeeta devotes a major portion of her day to studies. A typical day involves attending college from 8 o'clock in the morning till 2.30 p.m. (the timings are extended from 8 a.m. to 5 p.m. – twice a week). After a quick lunch, she heads for Swapna Classes, where she undergoes exclusive coaching in her core subjects.

In the 6th std. in Khernagar school, she was quite average at schoolwork. The family ambiance not being conducive enough, the child would be least interested in studies. Then one day, she came to know of Sunbeam and its intervention program through a friend who was enrolled there. Upon request, the friend put her in touch with our staff, and so – she says – her life changed course. "It was amazing being here. Our didis fulfilled all our basic needs.....gave us all that a child's heart can desire. Sunbeam provided the facilities which I had only heard of until then – besides being coached in tough subjects, I was showered with utmost care and affection. What I could not share with anybody, I could confide in my didi," she reminisces warmly.

The didis at Sunbeam have always showered all their students with unrelenting love and support. Sangeeta has fond memories, especially of the days when there would be picnics because – "We could get to meet all the didis from the different centers, together at one place. It was such fun!"

When asked if ever there was something that made her sad, she recalled, "Khurshid didi, you had met with an awful accident in February '08. All of us students longed to meet up with you, but we didn't have your address. That period of uncertainty was the most agonizing one I've ever felt during my tenure with Sunbeam. You have always mentored us during our troubles, and yet we could be of no aid when you were in pain."

Like any other teenager, she enjoys college life. Despite having made quite a few friends belonging to varied income backgrounds – ranging from the middle to the elite class, she makes it a point not to bunk lectures to be with them. "Meeting friends outside of college, or going for movies with them, is alien culture. The only time I spend in their company is during intervals between lectures, at break-time, or while returning home," she explains.

What draws her to college is her faculty. She admires the fact that the teachers are good friends to them and extremely supportive. When asked about her participation in Personality Development and Environmental camps organized by the college, she chirps enthusiastically, "We had been to Nerul on a 3 day camp in November '08. The pollution-free environment was extremely appealing. We were given short insights into the finer aspects of one's persona – proper presentation of one's self, checking one's behaviour during significant circumstances, the importance of body language, and so on. I was also a part of a group that staged a dance and drama program regarding the citizens of India's younger generation."

An artist by nature, numerous creative activities catch her fancy – singing being on top of them. Being a part of the singing classes that operate in the vicinity of the Sunbeam center is on her wish list, but she barely has any time left to pursue her passion after a hectic schedule. She deems the inter-college festivals as stimulating – participating in the mehndi competition during the first year of Degree College was refreshing.

Once done with the final exams in March 2009, to brush up on her conversational skills, Sangeeta wishes to join the 80 hours Spoken English classes during April – May '09 (sponsored by Sunbeam). Her words unknowingly justify Sunbeam's recent initiative to chalk out a considerable chunk of staff budget towards hiring Conversational English faculty. "When I had joined college in 2006, I spoke little English. I would be at a loss to understand most of the portion – during lectures as well as from the textbooks. Words such as 'verb' and 'proverb' were out of my comprehension – because Hindi was the medium of instruction at my school where English was the third language." But not one to lose courage, the confident one soaked in all that she could grasp with the help of peers. "Friends and teachers were a great help. I face almost no problem now in this regard – my vocabulary has improved a great deal. I wish I'd taken this kind of coaching earlier."

She is a girl of courage and determination. "I'm definite of receiving parental support at least till I graduate. Beyond that, my will power shall hold me in good stead," says Sangeeta. As a volunteer, she had tutored one of our primary batches of students for nearly 9 months. "After being at the receiving end, I desired to do something for the organization that had filled my life with joy. By coaching younger children, I could help educate them in my own little capacity. Even in the future, given the time and the opportunity, I would not hesitate to play 'didi' to our fresh Sunbeam attendees once more."

"My prayers have been answered in the form of Shanta, Ujwal and Bakhtawar didi", says Ganesh!

Sunbeam will always remain indebted to Shanta Koli, Manager – Counselling and Community Development, for her countless acts of love towards our beneficiaries since the past 10 years that she has been with us. Our beneficiaries are indeed privileged to have access to didis like her who have a tremendous capacity to nurture them. She goes about developing character traits in the children that will enhance their success in life. She has always had an instinct for what is right, and the self-confidence to do it.

Whenever I made an attempt at thanking her, in all modesty she'd say, "Being a staff of Sunbeam has been a meaningful profession of my own choice. I enjoy every moment of it and gain rich insights, that make me a better individual. I believe, everyday is an opportunity to be a mother to our children who, more than anything, simply need love." Listening to Shanta, I discover the wonderful human being in her and I feel a surge of warmth welling up in me. By her love in action, Shanta never fails to remind me that true mothering isn't reserved for mothers alone.

One late evening, during our telephonic conversation, she mentioned that she was in too much pain. Her foot had slipped and she had had a bad fall from the railway bridge which had hurt her spine. I coaxed her to take medication and bed-rest for a few days and she even agreed to do so, much to my relief.

The next morning Shanta was again on the line, but her voice was cracking as she mentioned that she was calling me from the Kamala Mills Education Center. To my shock, my brave, ever-confident friend was sobbing like a child, and I assumed that it was pain that made her cry. The talk that followed clarified that Ganesh Mulwad, one of our 7th standard students, despite her warnings, had climbed the roof of the makeshift classes in order to remove the tarpaulin sheets. This was because now the monsoons had come to an end. He slipped and had injured his wrist and elbow very badly. She was rushing him to the hospital. Within hours, she called back to say that Ganesh would just not hear of hospitalisation and the subsequent operation that the doctors were scheduling for the next morning. The idea uppermost in his mind was not to miss out on his mid-term exam final paper (that of Social Science). Hence, the doctors had no choice but to place his hand in a temporary plaster and let him go to school.

When I paid him a visit at the hospital, I had expected him to be resting. But since as per hospital rules, he wouldn't have been allowed to leave the premises prior to the operation, he had not been admitted during the day, and the bed meant for him in the children's ward had been given away to another patient.

Our child offered me apples saying, "Please have some. You must be hungry and tired after a hectic day at Sunbeam. I'm very concerned about Shanta didi. She seems to be unwell. She hasn't eaten anything since morning and I don't like the way the receptionist has been talking to her in a rude tone." Ganesh, an exceptional child, as usual concerned about others' problems, was indifferent towards his own pain. Looking around, he reasoned, "Didi, a municipal hospital would have cost much lesser. Shanta didi didn't have to bring me to a private one. But she has had a word with the doctor and the hospital authorities have decided to waive off all charges, including operation fees."

We were told at the reception that it would take another half-an-hour before Ganesh could be moved to the children's ward. In the meanwhile, I sat reading. Ganesh inquired what the book was all about and I asked him if he felt confident to attempt reading a paragraph in English. He obliged and we opened a page at random. In a clear voice he read the following lines, stopping every now and then, asking for the meanings of the words that he couldn't follow :

> I asked God for strength that I might achieve.
> I was made weak, that I might learn humbly to obey...
> I asked for health, that I might do great things.
> I was given infirmity, that I might do better things...
> I asked for riches, that I might be happy.
> I was given poverty, that I might be wise...
> I asked for power, that I might have the praise of men.
> I was given weakness, that I might feel the need of God...
> I asked for all things, that I might enjoy life.
> I was given life, that I might enjoy all things...
> I got nothing I asked for – but everything that I had hoped for.
> Almost despite myself, my unspoken prayers were answered.
> I am, among men, most richly blessed!

The words Ganesh had read out could not have been more appropriate for the special moment. Coming to the last lines, once I explained to him the meanings of the words 'despite and unspoken', words that he hadn't understood, his face lit up. His spontaneous remark was, "Yes, it's Shanta didi. That's it. HE has indeed answered my unspoken prayers by sending caring didis in my life – Shanta didi, Ujwal didi, Bakhtawar didi and you." My child had uttered the loveliest words I had ever heard and it was such a humbling experience. When Shanta, Ujwal Mankar (a volunteer) and Bakhtawar Mistry (English teacher) had gone about sowing seeds of kindness, they had acted as positive forces in his life.

As my faith and trust in children deepens, I see that indeed we are their students and they, our teachers. Caring, confident and humble to the core, Ganesh has high expectations of himself and very less of others. Ganesh will always have a special place in my heart. That evening, and the next 2 days in the hospital, he taught me that gratitude can be found in our darkest moments. He taught me also about courage and trust and above all, consideration for others, even in one's own moment of pain.

Friends, you may attribute his success and his positive attitude towards life to many factors. It's true that he has been blessed with loving didis like Shanta, Ujwal and Bakhtawar. A nurturing family, that he has, too could be one of the factors because both his parents and older siblings take great care of him and he is the pet of the family. All these conclusions are valid but, I believe, it has also much to do with himself :

- his determination to overcome obstacles and reach his goal, come what may.
- his understanding that he can't control all the events in his life, but he can certainly control how he handles them.

Shanta's love for children is too deep for words. She pulled on despite her own pain and illness right through the operation two days later, and till the time that she personally saw Ganesh back home at the construction site where his parents work. The next 15 days saw her in bed, down with fever due to exhaustion. Her body could no longer take the strain. At the Aksa overnight camps, we all missed her terribly.

Despite his hand being in plaster, Ganesh took part in all the events (including sports) at the camp. At the prize distribution on the last day of the camp, there was a loud applause as his name was called out for the second time. In the trophies that he received, I clearly saw the reflection of Shanta's, Ujwal's and Bakhtawar's selfless service being manifested in every action of his.

On Ganesh's Compassion taking Many Forms

The first memory I have of Ganesh is of a 7-year-old child bubbling with life, walking into our education center at Arthur Road. This was sometime in 1998.

Friends, after years of timetabled work of 12 - 15 hours a day, in April'06, I was, for the first time in my life, confined to home. It was sudden physical decline that I seemed to be inflicted with. I was suffering from severe osteoporosis. When, despite medication, the pain in the fractured ribs and injury in the spine crossed the enduring capacity, before my mind's eye floated the pictures of all my unfinished writing work. I still had to embark on the mammoth task of writing a book on children titled 'The Sunbeam World' (The Vistas of a child's mind). With failing health and being in constant pain, I wasn't sure of completing this sacred task.

But only until one day when the doorbell rang. Ganesh, now a 9th std. student (whose dream in life is to be a CID Officer), stood at the doorstep and in a resolute tone said, "In my family, all of us are praying for your speedy recovery so you are bound to get well. Didi, you're never alone. Whenever you need any support, call out to me." And I did just that. That was the first of the many lessons I learnt from Ganesh, that help was at hand – I just needed to call.

In a loving tone, Ganesh addressed me thus, "Allow me to key in some of the data of the book. My typing speed may not be anywhere near yours, but I can type while you rest once in a while, or while you're at meeting up with children and drafting out their case stories."

All these years, I had rejoiced in his progress - academic and otherwise. Now he had taken it upon himself to spur me on. When he asked me, "Have there been occasions in life when you've felt you can't succeed at doing something that you've taken on?" I could hear him saying, "Didi, you've always made it. Don't give up now. You've got to fight it."

I assimilated many lessons from Ganesh in the past quarter spent in his company. If I have discovered anything about compassion and selfless love, I have learnt it from him. His regular presence at home during the pain-filled period (end April '06 to June '06 – his school vacation period) gave me the soothing feeling of being where I belonged – with children.

"Come, let's go for a brisk walk," he suggested one morning. Not being confident of managing on my own, I hesitated but he didn't allow me the luxury of self-pity or any excuses at not being able to move out of home. Soon I found myself walking with Ganesh, enjoying the sun and fresh air, jubilant that I was getting better. My child gazed at me lovingly, protectively, each time I stopped for breath.

Back home, I told him how elated I felt that I could walk so fast – just as prior to my illness. That's when he cut in gently by saying, "Didi, normally I walk at the speed of 38 but with you by my side, I had brought it down to 5. But don't feel discouraged. Over time, you'll be able to walk faster." In the next month or so, he kept building on my confidence. "Oh didi, you've made commendable progress. You walked at the speed of 10!"

Ganesh taught me to once again celebrate little successes.

He also encouraged me by sending me a beautiful email on May 4, 2006. It read as follows:

Dear Khurshid didi,

Hello! Hi didi! How are you? I give you one beautiful speech please read this speech.

Parents Prayer
Lord please guide us daily

Grant us wisdom, strength and love
As we guide this precious child of yours

Give us patience and control
To not hurt or neglect,
But instill with loving firmness
The behaviour we expect.

Help us teach by good example,
That your laws we must obey,
For children learn from what they see
Not what we say.

Oh Lord, we need your guidance
We cannot do this alone,
Lord, may we have raised a worthy citizen.

I think you will feel better and therefore I am writing to you. Read this message and when you feel better, write a letter to me. I'm waiting for your reply. If you reply I shall know that you are feeling better. I pray to God that you will get well soon..

Best wishes for my best didi

From,
Ganesh Mulwad
(Worli center)

A Vacation Spent Differently

Ganesh did us all proud by scoring well in his 9th std. exams in 2007. Foreseeing the need for extra coaching for the upcoming Board exams in his next academic year, we had enrolled him for Private classes. Nevertheless, vacations remain one of the most important sources of relaxation and enjoyment – almost indispensable – to a child. He subdued his Sunbeam teacher's curiosity, as to how he had spent the most-awaited for holidays, by narrating the following:-

"Like any other child, I look forward to vacations to relax, have fun, and, spend time with friends. But having been with

Sunbeam, since I was 7, vacations have come to mean more to me. Last year, after securing 72 % in Std. IX, Sunbeam enrolled me in private tuitions for the all-important Std. X exams. The classes began during the vacations itself from 7 to 9 every evening. But I had the entire day to myself, and I thought what better way to spend it than to volunteer at the Sunbeam office.

I felt pride in telling friends I was volunteering for Sunbeam. When I heard Khurshid didi mention that Sunbeam desperately needed volunteers to teach English, Computers, Arts and Crafts, etc. I knew I'd found my vacation homework.

I scanned websites and came across an organization called 'Karmayog' that creates networks between voluntary organizations. From their database I looked up volunteers who wanted to put their talents to good use. With this information, Sunbeam contacted the volunteers and found almost 20 of them, all of whom were oriented and began working with Sunbeam in the next academic year.

Once that was done, I was restless again, and I overheard Khurshid didi telling the staff to find out information about colleges for those students who had passed SSC. I put didi at ease by telling her I could find that information on the Internet. Soon that task was accomplished too, and I started looking around for the next project to work on. Actually, it wasn't work at all. It was the most fun I've had on a vacation."

The Manager in Ishrafil

Ishrafil Jainal Shaikh – that is the name his parents gave him at the time of his birth in Lalgola village. At Sunbeam, he is fondly known to everyone as Fakir. Today, 21 year old Ishrafil, an ex-student of Sunbeam and a school dropout at that, has his own success story to tell. He has a workforce of 85 labourers working under him. But his childhood was spent in poverty and hardships.

As a child, Fakir attended the village school; but an unfortunate incident at the school compelled him to discontinue with his studies. Income being scarce, the family had to live a hand-to-mouth existence. So, the father decided to travel to Mumbai to seek gainful employment. He found suitable work as a mason in a building under construction at Currey Road. He worked hard and earned a reasonable income. A few months later, Fakir and his mother too followed him to Mumbai.

In Mumbai, Fakir was enrolled into the 1st std. at Ganpatrao School. There, he met Ganesh, who was a Sunbeam student and had moved with his family to the Currey Road construction site. Through Ganesh, he came to know of Sunbeam. From then onwards, Fakir regularly attended Sunbeam classes with Ganesh, in a building at Arthur Road. His mother too approved of Sunbeam and she was positive that her child would make commendable progress. The bond between the teachers and children grew steadily, and Fakir fondly remembers his Anushree didi who used to teach him in the 2nd std. Much later, Fakir shifted to another formal school because it was closer to his residence and to Sunbeam classes.

Sunbeam had to close down the center at Arthur Road, and shift the education classes to the construction site at Phoenix Mills because the number of children grew steadily as we took on new entrants from the construction site itself. By then, Fakir had reached the 6th std. Unfortunately, due to the sudden death of an acquaintance, the family had to move back to the village. He had to stay back in the village for 6 months; and when he returned, he found that he had failed his exams. Much to his dismay, all his friends had moved on to a higher class, and unfortunately he had wasted another precious year.

Although deep down in his heart Fakir wished to continue with his studies, he felt terribly embarrassed and a misfit as he appeared much older than the other children in the class. He decided to stop attending school and Sunbeam classes as well. But he always kept in touch with Sunbeam. "I will always remember Anushree didi and you, Khurshid didi. Both of you have worked very hard for me and for the rest of the children as well," he said.

Steps towards a brighter future

After Fakir left school, he decided to accompany his father to get an overall idea of what work at a construction site is like. His father remains his role model, who had started his career as a mason and gradually moved up to being a labour contractor.

Fakir understood his parents' displeasure at not being able to fulfill their ambitions. But he was determined to make up for their lost dreams that he could not help achieve. Today, although he still has some regrets, he is reasonably content that he can help his father earn a respectable living. Together, they earn in the range of Rs.10,000/- to Rs.15,000/- per month. They started in '05 at a construction site at Virar, with a team of 85 labourers. Having come up the hard way himself, Fakir understands the difficulties faced by those working under him. He makes certain that the workers are paid their monthly dues on time. If, due to unavoidable circumstances, work is stalled at the site, the labourers are allowed to seek temporary assignments elsewhere. But, in one instance, it was gratifying to know that not a single worker went to another site, even though they did not receive any payment for the days that the work had stopped. The workers remained loyal – because they know that they are well looked after. Fakir and his father also ensure that suitable accommodation and water / electricity facilities are provided. Medical assistance is promptly arranged for whenever the need arises – and that too without any deduction in their dues.

The empathetic employer...

Calamities and catastrophes are frequent and are a part of the occupational hazards at any construction site. Once, a worker fell to his death from the 8th storey of a building under construction. The funeral expenses were taken care of by Fakir and his father and they even convinced the builder to pay adequate compensation to the mother that would in turn enable her to receive a reasonable monthly income. Whenever the time comes for another assignment at another location, they would want the same team of workers to join them at the new site. Theirs is one big, happy family!

Later, Fakir worked as a supervisor at a site in Kurla. After the completion of the work within a few months, the family intended to go on a 2-month trip to the village, as the next contract would commence only after 6 months. They were planning to invest their earnings in a flat – but that would prove to be a bit too costly. Instead, Fakir has decided to invest in a Tata Sumo which would be more cost effective. The car would be kept in the village, and they would rent it out on occasions such as weddings and other similar functions. This arrangement would fetch them a steady income on a monthly basis.

Even though Fakir is now at a reasonably comfortable level, he is completely at ease with the labourers who work for him. He has grown up amongst the workers, and has never considered himself separate from them. When his family was going through rough times and money was hard to come by, they were often ill-treated and despised, and Fakir vividly remembers the humiliation they had to face. But he ensures that his employees are treated with the respect and dignity that they deserve.

Self-satisfaction

Much earlier, the parents had lost 2 of their children at a tender age. And Fakir could not study further, nor could he become an engineer or a police officer that his parents had hoped he would become one day. But today, they are proud of him. What makes them even happier is that despite their recently acquired affluence, their child remains totally unassuming and humble.

"After about 5 years when I have made enough money, I will go back to the village and settle down there. It might be a good idea to open a small shop to generate a steady income." This is what his father has to say when asked about his plans for the future. Fakir is now married, and stays in the village. His dream in life is to directly be able to deal with the builders (rather than via building contractors) to acquire bigger and better contracts in the future.

Fakir also has another dream – this one for Sunbeam. "I will definitely do something for Khurshid didi and the children of Sunbeam because Sunbeam has done a lot for me. I know that the didis are proud of me and I want to make myself worthy of the faith they have placed in me. I want that all Sunbeam children progress in life, especially Ganesh. Because it was through this friend of mine that I came to know of Sunbeam."

Even though Fakir is a school dropout, he is a role model for many of the other children. He has learnt and received a great deal from Sunbeam – that hard work will always bring good results even if it takes a while; a growing confidence and self-esteem; leadership skills; to remain steadfast while facing difficult times; and much more. Very often, he joins the other kids as a volunteer on Sunbeam outdoor camps, encouraging and inspiring the rest of the children to dream high and then work hard towards fulfilling those dreams.

Fakir may not have progressed academically or attained elaborate qualifications, but his remains a success story at Sunbeam. He has succeeded in life on merit and consistent efforts, and remained humble in all his achievements. Like his parents, everyone at Sunbeam is also proud of him.

Suraj Reaches for the Light Beyond his Dark Tunnel

Adversity is a way of life for the children who Sunbeam works for. When I think of Suraj (name changed), one of our earliest beneficiaries, I cannot help feeling that all of us (who feel as if it's the end of the world if a slight untoward incident were to occur in our comfortable lives) could imbibe quite a bit of courage from him.

Suraj is currently 17 years old, and is pursuing a 2-year Certificate course to qualify as an Electrician from ITI (Industrial Training Institute), Gandhiganj. As I dwell on the conversation that I last had with him over the phone – when though slightly dejected, he had sounded optimistic about his future – the 8 years of his association with Sunbeam begin to come alive in my mind's eye.

Suraj, is the eldest of the 3 siblings – who were among the first few occupants of our Kamala Mills Education center in the year 2000. With his younger brother Kunal, and sister Sonali, in tow, he would attend the bridge course regularly. Their parents were encouraging, as the children had never had an opportunity to literacy earlier. Within 5 months, Suraj learnt a good deal, and was able to secure admission into the 3rd std. at the formal school on his merit! Later Kunal and Sonali started going to the same school as well.

As life unfolded....

Like the rest of the beneficiaries, Suraj attended the school as well as Sunbeam support classes each day. A diligent student, he went through the years with a consistently good score. Sadly, a few days prior to his 9th std. exams, Suraj lost his mother. Confusion pervaded the innocent children initially. It was a couple of days later that they realized that she had committed suicide at the railway station. The knowledge gave way to shock and grief. Suraj had always witnessed their parents get along really well. The child's mind could fathom no plausible reason for her to have taken this extreme step.

After the tragedy, followed the blame-game. Their maternal relatives threatened them with dire consequences if they did not depart from the city. With little or no local support, the family was left with no option other than moving to the native village – Nanded in Maharashtra.

The children were enrolled into the local 'Shanti Vardhak High School'. The sudden switch in the medium of instruction from Hindi to Marathi was a little tough for the children to cope with. Moreover, they did not have the support of Sunbeam classes anymore. Still, Suraj scored a commendable 73% in the SSC Board exams from his village school. Through this ordeal, I played a small humble part of being a sounding-board, an outlet for him to vent his anxieties and emotions.

The 3 children had not yet come to terms with their mother's loss, when another misfortune befell them – their father left home, within a year, on the pretext that he'd secured a good job in another village. Amidst sobs, Suraj admits, "Didi, it was a month later that we came to know that he had remarried." The unassuming children had trusted their father when he had promised to take care of them always.

On the brighter side, Suraj is fortunate to have a generous uncle. He took all 3 of them in his shelter, and saw to it that they continued with their education. He pays partly for the ITI course (the rest is sponsored by Sunbeam). "Since the institute is in Bidar, which is 50 kms. away from Nanded, my uncle has arranged for me to stay in a room near the college, which I share with a friend for Rs.300/- a month each. This spares me the daily tiring and time-consuming travel. Uncle also bears other costs, which come to around a thousand rupees at the most, every month," Suraj explained. Their father visits them once in a month and, Suraj believes, provides a certain amount to their uncle, from whatever he saves of his Rs.120 – Rs.150 daily wages as a mason.

Despite the disturbing state of affairs, the children are doing well for themselves. In Suraj's footsteps, Kunal too secured a decent 69% in the SSC exams. Sonali is currently studying in the 7th std. Both of them stay with their uncle in Nanded.

A child's dilemma

Even after leaving Mumbai, Suraj has been in touch with me regularly. Though I cannot be with him in person, he calls up at times when the situations become too much to contain; all the child needs is someone who can hear him out patiently. His last visit to me during the Christmas of 2008, when he'd visited the city to meet his friends at Kamala Mills as well, left an indelible impression on my mind. His tears told the story of a child's vulnerability – his need of being cared for, that of feeling secure, behind the facade that he might put up to the world, lest it considers him as weak.

"Life has been unfair to us, didi. Regardless of my father, the responsibility of my younger brother and sister rests with me." "Your present might be bleak dear, but I'm sure the future holds immense promises," I tried to give him hope. "It's the present that I have to consider as of now. It's extremely tough to come to terms with the insensitive facets of life. When I begin to earn, I would like to repay uncle's kindness in whichever measure I can. It is also my duty to start saving for Sonali's wedding, as I am the eldest in the family now..." his voice trailed off. He continued, "Yet, I haven't given up hope. I know that Sunbeam and my didis are always with me, as my everlasting moral support."

And unquestionably, Sunbeam will not only sponsor part of his training, but also make all efforts to have him placed in a suitable job.

Aspirations over Gender

Anjali adores Kiran Bedi, and wants to become a Police Inspector. Even as she watches her black and white television, the FYJC student doesn't stop weaving her dreams. Anjali is one of the few remaining students out of the earliest 15 who had joined Sunbeam when it started classes from the Kamala Mills premises in the year 2000.

A construction labourer's daughter, she empathises with her father's rigorous slogging that fetches him a mere Rs.100/- per day. "His body aches because of doing labour work all day long. He has acquired kidney and skin problems due to working with cement." Her mother earns Rs.1,500/- per month by sweeping the offices at Kamala Mills. Anjali has 5 sisters – the 3 who are elder to her are married, to a building-painter, a farmer, and a construction supervisor respectively. "None of them have schooled beyond the primary level. But due to Sunbeam, which entered our lives in 1999, I have been able to succeed at the S.S.C. exams, and even my younger sisters are attending formal schools besides Sunbeam classes," she says fondly.

During the past decade, the family's tin-built shanty has been shifted more than 8 times in the sprawling Kamala Mills compound. As the skyscrapers multiply, the workers' kin are pushed out to the farthest vacant piece of land. Ultimately, when the construction work in the compound is completed, their family, along with many others', will be exiled forever from the property.

"Yet, we have the plus points for which we are thankful. Availability of free electricity during the night, besides free water facility and accommodation, are the incentives!" Optimism surely is the key to satisfaction!

The diligent student:

When in school, Anjali would always attend the Sunbeam classes without missing a day, even though it meant carrying her little siblings, and taking care of them while the parents were away at work. She would become the self-appointed monitor, making it her responsibility to ensure that the mischievous children were in class and in their seats on time. Education, to her, is an adventure – one that she enjoys most.

She secured a laudable 84 % in the SSC exams and did us all proud. Besides attending Hinduja College in the afternoons, she spends her mornings at the Aman Classes, for intensive coaching in Maths, Accounts, English, Economics and O.C., the fee for which is partly borne by Sunbeam. The same classes also tutored her during the 10th Std. "Their approach is very professional, and they impart quality education. They had taken great pains in preparing us for the Board Examination. The lessons explained to us at college are better understood here. Also, what I hesitate to ask the professors, I can inquire freely at the classes, and am able to describe the concepts in my own words later," is what she has to say of them.

In college, her scores suffered drastically. There's a reason for the low marks, she agreed – her less-than-average English vocabulary skills. "There were volunteers at Sunbeam who took great pains in trying to create an interest in us towards Conversational English, but none of us understood the importance then. I used to get away with the excuse of filling water at home! At college, I have to struggle with the medium of instruction. Lots of times, I am unable to understand the theory, and even if I do, it is tough to write using sensible sentence-formation."

"Though I realize it's late, it's never too late to learn from mistakes. I shall speak to you in English within a year," she declares, confident of challenging her handicap.

Apart from English, Accounts is her favourite subject. Her most enjoyable moments at Hinduja college are spent during the O.C. lecture, as the professor's teaching is sprinkled with humor. She is embarrassed at times when she is unable to communicate effectively to the teachers. Nevertheless, she has friends who speak fluent English, and help her out patiently.

Leisure

She loves to sing, dance and participate in sports. She enjoyed painting diyas, and practicing drama during her early days at Sunbeam. She reminisces, "We were taught embroidery and tailoring too, and those classes were not only for the interested children, but for the mothers and sisters as well."

Life as a girl

Most of her friends from the 2000-batch are now married and settled in the village. She remembers them at times – some who studied up to the 4th std. and others who sustained till the 8th std, before being wedded off at the tender ages of 13-14 years, as per their customs. "One of them, barely 16 years old, is already a mother of 2 children!"

"Did the topic of marriage not come up with you?" I questioned curiously.

"It did, once when I was in the 6th std., but I put my foot down. Even the Sunbeam counselor convinced my parents against a wedding at that young age. Then, when I secured 70 % consistently at school, they realized I was serious about studies."

Sunbeam means....

Anjali feels lucky, that circumstances brought her to the Kamala Mills in Mumbai from Lindsur in Karnataka." Otherwise I could not have been a part of Sunbeam and experience the vast expanse of knowledge," she adds.

Her happiest memory is of the Navratri festival when all Kamala Mills students were taken to the Phoenix Mills center, and she had participated in the cultural programme.

"I remember that every Saturday we used to celebrate students' birthdays. On Independence Day, all labourers would gather for the flag hoisting ceremony at the site," Anjali remembers those days with pride.

Life ahead

Presently, she also serves as a Compounder at a doctor's clinic from 7.30 p.m. to 10.30 p.m. every day, for a salary of Rs.800/- per month. This, she feels, helps her bear the costs of her additional expenses on travel, fees or books. Though I feel that, that time could well be devoted to effective self-study.

She wants to join the police force but is unsure of continuing much further, owing to her father's ill-health, and to the fact that they might have to shift residence soon. Sunbeam has agreed to look into the matter of providing her accommodation in a girls' hostel (as and when her parents move back to their hometown), to aid her in fulfilling her dreams.

Salman's Engineering Dreams

Distinction in S.S.C., a first division in 12th Board exams, and entry into the 3-year B.C.A. (Bachelor's in Computer Applications) course – these are the academic credentials of Salman, a Sunbeam beneficiary since the past 4 years, the son of a cloth-shop manager, and, not to mention, an aspiring engineer.

Salman's father had moved from Allahabad to Mumbai in search of a steady and profitable source of income, leading to better future prospects. After trying his luck in diverse fields – driving, marketing, etc – eventually he found a satisfying job in a matching center in Bandra, owned by his friend. It is 13 years now, and Rashid Khan has been shouldering the entire responsibility of running the business with sincerity, faithfulness, and accountability to his employer. The assurance of a steady income of Rs.5,000/- per month generated the much-needed security for the family, paving the way for economic stability.

Salman's mother is a home-maker. Caring and loving, she unobtrusively encourages her child to give his best. The younger of his two sisters studies in the 3rd std, while the other sister prepares to appear for private SSC exams. The family has been extremely supportive during his preparations for the crucial exams that would decide his career.

The point of Salman's transformation was the year 2004 as he joined Sunbeam, when in the 9th std. at the Kherwadi Municipal School in Bandra. He was an average student, until the interaction with the didis at Sunbeam enabled him to dismantle his self-image of mediocrity and re-invent himself. Motivation and the feeling of being significant brought about a surge in confidence, and thereafter he was unstoppable.

Salman secured a brilliant 74.8 % at the S.S.C. exams, and topped it with a first division (62 %) in the 12th Board exams, in the Science stream, which he appeared for from Kirti College. He has an innate aptitude for Science, and May 2008 saw him take the coveted MH-CET (Maharashtra Common Entrance Test) for admission to an Engineering college. Currently, he pursues a 3-year B.C.A. degree from St. Andrew's college in Bandra, and wishes to be a successful software engineer.

Salman is a boy of multi-talents. After the college gets over at 10 a.m., the remaining part of his day is spent learning Accounts, Tally, and Programming on his personal computer at home donated by Sunbeam. Earlier in 2008, he had taken up a job at an A.C. shop, "There I learnt the process of operating, servicing and starting up an Air Conditioner. The extended work-timings (11 a.m. to 11 p.m.) left me with hardly any time for home-study, though the Rs.2,500/- earned lent a sense of supplementing the family income," he explains. Hence, a month later, he resigned. He plans for taking up a course in Hardware and Networking, which would assure him a job 3 months later, and would also be beneficial in the field of software.

Music and movies are part of his hobbies but "cricket takes the icing", enthuses Salman. The 'Mumbai Mirror' keeps his spare hours engaged and fruitful. The source of entertainment for the family usually is the 'Doordarshan' channel on television.

The family stays in a room in Bandra (East) provided by the owner of the shop where his father works – so electricity and water charges are the only expenses they have to worry about, which comes to an approximate Rs.500-a-month. That also remains one of the reasons he is able to persist in this city, unlike many who have to re-locate due to high accommodation charges.

Each year, Salman visits his grandparents in Allahabad. He prefers this city to Mumbai, and hopes to settle down there sometime in the future.

Salman credits Sunbeam and Aman Classes for his success at the SSC exams. "Sunbeam has helped me through all my exams, and is still with me in my efforts." The picnics and camps are the major sources of excitement at Sunbeam for him.

The child is industrious, kind and loving. It was his selfless disposition that urged him to offer sponsorship of one Sunbeam beneficiary. One day he made some quick calculations, and hit upon an idea – "Didi, I shall begin saving Rs.10/- each day, so that some day I accumulate the amount needed to take care of at least one child's education."

6

People Who Built Sunbeam (Staff, Volunteers, Donors, Well-wishers)

HUMAN RESOURCE – OUR GREATEST STRENGTH

I. Our dedicated staff - 2006 - 2009

People often come to Sunbeam with the intention of offering something of themselves. Inevitably, they come away with their purpose defeated. For they end up accumulating a monumental debt of gratitude to the children whose lives they come to enrich.

Given below are the experiences that some of our staff have shared with us :-

Rashida Karachiwala– Education Manager

"Working at Sunbeam changed my life tremendously. Not only was there a change in my lifestyle but my working here has also affected my demeanour, behaviour, thinking and many other aspects of my personality. It is not possible to use words to fully express the joy, gratitude and affection that I have felt and received during my tenure here. Each day brought with it a new set of experiences. Be it the children or the staff, each one has added a greater meaning to my life. I have blossomed to become much more seasoned as regards to my career and even my personal life.

We all have our shortcomings and I (unfortunately) had no experience of working in an NGO. Fortunately for me, and many others who have joined Sunbeam, every query was answered by Khurshid, Aban, Shanta and Mohini. I just had to ask and I was given. They have been mentors, friends and much more than that.

Where people talk about job satisfaction, Sunbeam has ultimate levels of satiety to offer to me. I wish I could have worked here for a longer time, Unfortunately, uncertainties in life do not allow us to always do as we want. What I would like to say is that I feel immense gratitude for all those who have been with me while I was at Sunbeam.

Each staff member and child, that I have come across, has touched my life in some special way or the other. A child may be traveling for a long distance to ensure that he comes to the education center on time and that too regularly. A teacher, in spite of having her own family member ill at home, will come for her work because she realizes that her responsibility is much more towards her work even at the cost of leaving a loved one in a state that needs someone to take care of him / her. I have seen sacrifices being made which I could never dream of doing. It just is extremely inspiring and provokes one to instantly be grateful for all the ease and pleasures that life has bestowed on us. Working at Sunbeam has ensured that my feet stay on the ground. And what I have learnt from the children is that no matter what your circumstances are or what situation you are faced with, there is always a silver lining in every cloud. There is always someone to whom we can render a helping hand and we should. There are more people who give us rather than take from us, it's just a matter of perspective. There is always someone who we matter to, even though we may not be aware of the fact. At some point in time, whatever you have done is going to return to you many fold. It is this ideology which always drove me to give my best.

I am and will always be grateful for all that Sunbeam has given me. It amounts to much, much more than I would ever be able to give back to it. Thank you everyone once again."

Swapnalee Gurav – Education Manager

Destiny brought me to Sunbeam. I did not realize that my one step towards this organization meant hundreds of steps towards me. The very first class that I took inculcated in me a special bonding with the children. Thereafter I didn't realize how time flew! It was not difficult for me to adapt to the culture or the children. The children are very loving and affectionate. They created in me a new Swapnalee who is now a sister, a mother, a friend and all that a woman wishes to be.

My giving to Sunbeam is petty as compared to what Sunbeam has given me. My greatest challenge was to instill in the students the liking for English, which I have successfully accomplished. But it would not have been without Khurshid didi's help. The children are now eager to learn English, so much so that they now request me to take extra classes on Saturdays so that they can master the language and try to speak it fluently. This attitude of the children taught me to be focused and never say die for any challenges. There was a time when I was totally demotivated. But it was the undying spirit of the children that rejuvenated in me the zeal and enthusiasm to teach them.

The children's love for me cannot be expressed in words. There was an instance where a child named Kunal was told that I would be leaving Sunbeam. He was very upset and started crying. He came up to me and said, "Didi, I would offer you tea everyday but don't leave and go." I was very touched by that innocent gesture. After his explanation I realized that he had been fooled by one of his classmates. I consoled him and told him that I was not leaving Sunbeam. The smile that I saw on his face was worth a million dollars.

I thank God for having blessed me with such beautiful and lovely children. I will try to do whatever I can for them. I would like to see Sunbeam shine not like the many stars but like the moon which shines brightly in the night sky. The children at Sunbeam are like my own kids and I am proud to be their mother. I would like to stay on till each child of mine starts speaking in English. It is a dream which I know I will be able to fulfill.

Sheetal Nazare – Secondary Section Vernacular Medium Teacher

When I had started working here, the final exams which Sunbeam conducts were going on. I was taken on as a teacher for the 4th Std. It has not been long since I have joined the organization and yet, what I experienced has left a lasting impression in my mind. In one of the exam papers there was a topic in which the children had to write an essay on 'Meri Ma'. Three to four children had compared me to their mother. I vividly remember what one child had written. His name is Suraj Shaikh. And even though he no more studies with Sunbeam and has dropped out, what he had written is something I'll never forget. He had written, 'Sheetal didi is a mother to me.' Some of the children who were taught by me at that time, and are still with Sunbeam, sometimes come up to me and say, that they wish that I was myself their mother.

I've taught various classes in my tenure for the past 3 years. And the children who have been in my class want me to remain as their class teacher. They insist that I should teach them. Sometimes the children even argue with me as though they are fighting for their right - that when I can teach the other classes, why not theirs too. It is these children for whom I would forever stay in Sunbeam.

Mitul Bagchi – Higher Secondary English Teacher

With a Master's degree in Computer Application, an exciting career beckoned me. But my own health and the onus of raising a young child meant that I had to refuse that call. Once my son grew up, I longed to be part of the country's workforce again.

I responded to a Sunbeam ad and worked out a part-time opportunity with the organization. As I got oriented to the work, I was a bit shocked to encounter first hand the gender bias among parents. They were keen to educate only the male child and it took much coaxing and cajoling from Sunbeam to make a few inroads into that mindset.

I am happy to note that there is clarity of purpose at Sunbeam – both at an organizational level and in terms of the expectations at each level of the staff. The organization has understood that English is an important component to ensure future employability, and there is one level of staff that is devoted to just teaching the language. I'm happy that a laudable objective has been identified and implemented in a holistic way.

I feel that if I am able to help children feel confident about themselves by learning English, thereby improving their opportunities in life, I will have contributed in my own way. India is in an exciting phase of growth, and despite the population, there is a shortage of skill all around. If in my own small way I can match the two, then may be I will have contributed to the larger good of the nation.

Kumudini Kamble – Community Worker

The toughest part in my role is convincing the parents and making them understand the importance of Education. I mainly do community work for the primary section.

I sometimes come across people in whose house the eldest child is not allowed to study. They're made to do work. They need to take care of their younger siblings. They need to attend to the household chores. Also the girl child is not allowed to study. She too is made to perform the household duties and take care of their other siblings. Their childhood is lost.

For about 4 to 5 hours a day, I move about in the slum community doing my work. Whenever a teacher is on leave, I end up playing the role of a substitute teacher. I also help the children when it is time for them to serve free lunch provided to Sunbeam by Ratna Nidhi Charitable Trust.

I've stayed on with Sunbeam for 3 years and I would want to stay on forever – only because of the children. I'm very attached to them. I've learnt a lot during my tenure in Sunbeam.

I've 2 children of my own - one in the 2nd and the other in the 5th. They too are Sunbeam beneficiaries. They study at the Worli center. I'm seeing a change in my children since they have started studying in Sunbeam. They are becoming more and more independent. I need not worry about them any longer. Just like I'm a mother to the children at the Bandra Education Center, the didis at the Worli Education Center are being mothers for my children. They discuss their problems with Sumegha didi and Mohini didi.

Pramila Parab – Education Manager – Vernacular Section

I've definitely gained a lot working at Sunbeam. The children have taught me so much and also I've been able to introspect my life through them. A boy named Ramesh Shireddy, studying in the 8th Std. (Hindi Medium), helps in household work besides doing his regular studies. His duties include cooking, cleaning the house, and attending to other responsibilities when his mother may not be well. This has led me to think how difficult life must be for this boy. When I was his age, I had never helped in any of my household responsibilities, even though girls are normally expected to do so. But, Ramesh, being a boy, takes care of things and helps his family. I only had to study and was enjoying my life. I'm certainly inspired by this boy and his perseverance.

There is another girl whose grit and determination is awe-inspiring. During the rains, their house gets filled with water. The water seeps in through the ground itself and worsens when the rains are heavy. But what she has to say has completely amazed me. She let go of her beautiful dress in the water once - but saved her books which she needs to take her education ahead. This statement of hers has completely humbled me. Those of us who live in plush and comfortable homes worry so much when we are faced with the slightest of problems on the material front. Firstly, she is a young girl and, as a young child, all girls love new and pretty dresses. Also, from the background that she comes from, it is seldom that she receives such clothes. But in spite of that, she has the heart to let go of something that gives her pleasure rather than shirking her duty. It makes me feel really humbled and I feel that it is a great learning from her for me.

In the past, I had even applied for a teacher's job in a government aided school that was in Ghatkopar. The salary offered was double of what I was drawing at Sunbeam. But my attachment to Sunbeam is such that I had to refuse the offer even though my mother was in favour of my taking up the job. It is very difficult for me to leave Sunbeam even if it is for better prospects. I would like to be a part of this organization for as long as my personal life permits me to.

Zaineb Lokhandwala – HRD and Communications Manager (w.e.f. 15.9.08)

Have you had the fortune of digging into a scrumptious, generously-iced, mouth-watering piece of chocolate cake? I'm sure we've all had. It looks irresistible and just melts in the mouth ....effortlessly. That's exactly what I feel Sunbeam is – effortlessly likeable.

I am a Science graduate. Marriage and a young child left me with hardly any time to pursue my interests. As my son grew, and started school, the urge to bring about a constructive change in life led me to look for a proletarian field of work. My search ended with Sunbeam. The day I met her for the first time, I was struck by Khurshid Ma'am's incessantly-operating mind – functioning sensitively and intelligently by the moment, churning out ideas at the drop of a hat. As she explained to me the assignment, and Aban joined in, the sheer energy and aura around them made the decision for me.

Though not at the field most of the time, I live the joys, cheers, tears and pain of our beneficiaries through the case stories I draft about them. Whenever I meet some of them, I come away impressed with their spirit and resolve – their enthusiasm is infectious. Not to mention, the way they greet you warms you to the core. They are, in most respects, like children usually are – naughty, fun-loving, and curious. Just unlike their well-to-do counterparts, some of them have faced the unkindness of nature too early in life. Many of their tales wrench my heart, and many still, speaking of the tenacity of human nature, surprise pleasantly. Like the proverbial ant, they never stop trying!

Being a part of the HR department, I know that there are several hurdles to cross if one is to overcome attrition. And Khurshid Ma'am goes all out to make the staff feel comfortable, aids their smooth functioning at all levels she can – she values talent and intentions. That's what is instrumental in keeping the employees in one close-knit family.

I love being a part of this life-transforming venture, and would continue to serve here for the oneness I have come to feel with the organization in a short span of time.

Shirley Hira – Manager Administration

I work part-time with a Research College, and also volunteer with Akanksha. So when SOSVA, the organization that provides volunteers to NGOs, asked me if I could be of help to Sunbeam, I was a bit reluctant due to my busy schedule. But when I visited their office, I felt almost drawn to the place. While speaking to the staff, I felt a unique selflessness and work culture with a missionary zeal.

I intuitively said yes, and have never looked back. Challenges are rife, as in any other organization. But the positive approach of the managing staff is exemplary. It's only been a month, but I feel like I belong to Sunbeam.

(The above write-up was done by Shirley over a year ago. She still continues to serve us selflessly.)

Vinay Trilokekar – Resource Generation Manager (Ex. Education Manager)

Although now I am into Resource Generation – part time (due to health reasons I could not continue in the field of education. Moreover, there was this vacancy that had to be filled), 'Education' has been very close to my heart. I shall always be thankful to Khurshid didi for giving me this opportunity after retirement from the corporate world to work with Sunbeam, which has enabled me to 'give back' to society in my small way.

I've been giving tuitions right from my college days and still continue to do so. Hence, when I joined Sunbeam, I thought it would be a cakewalk for me. But teaching here has been a different experience for me – both challenging and fulfilling. Even at this age of mine, it has been a learning experience.

A teacher has to be a 'role model', a 'philosopher' and a 'guide' to the child, especially when the latter has no one else to turn to. This has always been at the back of my mind. I have made conscious efforts to be disciplined, punctual and a better human being.

Both as a teacher and then as the Education Manager, I know how our Sunbeam children surmount the hurdles placed in their path without getting bogged down by them. Some of them do not even have a proper house to live in, others have to travel long distances to get education, while yet some have lost their fathers or mothers or both and long for that loving and protective hug of a parent. Despite these reduced circumstances, they work very hard towards fulfilling their dreams.

I too have a dream. I dream of a day when all our Sunbeam beneficiaries are able to walk tall and speak well, when each of them has the confidence to compete with the best, when their intelligence manifests itself not only in academics but also in acts of truth, righteousness and benevolence for the betterment of society at large.

II. Individuals who've volunteered their time and talent

Our Sunbeam family comprises not just of our regular staff members but encompasses the volunteers as well. There have been numerous organizations and individuals who have given their services to Sunbeam, without expecting any monetary rewards. *Whether as a part of college projects, or as their Corporate Social Responsibilities, or simply as a fulfillment of a personal desire to serve, the time and resources lent by them have been of great value, just like the vast amount of learnings that they must have carried back home. Here are some of their experiences, in their own words.*

"It started as a 'social service' project, with all the baggage associated with that label, but then it grew into something that would touch my life in unimaginable ways. The Sunbeam experience has been humbling. I went into it thinking, perhaps a little patronisingly, that I would be the change-maker. But roles were reversed and they changed me in many ways..... they made the difference!" **Avanti Maluste, 16 yrs, student – Cathedral and John Connon School**

"I've yet to come across a glum and reticent child. Each one of them loves you and wants you to know it. They have so much happiness to give." **Sharon Lewis – Freelance Writer**

"Despite being a deprived lot, I have experienced them as children who are happier than their counterparts I meet in 'my world'." **Mrs. Ujwal Mankar – Retired Teacher – Alexander School**

"My association with Sunbeam dates back to around the year 2000. I began with writing books of accounts and later went on to coaching the office accountants, preparing teaching aids, teaching English to the children at various centers and mobilizing resources.

Starting from the one room office in a tenement to the current layout, Sunbeam has really made great progress, and I feel good to be associated with this institution. Dating back 8 years, I remember the painstaking efforts put in by a volunteer in getting an output from the only dilapidated printer that was donated to the office. What has impressed me the most is the honesty, dedication and perseverance of Khurshid and her team. I'm convinced that every penny invested by donors is well-spent and that's what inspires me to continue with Sunbeam.

Another thing worth mentioning is the love and affection of the children. Their shouts of 'didi ayee', a toffee quietly sneaked in my hand, the delighted faces of children being able to dabble in English, are some experiences etched in my mind. Once at the Bhuleshwar center that catered to street children, I disclosed my residence contact number in response to an innocent query. I was sure that the child would not spend more than a rupee once, to contact me. However, I was overwhelmed by the barrage of calls that I continued to receive every evening till I had to firmly put an end to this.

My active association with the institution has slowed down due to other pressures, but I continue to brag about Sunbeam and share my experiences whenever possible. I can now convince and inspire potential donors to continue with Sunbeam, with a greater level of confidence.

Thank you Sunbeam! Good luck and good cheer." **Coomie Kapadia – Chartered Accountant – Volunteer and Donor**

While on the topic of volunteers, I'd like to take the opportunity to acknowledge two special volunteers, ***Mrs. Vinod Chopra and Mrudulaben Shah.*** *These individuals have walked with us over the past decade and continue to give of their time in teaching our children.*

From the above write-ups of the volunteers, you must have noticed how enriching an experience it can be to partner a deserving cause. At Sunbeam, we have a wide range of individuals of different ages, with diverse lifestyles, economic, educational, and social background, ranging from college students to working people to retired school teachers to social workers to professionals.

III. Individuals who've selflessly served Sunbeam 1997 - 2009

Aban Bharucha, my dear friend and Ex-Managing Director

In my life if there is anyone who I can call my best friend, it's been Aban. I could never have dreamt of Sunbeam without her, and yet, I respect her decision of taking a breather, owing to the indifferent health of her elderly mother who needs more attention. I have always asked her for something or the other all my life, since the day we met almost 17 – 20 years back. And she has never refused to accede to any of my requests.

"Thanks Aban for giving me unconditional support. I'm so proud to have a friend in you, who, upon my request, quit CRY, to be full-time with Sunbeam at a much lesser salary as compared to what CRY could offer, and for having assisted me at all levels in matters concerning Sunbeam, since the past 8 years."

During my 3-month long period of illness (critical osteoporosis) in 2006 and again during my equally long break (due to an accident followed by spontaneous multiple rib fractures) in 2008, Sunbeam's smooth functioning was ensured – by Shanta at the field level, and by Aban at the office. The pain-filled days were made bearable because –

She stood by me day and night (in turns with Shanta)

She spent each Sunday editing this book, and weekdays, doing Sunbeam work in my absence, from the office.

She has been a moral support, and gives me the courage and confidence to carry on with life despite the agonizing pain I'm in oftentimes, due to spontaneous multiple fractures.

Above all, for 8 long years, she let me place the entire responsibility of Resource Generation, Communication and interaction with Government authorities at an organizational level on to her.

For all that she has done for Sunbeam, I'll never be able to thank her adequately.

"Aban, I have no idea whether I had any right to expect so much from you, especially the immense responsibility of the 2 divisions that I had placed on your shoulders, and your willingness to take it on. I'm also aware of how unsure, inadequate and ill-equipped you felt at times, but trust me I have always felt you have done a good job at all tasks you have handled."

With her around, every time I thought of Sunbeam's future, I was certain that it was bright. Sunbeam couldn't have had better individuals than her, Shanta, Mohini, Swapnali, Jyoti, Pramila, Seema, Zaineb, Shirley, Vinay and Ganesh (Functional Heads). The organization's responsibility lies in worthy hands, hands chosen by the Lord Himself. (And the same holds true for the rest of our staff members working at the field level as well.) However, with her resignation, I feel tested once more, and apprehensive of being able to handle everything at the office level as effectively as she did – attending to every detail, following up ardently on all issues. I hope and pray that the Almighty would continue to assist me in these philanthropic efforts.

Aban, finding your replacement would be a monumental task in the least, if not impossible. Sunbeam has been tremendously advantaged to have you as a friend and moral support at all times – of joy and crises.

Shanta Koli, my dear friend and Manager – Community Development and Counselling - Bandra

10 years ago when I met Shanta, I had never known her immense potential, I had never imagined her to be capable of evolving in her own role to the extent of being able to handle all field level jobs from a to z – in my absence (each time that I was confined to home / hospital because of spontaneous fractures caused due to severe osteoporosis). But that's what she has been precisely doing, being a major support at the field level.

My gratitude for her consistent, selfless service of 12 to 14 hours a day in the past decade cannot be expressed in words. Because I can say with conviction that she has lived just for Sunbeam and its beneficiaries.

Today, the team of community workers and counselors, as well as the primary teachers working under her is an extremely motivated and dedicated set of individuals, because she has been their role model.

It's been Shanta who has assisted me in recruitment, orientation, setting each staff member's Key Focus Areas for the year – giving them role clarity, working on building upon their capacities, monitoring and acknowledging their efforts, and so on.

Shanta, my dear friend, you've always demonstrated your love for our children in action. You've been their friend-cum-mentor. Thanks for standing by them in times of need, rejoicing in their progress, staying with them in the hospitals whenever they've fallen ill or met with accidents. By example, you've shown them a way of life, also been their mother and dispelled the darkness that surrounded their lives prior to joining Sunbeam. You've groomed many more staff members to be friends and mothers to our child beneficiaries. Sunbeam is blessed to have someone like you walk with us. I've one small request to make of you, dear friend. It's nice to know that you feel there is still so much more to be achieved. But once in a while, do learn to give a little credit to yourself for our modest achievements. You deserve it.

Shanta, I'd like to take this opportunity to acknowledge you by quoting Sameer, one of our Trustees who has this to say of you : "Shanta is a one man army by herself." Shanta, I couldn't have said it better. I'm in awe of all that you've done for our beneficiaries, and consider myself privileged to have you partner us in our efforts at Sunbeam.

Once, sometime in mid 2008, when many of our senior staff members put down their thoughts on paper – on what made them carry on with Sunbeam despite innumerable challenges, this is what Shanta had to share:

On 13th August '08, I'll be completing 9 years at Sunbeam! It's been a struggle throughout and the role becomes extremely unmanageable each time the teachers quit, leaving the load on the balance few who have dedicated their lives to Sunbeam. But still what I know for sure is that come what may, I'll forever be with Sunbeam because I've received more than what I've ever given or will contribute to the organization.

What makes me carry on despite challenges that go with my role?

Love from the children

A high sense of self-esteem

- A high sense of self-confidence
- An identity for myself that I got from Sunbeam
- Full support and guidance from Khurshid didi at every step in the different roles that I played at Sunbeam, getting promoted from an Assistant delivering letters to donors/ Trustees, to a Community Worker, to a Coordinator, to the Manager that I am for Community Development and Counselling (and also in charge of overall Education at the Bandra Center each time in the absence of an Education Head).
- Whenever there have been lapses on my part, didi has never failed to point them out to me and yet her reaction has always left me reassured. She has made me understand that it's human to err and that I never need to lose confidence in my ability to play my role effectively.
- Any time that didi has delegated new work to me or has taken decisions regarding a management role, she has never just dumped her decisions on me but has gone to great lengths to explain to me why that assignment needs to be done and how it would be beneficial to the organization.
- If any emergency work comes up at the office, didi has sought my support in Admin related functions. Why don't mind stretching myself beyond my role is that did requests and does not ever demand that I do it. And s that it should never be at the cost of my own field relate work, she first ensures that she provides adequate suppor staff at the center.
- For all organizational level decisions, didi has always mad it a point to seek my opinion and views (just as she check with Aban and Mohini).

- Most of the times, my suggestions and inputs are accepted by didi. On rare occasions when she can't accept them, I don't take offence or feel rejected because she makes it a point to justify the same as to why it may not be feasible to implement my ideas at that point in time.

- It's nice to know that didi trusts me to do a good job at whatever she has put me in charge of. And I get immense satisfaction when I'm actually able to fulfill my duties and see tangible results.

- Not 100 % of the students whom we began with in 1999 are still with us, many dropped out on the way. Yet, seeing the progress of those who lasted, completed schooling and moved to colleges, makes me feel that – my 10 to 12 hours a day – 365 days of the year – for the past 9 long years with Sunbeam – have not been in vain.

- Had it not been for the few dedicated members of my team who've lasted with Sunbeam and, overstretched themselves to ensure child retention, it would have been next to impossible to meet my targets.

- I've been in charge of the Bandra center. Yet, at times, when Bandra has been short of staff, thanks to Mohini, she has never hesitated to send a staff of two (temporarily) from the Worli center of which she herself is in charge of. That's always been a big support to our center.

- As I didn't have any social work background, didi had sent me and my team members for Para Professional and other relevant trainings which have also been responsible for the effectiveness of my role.

- There is a special bonding that I have with children that can't be expressed in words. In order to discipline, oftentimes, I've had to adopt a stern tone with them. What makes me feel happy is that they understand that it's my love that makes me strict with them. Hence, instead of getting angry with me, they've always moved even closer.

- Children have such forgiving and loving hearts that their innocent behaviour humbles me.

I'd like to end the note with a small confession:

There have been times when despite all that I've said above, I've felt utterly helpless to bring about the desired amounts of results and at such times (at least twice in the last 2 years) I've put in my resignation. But I'm also very thankful to didi that she never accepted the same. Because she knows that it's a passing phase and I can never live without Sunbeam.

Mohini Pawar, my dear friend and Manager – Community Development and Counselling - Worli.

This is what Mohini has to say on what makes her carry on with Sunbeam despite innumerable challenges that she has faced in the last decade that she has walked with our children:

If I joined Sunbeam (in 1999), it was because it fulfilled my need for a job. The center where I began working in those days was the Arthur Road Center. From there I moved on to many more Education Centers i.e. Phoenix Mills, Kamala Mills, Charni Road and Bhuleshwar, till I finally was put in charge of Worli. At each of these centers I've worked with children. I've had numerous sweet and sour experiences, encountered endless problems, learnt a lot.

Honestly speaking, it's only after coming over here that I became a real teacher. Prior to joining Sunbeam, I had no teaching experience. Yet, when I was able to teach well and bring results, especially with the bridge course children, then I felt a deep joy within. 'Oh, I can teach!' At the same time if I did manage to succeed in my role, it's because of the support and guidance that I received from Khurshid didi. I never had any self-confidence in achieving results. But here one name clearly stands out in my mind – 'Shanta'. She always made efforts in the direction of making me go ahead and built on my self-confidence. And as a result, I moved on from my role as a teacher, to that of a Community Worker, a Center in Charge, Child Counselor and, today I'm a Manager for Community Development and Child Counseling.

Once again I go back to my sweet and sour memories: at times, some parents were unwilling to send their children to our study centers, some children themselves never reached classes in time. On other occasions, despite best efforts, I couldn't succeed in making timely arrangements for space to conduct our study classes. When parents didn't cooperate, it hurt a lot. At such times, I lost my self-confidence and wondered if I'd ever be able to get results. But Khurshid didi and Shanta were always there to boost my sagging morale and give me back my lost confidence.

On how to handle children? How to make them understand things? In what manner to talk to the parents of our beneficiaries? On how to understand children's problems from their view point and then talk to them? I learnt all these aspects of counseling from Khurshid didi. I used to make a lot of errors but always got an opportunity to rise above my limitations. It took a lot of time for her to make me understand each role, each time, but she succeeded in doing so.

No doubt, I'm doing a job at Sunbeam where I've been allotted the Worli center. But I've never felt that I'm working for Khurshid didi. I feel it's my organization and I've to perform well. It's an organization that I've, rather we've created together.

Problems kept cropping up, problems such as:

- Inability to get adequate space for conducting education classes.

- A center would begin but the children wouldn't be regular.
- Parents' meeting with us (in the early days) went on till 8.30 - 9.30 p.m. because the parents then happened to be construction labourers who couldn't make it earlier than 7 p.m.
- During monsoons, our classrooms would get flooded (because in those days we used to operate from hutments).
- During summer, with no space to accommodate children, the frantic search for a large shade-giving tree, rounding up kids and making them sit under that tree that was our classroom. All these were some of the challenges that came my way.

I had never worked elsewhere. Sunbeam has been my first job. Would I be able to carry on or not, I knew nothing those days. But yes, I still am with Sunbeam; will continue to be with Sunbeam and will stay here forever. Regardless of the problems that life may bring on in the future, I'll continue to be with Sunbeam.

Oh yes, we had even given it a try working with street children. My experiences at those two centers (at Chandanwadi and Bhuleshwar) have been the most moving and sweet ones. The love that I received from those children, I've never received elsewhere. They may have been street children, but their love came straight from the heart. Today, those kids have dropped out of Sunbeam, but their memories are still fresh in mind, vivid as before. I had faced a lot of problems to start and run those education centers; but each time a new door opened to lead me out of the problems. Those centers too went on for years before we had to close them down due to circumstances beyond our control.

7

People Who've Walked With Us On Our Journey

Special Friends of Sunbeam

Dear readers, the establishment of Sunbeam during the earlier days seemed a big challenge. Having individuals who had faith in our cause made a lot of difference. The few dear friends of Sunbeam – **Sangeeta Kapila, Leela Alvares, Ashish Sheth, Rajnish Agarwal, Pervin Varma, Puja Marwaha, Janaki Venkat, Leena and Sameer Koticha, Kanan and Asit Koticha, Rashmi and Vivek Gour, Narasimhan Narayanan and family and the CRY staff members** didn't have to make any speeches. Just trusting my ability to handle the organization's management, and demonstrating that belief in high value, consistent, unconditional moral and financial support was enough for me to face, with courage, the numerous obstacles in the path of raising my brainchild, Sunbeam. These individuals have walked with Sunbeam for quite some time now and are kind-hearted people. Compassion, love for the less fortunate, simplicity, humility – they had all these in good measure. Every kind gesture of theirs only reconfirmed that none of them entertained the sense of doership in doing their good deeds. In them, I had found true givers whose single motive was to benefit others without any thought of themselves, without expectation of any mileage of any kind.

Knowing them the way I do, I know none of them would want to be acknowledged. Yet, I take the opportunity to do so.

Leela and Sangeeta

Dear Leela and Sangeeta, I'd like to take the opportunity to thank each of you, dear friends. It's not just funds that have made a difference to my life at Sunbeam. I'd like you to know how proud I have always felt to have you two to turn to, whenever I needed moral support. Thanks also for sharing perspectives, principles and values on the various issues at Sunbeam. My guru Himself had recommended your names when I had sought His guidance (in 1999), as to who could I request to join me on the Sunbeam Board. Hence, I consider myself privileged to have both of you partner me in fulfilling my dream of a brighter future for our child beneficiaries.

Dear readers, Leela and Sangeeta (who worked in the Communications Department of CRY – Child Rights and You) supported Sunbeam and me as the first Trustees of our fledgling organisation. They put faith in me and in the project even when Sunbeam had no achievements to its credit.

Over the years, Leela would draft and design the annual report of Sunbeam and continued to do so even after she migrated to Dubai.

Dear Leela, thanks for being my friend. Also for your consistent moral support and for all that you continue to do for Sunbeam. I'm taking the liberty to quote a part of one of your emails to me.

7th January, 2003

My dearest Khurshid,

I want to share with you that Sunbeam has been the most beautiful part of my life. I have never been able to love more unconditionally, give without expectation and feel more deeply than I have when we first started out with the Neighbourhood Project. Being with our first children really put me in touch with the best part of myself. In fact, I can truly say it made working at CRY meaningful because I could actually 'be' what I wrote in all my communication.

I'm glad we started out together, stumbled together, found our footing together... but most of all I'm glad to have a friend in you.

With you, in faith and love,

Leela

At various levels, Sangeeta too offered her valuable inputs in all matters relating to Communications, particularly on the Sunbeam website. Also, on matters at the organisational level whenever I sought her assistance.

Dear Sangeeta, I want you to know that your encouraging messages always lift my spirits and I'm grateful for your thoughful words that have helped me get over the disillusionment, that takes over at times when things don't go right in the lives of our child beneficiaries. Also, when I feel low when a staff member can't fit into the Sunbeam culture. Sangeeta, I take the liberty to quote one of your lovely emails to me (dated 11.1.06).

Hi Khurshid,

Know I had to call you the other day ... but instead am writing as I do not want to butt in your time at work ... have read the mails and all I can offer you is do not get disillusioned... He has given you the strength, patience and energy and will continue to be with you in this journey ... yes, as a human, it's natural you experience the ups and downs ... go thru' the flow. You are a rock Khurshid for Sunbeam and for each of us... If all your teachers were like you, there would be no need for a Sunbeam ... or any other NGO for children ... You are strong and will continue to be that force .... have a plaque with Rippan's words – "I have always believed that no matter how seemingly insurmountable the obstacles, they can be overcome. Sometimes it's exhausting to confront problems over and over. But when you see the results, you feel it's worth it. Our work is difficult, sometimes it's very hard but knowing who it's for makes it easier."

Love,

Sangeeta

I am indeed indebted to Sangeeta and Leela for their everlasting companionship.

Ashish Sheth

Ashish has been our supporter since 1998 when our newly founded project was known as the CRY Neighbourhood Project. (It is much later, i.e. on 10th December'99 that it got registered as Sunbeam.) Though our outreach was limited to 18 - 20 children those days, it was never easy for me to convert the mindsets of the parents of our beneficiaries. Perhaps, my feelings of helplessness, of inadequacy at handling the project and of giving up on myself were conveyed in one of the newsletters. Ashish could sense that and, being his usual kind self, wrote one of the most encouraging letters - something that made me resolve never to give up on myself.

Ashish, I wish to thank you for what you did for me then, and for your consistent support to Sunbeam till date. And I'm taking the liberty to quote your letter to me dated 17th July 1998.

Dèar Khurshid,

Thanks for the newsletter. I do understand that many-a-times when things don't seem to be going right, there are feelings of despair, but then you are on a path where even angels would dread to tread on. You and all the CRY volunteers are a ray of hope not only to the children you support but to so many of us also.

You're making a difference. That's important. That is what matters.

Further what is also important (you may be a CRY employee) is that you are one of the very few people in today's world who CARE and reach out to such children and who, for them, is the only flicker of light which makes them go on.

PLEASE therefore for their sake and ours, think at least a thousand times before giving up. I am ready to offer whatever help needed within my abilities.

Further, in the newsletter there is a very hopeful sign. That of Sailesh's wish to study. He has pointed out that he wishes to go to a Boarding School. Is it possible that some arrangement can be made? If yes, do let me know what can be the yearly cost and I will positively try to do something about it. This goes for other children too. It is very heartening that in spite of the way they live, there is a wish to study. Let's try and see this through.

Another heartening news is that of Nirmala's father rejecting a proposal for her. Is she studying?

Is anything else required for the Neighbourhood Project? Do let me know without hesitation.

THANKS to all of you at CRY.

Sincerely,

Ashish Sheth

Rajnish Agarwal

Alpana Tandon, my colleague at CRY, recommended Sunbeam to one of her friends, Rajnish. He happens to be one more wonderful individual in whose form God sent us timely help.

Rajnish, your visit to India and to Sunbeam (sometime in 1998 / 1999) was just at the time when I needed more funds and someone who could trust me at a personal level so much so that he could give me funds in my name, as Sunbeam was not registered as yet. Your one visit to our center and an unexpected commitment of consistent funding of Rs.10,000 / - per month (to meet the requirements at that point in time) so that I could reach out to more children and take on two more dedicated full-time staff for them, overwhelmed me. Thank you so much for sharing my dream of reaching out to the underprivileged, and your complete trust with your funds being given out in my name month after month. Thank you for keeping in touch and giving us encouraging feedback on our monthly reports.

Puja Marwaha, Pervin Varma, Janaki Venkat

I had served CRY, for the period 1989 - 2001. Till 1993, it was in the capacity of a Secretary to Rippan Kapur, Founder Trustee of CRY. Later on I worked in the HRD division as a Coordinator, under Puja, All India HRD Head. Puja was a wonderful human being – a friend who always built on my self-confidence and self-esteem. If there was one thing that I was always unsure of, it was my own writing ability. Therefore, I depended on others to do my quarterly newsletters for Sunbeam. Sometimes, the staff concerned expected to do so for me would be too tied-up with other assignments, and our newsletters got delayed by months. Puja insisted that I wrote well and my write-ups had a personal touch which gave insights into the lives of our child beneficiaries, that my writings always moved her to tears and inspired her to take that extra step. While I was still at CRY, she gave me the flexibility to work part-time to enable me to devote quality time to Sunbeam.

My dear friend Puja, you may have moved out of India but will always have a special place in my heart. You have left behind warm, loving memories of the time we had spent together. Not only were you a wonderful boss to work with but I hold you in high regard for the innumerable ways in which you demonstrated your love for our child beneficiaries during the period 1997 - 2000 that we were together.

Eventually, Sunbeam work took over and I resigned from CRY with effect from May 15, 2001. It wasn't easy for me to move out of CRY. This was an organisation where I had spent almost a decade. Yet, I knew Sunbeam needed me more; that's what made the anguish at separating from CRY bearable. For over a year now, I had been working only part-time at CRY, so walking out of CRY wasn't that hard on a practical level. On a psychological level it was more difficult, because it meant abandoning the security of the close company of wonderful, selfless human beings like Pervin and Puja. Yes, even the enthusiasm to be able to spend all my time with Sunbeam paled in comparison to the difficult prospect of handling Sunbeam on my own.

At CRY, the association with Pervin, the then CEO of CRY, her accessibility and concern for the well-being of Sunbeam had made me the privileged recipient of her advice on matters that I couldn't handle on my own. It's without exaggeration when I state the fact that she was my friend, guide and counsellor so far as Sunbeam was concerned. Not once did she give me the feeling that I was imposing on her time.

Pervin, you're truly God's gift to Sunbeam and to me. You always built on my self-confidence. You trusted me even when I could not trust myself to start a project on my own. Way back in 1998, when I ran out of leave at CRY, you were the one to encourage me to take on our first full-time teacher-cum-community worker at Sunbeam, and sponsored her salary. Today, we have a staff-strength of 35 and hopefully, Sunbeam will continue to attract the right talent in the years to come. Thanks. Also by recommending Sunbeam to others, you've demonstrated your faith in our cause.

I have known Janaki Venkat and have turned to her for her support time and again, and I can say with conviction that Sunbeam could not have been blessed with a better partner than her. She works as an Organisation Development Consultant to Corporates.

Janaki you too are someone whom I've turned to for support, time and again, and I can say with conviction that Sunbeam and I couldn't have been blessed with a better friend. Thanks for your generous contribution towards recreation for all our kids since the past many years. Very few donors are inclined to sponsor recreation costs. Thanks also for giving of your time for building on our staff members' capacities as well as your substantial contributions towards their training and development programs.

The Koticha Family

I move on to another set of wonderful individuals, invaluable members of the Sunbeam family – the Koticha family. This is the family that has always demonstrated its faith in the organisation and deep respect for the cause. They've walked with Sunbeam for quite some time now.

Dear Sameer and Asit, more than being Trustees and donors, you've been my friends. Over the years, that has helped me face with courage, the innumerable number of obstacles in the way of fulfilling our organisation's mission. Your presence at Sunbeam has been very reassuring and your total involvement in our activities is highly appreciated. It's been my privilege to be associated with you.

Readers, the Koticha family, together and individually, demonstrated their commitment and belief in the cause of Sunbeam in many ways. Since 2001, they funded our entire yearly expenses till such time that Sunbeam could build its credibility and get other Corporates, Trusts, Clubs and individuals to partner us. For this unique support and the total faith that they had placed in me and in our cause, I'll forever remain indebted to them.

Asit Koticha, the elder brother, provided quiet and unstinting support for Sunbeam through his family's substantial financial contribution, and helping Sunbeam to pursue its activities and live its values without let or hindrance.

Kanan (Asit's wife) too visited our education centers and spent quality time with our children. Kanan, thanks for being with us.

Besides substantial financial contributions, Sameer Koticha always made time from his hectic schedule for our monthly meetings, and at times even for our community meetings. (These meetings were held with the aim of empowering the elders to take responsibility of their children's education and healthcare.)

Sameer, I want you to know of the debt I owe you. Besides being a donor, you've also been a great moral support. You are the one with whom I have had frequent interaction on Sunbeam activities and future plans. I owe you a big thanks for always allowing me to be myself. In your presence I have always felt comfortable, at ease. Thank you for considering me worthy of the trust you placed in me vis-a-vis my role at Sunbeam. In our monthly meetings over the years, you've made me feel valued, listened to and appreciated. I consider it my privilege to be associated with someone like you - humane in every respect. Your thoughtful gesture of meeting up with the Functional Heads and even field level staff on a fortnightly basis is highly appreciated by me. Besides, it has resulted in making them feel valued through the involvement shown by a Board member.

W.e.f. 2003, Leena (Sameer's wife) began to volunteer at our Worli education center and our children were privileged to spend time with her twice a week. Besides being a teacher, she was also a friend to our beneficiaries. She continues to do that even now. She has been regularly attending our staff monthly meetings, giving us invaluable inputs and suggestions on field-level challenges that we're often faced with. For our Annual Day function to be a success in 2004, Leena took over the entire responsibility of all musical items by giving her time and talents for months at end to ensure that the children's confidence level to perform before a huge audience was high. She has graced many occasions – be it a staff's farewell party or orientation meetings for new recruits.

Leena, I'd like to take this opportunity to say that I've always appreciated all your efforts and Sunbeam is privileged to have you partner us at all levels. Thanks also for having stood by me each time that I needed moral support. Special heartfelt thanks for standing by our children during the most traumatic periods of their lives. Our children have also felt valued each time that you've invited them to your home or joined them on their yearly camps at Aksa. Today, your idea of extending our Sunbeam activities to cover music, singing and dancing, etc. (i.e. going beyond academics) is actually taking shape and it's going to help fulfil our mission of their overall development. Thanks for befriending our children.

Vivek Gour and Narasimhan Narayanan

If Aban and Shanta have been my very dear friends, so have you been, Vivek. And I take this opportunity to thank you for having contributed to my evolvement as a human being who is able to reach out to others. Also, thanks for sharing your perspectives and ideas on our cause. I've always counted on your consistent support, fair criticism and reassurance. In moments of crises, you've been there for Sunbeam. Thanks for building on my self-confidence, thereby helping me realise my potential. Vivek, your consistent financial support and that of your friend, Nara, has not only been of high value but also has built upon the credibility of our organization, because both of you have contributed substantially towards the Corpus of the Trust.

Dear Nara, a growing Corpus gives me the reassurance that there are people like you and Vivek who care, individuals who have granted long-term stability to our effort. Nara, very often people prefer to partner NGOs that are well-established. By partnering Sunbeam at a time when we were an upcoming organisation, you demonstrated your complete faith in our cause. Thanks Nara.

If we wish to retain our employees, they need to be adequately compensated for their selfless service to our cause. Therefore, Vivek, your large contributions and that of Nara's towards staff salaries (till we could start getting funds from others) enabled us to raise the compensation package at least up to the bare minimal wages for the field staff, and to give better remuneration to the Functional Heads. This support has helped me attract and retain talent. Thanks, Vivek and Nara.

It was my Guru's will that Aban and you be the two individuals who should assist me in editing this book which is why I was glad that you acceded to my request to do the same. Thanks for giving me the larger perspective, for taking the time out of your busy schedule to work upon this book. Thanks for recommending the necessary changes in the book. By doing so, you've helped me bring the book up to the level it is today. Sunbeam and I are privileged to have you as a friend.

Even though you're based in Gurgaon, I've always been touched by your total involvement with our cause – your regular feedback on all Sunbeam issues via emails and phonecalls. Your inputs are invaluable and highly appreciated. Thank you for accepting the offer to join the Sunbeam Board of Trustees. Thanks for your appreciation letters to each of our staff members. It means a lot to them. They feel valued and motivated that their tireless efforts are not going unnoticed at the Board level.

Acknowledging some of our Invaluable Partners

The Education Department of Mumbai

With the support of the Education Department of Mumbai, we are privileged to have been allotted spacious and well-ventilated classrooms in the BMC schools in Mumbai, wherever we have our education centers. Our child beneficiaries are, thus, fortunate to have Sunbeam classes in an environment that is conducive to their overall growth and development.

Other Organisations

Magic Bus, an NGO devoted to mentoring children via sports and outdoor activities, has granted our children the much needed exposure at various levels – from one-day excursions, to visits to places of interest, and also trekking trips and outstation camps.

J.J. Hospital Nursing Association is the organisation that has, on a yearly basis provided suitable accommodation at the Children's Camp at the Aksa beach.

Ratna Nidhi Charitable Trust has been kind enough to extend its support to Sunbeam via their midday meals programme and donations of clothes in bulk for our children dwelling in slums and on the pavements of Mumbai.

LIFE, an organisation based in Rajkot, has always acceded to our request for donations of clothes in bulk – to cover our beneficiaries across the organisation.

SOSVA and St. Xavier's College are organisations who've put us in touch with wonderful individuals, who offer their time and talent on a voluntary basis.

Prestige Foundation & CORP (Community Outreach Programme): Their support has been equally invaluable – having taken the form of free medical check ups / medication facilities provided to our child beneficiaries on a regular basis, at the education centers itself.

Bachoo Ali Eye Hospital: Quite a few of our children have benefitted from their yearly checkup and free treatment for poor eyesight.

D'souza Travels: Their consistent support over the years, at providing their transport facility for weekly sports activity, excursions and overnight camps - at very reasonable cost - has helped us keep our recreation budget within limits.

Satyendra Vepari & Co. In 1999, a colleague from CRY put me in touch with Mr. Satyendra Vepari - Chartered Accountant and Auditor by profession. Right from guiding me on how to get the project registered as a Public Charitable Trust, to actually accompanying me to the Charity Commissioner's Office, Income Tax Office for 80G approval, helping me get through the FCRA approval procedure - he took the trouble of getting his office staff to do the finalisation of accounts instead of just sticking to his auditing role. He was a big moral support at all levels. Today, he is no more, but his sons, Bharat and Kashyap, are carrying forward his legacy and are equally supportive, and continue to be our auditors till date.

Corporate Houses, Trusts, Clubs and Individual donors who've Supported our cause

I take this opportunity to acknowledge some more of our invaluable partners who've provided Sunbeam with consistent financial support and made it possible for us to reach out to so many child beneficiaries.

Corporate Houses : ASK Financials, Cedar Management Consulting Pvt. Ltd., U.H. International, Zeeman Group of Holland, Edelweiss Securities Ltd., Piem Hotels Ltd., Deutsche Bank, Spenta Multimedia, Siroya Infrastructure Pvt. Ltd., PID Pvt. Ltd., Tata Services Ltd.

Trusts : K.C. Mahindra Education Trust, Pirojsha Godrej Foundation, Ammada Trust, J.M.Morgan Stanley Foundation, Lions Club of Bombay (Queensway) Charity Trust, Sohanlal Harlalka Charity Trust, SARRAM Trust.

Others : All Saints Church, West Wind Association.

Individuals : Mr. Sameer Koticha, Mr. Asit Koticha, Mr. Vivek Gour, Mr. Narasimhan Narayanan, Mr. Rajesh Chaurasia, Ms. Gitanjali Sriram, Mr. R.N. Wahi, Late Mr. Homi Sethna, Mr. Naresh Lalwani, Mr. Mustafa Nulwalla and friends, Ms. Janaki Venkat, Mr. K. Venkat, Ms.Pervin Varma, Puja & Ajith Narasimha, Ms. Anju Madhok and friends, Mr. Somesh Quadros, Mr. R. Hariharan, Mr. P. Ramani, Ms. Perviz Magrolia and friends, Mr. R. C. Padder, Mr. Anup Bagchi, Mr.Suresh Patil, Mr. Hem Agrawal, Mr. Noshir Desai, Mrs. Maneck Cooper, Mr. Prashant Sarkar, Mr. and Mrs. Amritlal Hirji Shah, Mr. Hrishi Modi, Mr. Z. Bhiwandiwalla, Mr. Alok Kakkar, Mr. Vikram Tannan, Ms. Roshan Mulla & family, Ms. Alka Puri and family, Ms. Coomie Kapadia and family, Mr. N. Srinath and an approximate 100+ other individuals who have joined us in our effort.

Even through all the support and recognition that we acknowledge and appreciate whole-heartedly, there are times when I am left wondering as to the recognition of Sunbeam's credibility, and its future. It is then that the partners' feedback such as the one that follows puts my anxieties to rest.

Given below is the write-up of Mr. Naresh Lalwani, one of our donors, who has partnered us unfailingly for 7 years now:-

"I've been associated with Sunbeam since the last 6 – 7 years. I came to know about Sunbeam through a one page article in Outlook Magazine, which carried a brief about the activities of Sunbeam. At that point of time, I was looking forward to doing something for the community. It is my thinking that if we do not have any feelings for our fellow human beings, then our existence as the most intelligent of species is not justified. We are not purely an instinct driven species and, having the capacity to understand the condition of fellow human beings, we should not only feel for but also do something tangible for them.

Financial help is one of the easiest things and the least one can do, living in a world where time is always felt in short supply. Many people are willing to provide financial aid but are afraid of their money not being put to good use. No one likes to be fooled. Trust is the key word. I have full trust in Sunbeam and that is one of the reasons I contribute to Sunbeam without any hesitation. The humility I see in Khurshid and Aban reinforces my faith in their ability to change the lives of the children of the slums and construction workers. I have seen Sunbeam grow from strength to strength in all these seven years from a few odd children to over 1000.

I hope I can do something more apart from whatever miniscule financial contribution I can make."

8

On My Role at Sunbeam as I Saw It (1997 - 2006)

Introduction

Friends, the pages to follow are a sort of a thanksgiving-cum-confession between God and me. An expression of my gratitude to Him for sending wonderful, selfless souls to serve our cause. Also, a confession expressing my sorrow at not being able to succeed at transforming a few of them into caring friends and mothers, besides being teachers, to our child beneficiaries. Here, I was left with no choice but to terminate their services.

At our organization, we've always aimed at creating conditions for our children to realize their full potential. We merely set up the ladder for them and they begin to climb. Yet, we've to ask ourselves on a regular basis, "Have the children accepted us enough to trust us with their inner–most feelings?" If some of them haven't, we need to promptly undergo an introspection and find out what holds them from doing so.

One of the promises that I had made to the children was that I'd join them at their overnight camps at Aksa. Given my schedule, it's always been a very difficult promise to keep, but I'm glad I've always put all the lame excuses to rest and have joined them on their yearly camps. I recall the days of our camp in end 2004 with gratitude, because it provided me with insights into what made our beneficiaries happy or sad at Sunbeam.

To have a successful process of receiving feedback from 5th-9th standard children at the camp, we had center-wise sessions with them. The environment at Aksa seemed to be just appropriate and conducive for these workshops.

We heard children freely talk about their joys, fears, aspirations, anger, achievements, love, friendship, isolation, shame, hurt, pain and sorrow. What made me feel really warm inside was when they spoke on what they believed they had received from Sunbeam. All the positive feedback reconfirmed my belief that kids, who, a few years ago had stepped into Sunbeam with dreams of finding love and unconditional support, had received it all in abundance. They had bonded so well with the didis and bhaiyas at Sunbeam. They had also finally bonded with their own parents. And all this was nothing short of a miracle.

Unfortunately, the thrill of the extremely positive feedback soon got overshadowed by the not-so-good feedback on Sunbeam – also provided by the beneficiaries themselves. Thus, this small report will give a picture of the gap between our ambition and the outcome - in the case of quite a few batches of our students.

To my delight-cum-sorrow, I could have access to that incredible and candid feedback that they gave without any reservations. Once you go through the same, you'll agree with me that their spontaneous feedback is priceless.

"This is why we Love Sunbeam," Say our Child Beneficiaries

Feedback in children's own words, on what they believe they've received from Sunbeam. (Following are the advantages/ opportunities that the children feel Sunbeam brings into their lives.)

- Hope for a better future.
- The value of formal education.
- An awareness of the world beyond the boundaries of the construction site where I was born and brought up without being aware of the existence of schools nearby.
- Knowledge beyond textbooks.
- Friends in the form of children at Sunbeam, volunteers, bhaiyas and didis.
- An identity for myself.
- Earlier on, I was an extremely shy fellow. Today I feel quite comfortable in the company of friends and colleagues.
- Have learnt to respect elders.
- An assurance that Sunbeam's support will be consistent and long term.
- At Sunbeam, they taught me so well that I gained admission into a private school - on merit.
- Feel a sense of belonging at Sunbeam.
- Facilities at Sunbeam to make education a possibility.
- When I joined Sunbeam last year, I was not even literate. Within 6 months, because of didi's tireless effort, I could gain admission directly into 3rd std. at the formal school.
- A high sense of self-esteem, self-confidence and faith in myself. Also support at all levels from didis at the center where I study.
- I've learnt that instead of always expecting the didis to be kind and forgiving, we ourselves need to be more disciplined so as not to give reasons to any of the didis to be upset with us.

- Exposure trips, dance and music.
- I love to come to Sunbeam classes, not so much for studies, as for the opportunity it provides me to meet Bharati didi whom I love. And also, Lalita didi.
- We prefer Sunbeam to formal schools because it has a comfortable atmosphere. At Sunbeam classes, we sit close to each other and to our didi.
- If at Sunbeam we fail to understand a lesson, our didi explains it to us once again.
- At Sunbeam, the didis prepare us for school exams by conducting our exams at Sunbeam a week prior to the school exams.
- I love to be at Sunbeam because of Shilpa didi and Bakhtaver didi.
- At Sunbeam, our absence is a cause of concern to our didis who will go out of their way to pay a visit to our homes.
- Didis care about us and are concerned about our welfare.
- Didis also tell us stories.
- At Sunbeam and at Magic bus we are taught values in life.
- At Sunbeam, each of us are made to feel valued and every single child's progress matters to the didis.
- Our didis love our company and enjoy playing with us. I believe that's the reason they are with us.
- We love to attend Sunbeam classes because we love Chhaya didi.
- We respect Vijendra bhaiya for teaching us English from scratch. We're already in 9th standard and believe it's too

late for us to master a new language, but Vijendra bhaiya doesn't believe it to be so. Hence, we see hope.

- Leena didi has made me aware that I have a good voice. I may not be a great singer but she understands that I love to sing and, with practice can make it happen one day.
- Khurshid didi, you've taught us never to consider ourselves as poor just because of our economic status in life.
- Khurshid didi, you've taught us not to think of ourselves in limiting ways. Today, we've got full confidence in ourselves - of leading a good, independent life, by choosing careers that will suit us best.
- At Sunbeam, there is no discrimination based on caste.
- At our school, the teachers go only as per syllabus - including English. At Sunbeam, Vijendra bhaiya understands our difficulties and helps us with basic language skills and grammar.
- Meenakshi didi is great fun to be with.
- I'm happy at Sunbeam because my best friend, Nitu, too is at Sunbeam. And I'm fortunate to have Meenakshi didi as our teacher.
- At Sunbeam the children are always supportive of each other. One day when my classmate, Vikas, fell unconscious, Manish immediately did all he could to bring him back to consciousness.
- I had never seen any life other than street life. 4 years ago, Shubhangi didi entered my life and I received only love and affection. Nilima didi, too, is someone whom I love a lot.
- Sunbeam classes are full of fun and laughter because of Nisha didi who dances with us.

- Didi, even though my school timing clashed with the Sunbeam classes meant for the other students of my class (who study in a different school), Jyoti didi specially made time out for me and taught me for an hour daily.
- Because of Sunbeam, my friend circle has widened.
- Earlier on, I was an average student. Today if I'm among the top rankers, it's because of Rashmi didi.
- Some of my classmates still go to movies on the pretext of school. I try to create interest in their minds towards studies.
- College, I believe, is a possibility. I'm sure most of us will make it to college.
- Because didis and bhaiyas at Sunbeam believe in me so much, I too have learnt to believe in myself.
- Sunbeam has taught me that I can do anything if I set my mind on it.

Summing up the Positive Feedback from Children

Friends, as you'd have gathered from the extremely positive feedback mentioned above, our children had recalled all the possible times when they had felt listened to and valued at Sunbeam. In all that they had said, indirectly they had expressed their gratitude for teaching them with love.

Some of the greatest moments of my life (at Sunbeam) have been at Aksa, those that have caught me off guard. Listening to this pleasant feedback was a truly rewarding experience for me. Never had I felt so proud of our children. I'll cherish these moments for more than one reason.

I believe that a fair share of the success of our initiatives goes to our staff. It's all a result of the labour of love on their part. The unconditional warmth and affection showered by the Sunbeam staff has made our classes a home-away-from-home for our children. I marvel at the kindness and patience with which our staff help the children emerge victorious from different situations in life. I am awed at the transformation coming about in most of them, at who they are becoming - children with a high sense of self-esteem. The pain-filled years that they had endured prior to Sunbeam intervention are now a dim memory.

Pooja was one of the few primary section kids who had joined this camp meant for secondary and higher secondary children. She ran up to me and hugged me in response to my query on what she had to say about her experiences at Sunbeam. Her face was beaming with joy.

Friends, all in all, the future of our children is bright and if all goes as per our plans, there's no stopping them from succeeding in life.

I feel most blessed to be given the job that I have - that of raising kids. I think no other job can equal it. Nothing could beat the paycheck that I had just received in the form of the feedback from hundreds of children.

"This is where Sunbeam let us down," say some of our Children

"Ours is an ideal organization where children are treated with dignity." Even while I was thinking on those lines, I checked myself. Because there were some children from specific batches at a particular education center - children who maintained silence during the entire session. These kids had nothing much to say on their positive experiences at Sunbeam. So I coaxed them to speak on their unfulfilled wishes at Sunbeam, little knowing what the response was to be. They mentioned about the lack of love and dignity as things they wished they had not experienced - at least not at Sunbeam.

Friends, I believe that by not sharing that feedback with you, I'd be depriving you of a complete picture and that would amount to distorting reality. So here is the not-so-happy feedback from those children.

- We would love to stay on with Sunbeam if our didis (teachers at Sunbeam) would stop beating us.
- We want to be loved by our didis.
- It's OK if our didis punish us. But only if they'd be a bit more forgiving then we'd know that they love us.
- When our didi beats us, we cry. And when we cry, she tells us to improve ourselves.

The children needed to know that it was all right to share their feelings. The teachers concerned needed to know how the children felt when treated with indignity. "Tell me, what do you feel when you are beaten. You said you cry. Is it because of the pain that it causes you?" I could barely bring myself to ask these questions. I sincerely hope that the answers that followed made the teachers realize their error of resorting to physical abuse, and the psychological effects it had on the child.

- I cry because I feel upset with didi. The physical pain is there, no doubt about it. But that never lasts long. It's the shame that doesn't leave me in peace. Long after the beating is done and finished with, our classmates and other children keep reminding us of it and the humiliation continues.
- "Didi, it's not just one or two of us trying to express the same expectation of Sunbeam didis. Please take note of it that 12 out of the 23 from our batch are saying that our didi has been raising her hand on us."
- "I do not like to be made fun of by the other students at my poor performance, for which I get a good spanking from didi."

My Reflections on Children's Feedback

Overnight as it were, the reserved, shy batch of students seemed to have vanished, leaving in their place children who wanted to share how vulnerable they felt at Sunbeam. I began to reflect on what I had just heard, trying desperately to make sense of it all. It was a very humbling experience for me. Our beneficiaries were bringing to my notice the grey areas of our organization. I sat there in disbelief. It wasn't an isolated case of punishment that the children had quoted.

Friends, in principle, I have always opposed punishment. Rather, I've been against punishment of any kind. Because there are other loving ways in which one can discipline a child. Unfortunately, our children, who spoke about being beaten by our staff, were not even an undisciplined lot, with whom our teachers could have lost their patience. They had merely performed poorly in their exams, or had fallen into the category of average performers.

Right from the time of orientation of the staff during recruitment, to mentioning it at the meetings, to bringing it to the notice of the concerned staff members at the very first instance, to warnings if the error is repeated - I've never failed to stress on the importance of treating a child with dignity, briefing every individual on our organization culture from time-to-time

Orienting and reorienting our field staff into the Sunbeam culture is no small task. It's been an ongoing process to which I've always devoted most of the working hours of the day - explaining to the teachers that it's the efforts (on the part of our children) that count, and that being an average student is not a crime. But given that the teachers lay greater stress on marks, incidents of insensitivity are bound to happen. I'm not saying that we shouldn't aim high, but our expectations of children have to be realistic, given their situations in life. In my opinion, if Sunbeam teachers do not focus on equally important matters such as their children's self-esteem, self-confidence, spiritual growth and their emotional well being, Sunbeam can never achieve its goal of their overall development.

The candid feedback from the children made me more alive than ever to my sense of duty – that of sensitizing the field staff in their attitude towards our beneficiaries.

When I say that I'm against the idea of punishing a child, not for a moment am I implying that indiscipline or unacceptable behaviour in a class should be allowed. I'm simply trying to convey that we need to balance discipline with love. Even when a child misbehaves, or is dishonest and resorts to cheating during exams, there are ways to mend such behaviours – one of them being loving counsel after gentle probing and getting to the root cause of the behaviour. Children, sometimes, resort to untruth simply to avoid being punished. Or, if for instance, a child does not take academics seriously and regularly bunks study classes on some pretext or the other but promptly turns up in time for the weekly sports sessions or outdoor activities / picnics, disciplining can take the form of withholding these privileges that would matter most to the child and therefore he can be prevented from repeating his error. Yet, we would have to ensure that this kind of disciplining was followed up with reassuring the child of our consistent support and faith in him - explaining that we love him dearly as before but that there were certain norms that we would not compromise on. We needed to set limits and let them know of the same.

Illogical as it may sound, I felt betrayed by the few teachers who beat their children, going against our organizational values. It is not uncommon for our children to be exposed to cruel treatment at the hands of adults who surround their lives. But the very idea of them having to face shame at Sunbeam broke my heart.

Most of our children are into the mainstream. They'll never see a day when they feel the handicap of want of school education. I've always yearned to save our children from tears and hurt – at least as far as life at Sunbeam is concerned. Painful that discovering the grey areas of our organization was, I'm so grateful that it happened. Children's feedback was God's way of giving me an opportunity to know of issues that needed my time and attention.

Based on what I know of the field staff, I could interpret their actions in many ways. But at its most elemental level it was just that they were unable to cope with the enormous challenges that went with their roles, combined with the problems they faced at their own home-front. By not giving up on the teachers who have also demonstrated, time and again, their love for our children and dedication to our cause, I adopt an attitude that has always brought about positive results.

My conscience does not allow me to consider it a matter to be ignored if a child is deprived of what is rightfully his – a secure, dignified childhood. But the teachers under discussion either didn't notice or chose to ignore the pain that the children had voiced. So I pondered over broaching the topic 'what kind of an environment at Sunbeam would enable the children to flower to their full capacity'. Though I had taken the teachers through this process umpteen number of times in the past, my duty towards the beneficiaries did not allow me to keep quiet. Doing so would have amounted to living a life inconsistent with my own value system. Unfortunately, when with a few of our staff members, despite counselling, I could not see the desired change coming about in their attitude towards our beneficiaries, I was left with no choice but to terminate their services.

On my Efforts at Moulding our Staff to our Organizational Culture

I. Self-esteem is Crucial to a Child's Psychological well-being.

If making a profound and positive difference to the lives of our children has been and will continue to remain Sunbeam's main focus, to make that possible, my own focus has always been in the direction of making a profound and positive difference to the mindsets of the field staff.

Passionate about her work and fiercely optimistic in spirit, Rashmi didi was a blessing to her students, incapable of causing them any pain. At least, that's what I had all along believed it to be. Hearing from the beneficiaries how insensitively she handled them, had left me feeling devastated.. This too was a part of Sunbeam, the existence of which I couldn't deny. Why did her students speak of facing shame because of her punishment? What kind of punishment did she mete out to them? As it turned out, it was not so much the beating as the labelling that caused them embarrassment.

Quoting an instance of a child who had cheated in the exams, Rashmi justified her behaviour by claiming that it was in order to teach him a lesson that she had given him a good thrashing and exposed him to his classmates. Her answer was not at all comforting. It was natural on Rashmi's part to feel upset if she found her students copying. But the means she had adopted to express her disapproval were wrong. While disciplining the children was necessary, all of us at Sunbeam had to keep the following rule in mind: Wrong doing, of course, has to be identified, but the means to correct it should always be positive and constructive, not negative and destructive.

I decided to make one more attempt but it was futile. She had no doubts whatsoever about the correctness of the way she had handled the erring child. I realised that changing the mindsets of our staff was no small task. Sometimes I had serious misgivings at my own ability to do the same. Unfortunately, Rashmi's was one such case where my efforts had met with polite indifference. I resolved to share with her one of my own childhood experiences that had had a big effect on the way I looked upon another's errors, especially if it happened to be a child who had erred.

Rashmi's words had awakened memories of my own childhood: One of the early recollections that is outstanding; and literally so, for I bore the scar for a long time to come. As I sat with her that day, our office rooms were filled with memories. (Friends, the place where the Sunbeam office is operating from, happens to be my residence where I had dwelled till 1997). Memories came alive as I related to her my own experience as a child in a similar situation, a child who had cheated in her exams and had got caught. A child who was not forgiven but severely punished and humiliated. In order that none of our kids at Sunbeam should have to go through similar humiliation I had as a child, I had shared my experience with our staff last year. Rashmi was a new recruit and perhaps hearing my tale could possibly help change her views on how to handle children who erred.

I must have been about 9 years old and in the 5th standard, an average student. At school, English was the medium of instruction. At home, we always spoke in Gujarati. Hindi, which was the second language at school, I had found easy to understand and speak. But with Marathi – the third compulsory language at school, I found myself completely at a disadvantage. The fear of failure led me to cheat, which I now see was wrong; but that was not how it had appeared to me then as a child.

I was caught by the teacher who made me stand up, declared me a cheater in front of the entire class, made me leave the room and gave me zero marks in that paper. But that was not the end of the punishment. Next morning during the school assembly, i.e., in the presence of the large gathering of children from all the classes, I was summoned on the stage and my misdeed was announced. I recall this as the first occasion in my life when I was put to shame in public.

That was the longest day I had gone through. The day just dragged on and on. I was scared of speaking about it to my parents though I had resolved to make a clean confession of it. Not that I was afraid of them punishing me - I was worried about the pain I'd be causing them. I was contrite and full of remorse when they took the blame of my error entirely on themselves. "We, as parents, should not have taken for granted that you'd be able to cope on your own with a language that's alien to you. It's our fault. We should have enrolled you into some tuition classes for Marathi." Mum held me in her arms all through. My parents had demonstrated by this forgiving act of theirs that their child's self-esteem was too precious for them and that nobody had any right to snatch it away from her. Their kindness made it easier for me to forgive myself. I could not disregard their trust in me and resolved never to cheat again. And I stuck to my resolve. Today, I cannot but think with gratitude of my parents.

My parents' words of understanding had brought healing to my wounds – those caused by the humiliation at the school assembly. But months passed before my classmates allowed me to forget the shame of being labelled a cheater. They made it a definite point to remind me of it and ridicule me.

After I had finished, there was complete silence. Finally Rashmi spoke, but her voice quivered and it was only a whisper, "Didi, I assure you that no child will ever again be made to feel small by me." She kept her word.

(In contrast to the above mentioned incident in which a child had cheated, I can also vividly recall a time when to our dismay, we found a teacher erring and misguiding the children. I was compelled to terminate her services for encouraging the children to copy from the guidebooks or from one another's exam papers.)

II. On Mentoring our Staff

Patiently, I continued to work upon the staff members' limitations by reminding them of their own commendable past contributions to the growth of our child beneficiaries. I reminded myself, time and again, that despite some of their negative personality traits, they were individuals who had come forward to partner us in our efforts for the betterment of our child beneficiaries.

Once I noticed that Shruti (name changed), a staff at Sunbeam, was proving to be a wrong influence on the other staff at the center. There had been instances of insubordination with her immediate coordinator. Her attitude towards work in general was becoming a problem. 'Should I transfer her? Sack her?' A multiple of such thoughts passed my mind. Fortunately, I did not immediately act upon these unpleasant options. Moreover, after a thorough introspection, these ideas underwent a radical transformation. My conscience said that other choices were available.

Her attitude problem, no doubt, had to be brought to her notice. But I did not have to let myself get mired in negativity. I needed to believe in her intrinsic goodness. What was needed was to bring about a change of heart, a change in attitude of these teachers and community workers. I had to also be practical and find out for myself if the loss of her transfer to another center - would outweigh the gains it would bring along. Shruti was an excellent primary teacher as far as her teaching skills were concerned. Therefore, a better solution would be to transfer Maya (name changed), a very balanced, mature, sensitive and effective staff from where she was currently, to Shruti's center, to fill in an existing vacancy. She, I believed, could be an extremely positive influence on Shruti as well as on the rest of the staff at the center.

Even though I was profoundly committed to the cause, if I wished to evoke that sense of commitment in others, I had to learn to express myself without that edge of anger that made it difficult for others to accept what I was saying.

I wasn't tolerating wrong doing on the part of the staff members, but simply appealing to their conscience. In the process of moulding them into our culture and helping them to rise above their limitations, rise to a new level of performance- I too was growing out of my own limitations and learning to find the better side of human nature.

III. On being a Friend-cum-Counsellor to the Staff

Some of our staff members are mothers themselves, and others have younger school-going siblings. The frequent abuse that they might have experienced as children, has turned a few of them into violent adults. Upon being told to give an explanation on their questionable behaviour and whether they would have treated their own children in a similar fashion, they calmly told me that I was mistaken if I believed that they would discriminate between their own children and ours. They claimed that even at home they taught with the cane!

It dawned on me that I had found the key to our problem. If I could gather my strength, and forgive and awaken those who had difficulty in forgiving our children for their small errors, there was a possibility that I'd be able to extinguish the bitterness that filled their own lives, at least to some extent. As a result, there was a likelihood of them being more humane in handling our beneficiaries.

Before leaving for my yearly vacation in December '04, I spent 2 entire days with the concerned staff – both individually and as a group. Alka (name changed), one of our teachers, needed help. By assisting her in undergoing an introspection, I hoped that she find the person deep inside, that she used to be. Experiences in the past had given me ample reason to believe that she possessed a mother's heart. Determined to make it easier to overcome her limitations, I decided to give it one more try. I shared with her what Sagar and his friends had to say of their experiences at Sunbeam (please refer case story titled 'Sagar's unfulfilled dream of finding a sense of belonging at Sunbeam' in one of the earlier chapters of this book). I also shared at length Mizba's extremely positive feedback on her (please refer case story titled 'Mizba's growing sense of self-esteem' too in the earlier chapters).

Alka promised to never again raise her hand on children, to love them for who they were and to ensure that they felt a sense of belonging to Sunbeam. In response I said I believed her and would appreciate her long term services if she could, once again, become the loving the didi whom the Dadar center construction site children remembered. I told her that I too had never forgotten any of her kind acts towards them - especially the time when she had taken the entire batch of students to her home and celebrated her son's birthday with them.

(In the past too there had been similar instances when Alka had been warned – verbally though – that spanking children was unacceptable. On another occasion, a disciplinary letter had been issued to her for a different reason altogether – that of insubordination to her immediate Supervisor. This time when her objectionable behaviour was brought to my notice by the children themselves, there was no other option but to give her a third and final warning letter, categorically stating that recurrence of such unethical conduct would result in her services being terminated.)

The above explanation is an indicator of the corrective measures that need to be taken at a professional level for any erring staff member. On the other hand, at a personal level, I continue playing the role of a mentor with the sole aim of bringing about a greater level of sensitivity in the staff handling children who are placed in our care.

A glimpse into the Key Focus Areas of our Child Counsellors

On 20th December '05, the Sunbeam Annual Day was celebrated with a difference. It was unique because on that day we decided to hear the voice of our 900+ beneficiaries, on what it was that made them happy or sad in life. Also, on what their expectations of Sunbeam were and what made them regular at- or alternatively stay away from - Sunbeam classes. They came up with the most touching and unexpected response. And we understood that the need of the hour was to have at least 1 full-time child counsellor at each of our 4 education centers. Soon we appointed from within our organisation, staff who had the aptitude and immense patience, love and understanding to resolve our children's innumerable issues.

Friends, let me give you a glimpse into one of the many Key Focus Areas of our counselling team. And the positive impact that the general counselling sessions have had on our children. The deeper issues of vital importance that the children have mentioned in their written feedback, such as the traumas that they face in their personal lives, are being addressed with each of them individually, with the involvement of the family members who are handled in an equally sensitive manner.

Objective / Outcome of Counseling Sessions Conducted Across the Organization (for the Reader's Benefit, we are Quoting at Random Jan '06 Sessions)

Based on the feedback obtained from the beneficiaries across the organization, it was decided to have class-wise weekly counseling sessions with them.

Session 1.

Topic : Awareness on Sunbeam

Objective: To create awareness about Sunbeam among 900+ child beneficiaries, especially the recent entrants.

Outcome: Children got to know of Sunbeam's birth and its gradual growth. Also, became aware of a Sunbeam beyond their own center, got an idea about the different categories of beneficiaries, the total outreach as well as the mission and objectives of our organization.

Session 2.

Topic : Academics.

Objective: To what extent could Sunbeam ease the pressure of academics on them? How could they overcome their fear of the same, especially the fear of exams? Moreover, to explain that it's the effort that mattered and not just results. That, one didn't always have to be excellent in all the subjects, though it's necessary to aim high and do their best.

Outcome: Children who had, in their written feedback, expressed their fears of falling in the sight of their Sunbeam didis just because they didn't stand first in the class or didn't get excellent results, now understood that our expectations of them were modest, and that they were loved and valued regardless of their academic performance. Because their didis took into consideration their efforts at studies and did not judge them by their results alone.

Session 3.

Topic : To treat others, especially one's own classmates, with sensitivity and dignity.

Objective : To make children understand that it's incorrect on their part to tease or bully their classmates, because of which those at the receiving end ultimately become irregular, or in rare cases, even drop out of Sunbeam. That it's OK to have fun but not at the cost of others.

Outcome : Children's quotes

• "Didi, after the session of last week, I confess, I haven't given up teasing others. I still do end up doing it once in a while but the moment I realize that it's causing them pain or embarrassment, I make it a point to apologize to them."

• "Didi, because so many of us made fun of Tejaswini's appearance, she stopped wearing glasses even during studies though she can barely read without them. But now we feel sad about what we've done."

• "Ajinkya has stopped attending Sunbeam classes altogether because we all used to poke fun at him. We're sorry, and regret our rudeness, which made him drop out of class. We want to make up for it. How do we go about making amends?" "What about writing an apology letter to him, letting him know how much you miss him?" their Sunbeam didi asked of them. The children did just that, and Ajinkya became a part of Sunbeam once again.

Session 4.

Topic : Celebrating birthdays

Objective : To make each child realize that he/she is special and that a birthday celebration for a child is an important occasion at Sunbeam.

Outcome :

• Children who had written in their feedback - that they felt extremely sad when nobody at home remembered their birthdays, let alone celebrate them - were touched and felt loved when each got a lovely birthday note from their Sunbeam didi and some of their friends at Sunbeam. Henceforth, birthday celebrations (without any expense) are going to be a regular feature at Sunbeam.

• Let me cite an extremely moving case story, that of Sony, whose father, upon getting to know that Sunbeam was planning to celebrate his child's birthday, himself decided to do his bit. He took a half day's leave from his work and requested the Sunbeam teacher to allow Sony to leave early, so that he could take her for a family outing on her birthday!

Positive action taken at the Organisational Level on Children's Written Feedback

Given below are a few of the hundreds of expectations of Sunbeam that the children 5th standard and above had penned for us. Almost all the problems were addressed with care and in time. Majority of these problems were solved, thereby making the children feel listened to – giving the children their due respect.

1. *Problem : Children irregular because of having to daily walk long distances.* "Our feet ache on walking long distances - all the way home from formal school, and back to the Sunbeam center - and that too in the scorching heat, to go home just to have food. We are too tired to attend Sunbeam classes, hence are irregular." (Feedback from 7th std. child)

Solution : Midday meals program extended to these children, besides the pavement dwellers to whom it was limited till date. Based on that one child's feedback, we managed to identify almost 65 students who were facing similar problems. Our proposal to Ratna Nidhi Charitable Trust was approved and 65 children now benefit from the same.

2. *Problem : Need for acknowledgement.* "Didi is not aware of it, but I love to come to Sunbeam." (This written response came from a child who used to come to Sunbeam all the way from Nalasopara to the Chandanwadi center – travelling more than an hour by train each way – and hence was late at times).

Solution : A new teacher is now orientated on each child's background – the ones whom she is supposed to handle - so that children who need to be appreciated need not be penalized for circumstances beyond their control. Here, the Education Coordinator explained to me that the child's expression had to do with the new recruit at Chandanwadi who might have scolded the kid for late coming, as she might not to be aware that he came all the way from Nalasopara (which is at the other end of Mumbai), as compared to the rest of his classmates who stayed at a walking-distance from the Sunbeam center.

3. *Problem : I want love from Sunbeam, and one good didi.* "I received stationery, toys, etc. from Sunbeam. I want love from Sunbeam, and one good didi. What makes me saddest in life is that there is no love for the country in anybody's heart but I still have love in my heart." This is what Sandeep (name changed), 6th std. wrote in his feedback.

Solution : These are the kind of cases that need gentle probing to know what a child is trying to convey. (Shanta, with her counseling team members, is looking into the many cases where it's only because of inability on the part of Sunbeam's teaching staff, especially the new recruits, that a child ends up feeling lost where there's a possibility of simple solutions changing the situation in his / her life.)

Friends, let me explain Sandeep's case and how we have handled it, for all of you to understand why sensitive counseling is required in such cases.

- Sandeep happens to be a kid whose mother, a year ago, abducted a girl-child from his neighbourhood, and was later imprisoned for it.
- Unfortunately, there was a vast difference in how his Sunbeam teachers viewed the situation, as compared to the very horrible trauma he was actually undergoing.
- We requested our teaching staff to share their feedback on problem cases where child counselors could be of help. In Sandeep's case, all that they had to say to Shanta and me was "Sandeep's having problems at home, for which reason, he, who had been an excellent performer in academics, managed to get only average marks in mid-term exams."
- Only on further probing from my end, they casually told me that up until 8 months ago, he used to plead that though, his mother had been in the wrong, he could be spared by the world and by his classmates. His only question to his Sunbeam didis was, "Why am I being mentally tortured, looked upon with contempt, or jeered at by my classmates?" Unfortunately, the didis hadn't felt the need to have counseling sessions with the entire class (during their free period or half-an-hour on the weekly day meant for sports) to make it easier for Sandeep to attend Sunbeam.

- Two months ago at the Lonavala camp, a community worker found him with a huge stone in his hand, and stopped him before he could harm another child. Now, Sandeep has reached a stage where he has become violent and cannot forgive the world for the pain it's unnecessarily causing him.

- In his written feedback that was supposed to be handed over to the teacher, he couldn't dare to voice his actual problem, which he was too embarrassed to share with his teacher.

- To Shanta he revealed that he wasn't pointing at love for the country but his classmates not being able to accept him. Now he knows he can count on didis like Shanta and Mohini to sensitise his classmates.

4. Problem : One of the family members is missing. The search is on with no result.

Bhavani (name changed), Sandeep's sister, studying in the same class as he does, has mentioned in her written feedback, that one of her family members is missing. The search is on but no one is able to locate him.

(Friends, with so many problems and traumas in Sandeep's and Bhavani's life unaddressed, it's not right on our part to expect them to be able to concentrate on studies or get excellent results in academics. We may not be able to solve each and every one of their problems, but that's not even what Sandeep or Bhavani are asking for).

Solution : Be a good listener. Let children have space to unburden themselves. Provide solutions wherever possible. Where it's not possible for the staff or Sunbeam to do anything about a problem, explain why so – to the child. He / she will understand and still feel loved.

- Unfortunately, this is what the Sunbeam didis have to say of Bhavani. "She is a very good girl. No amount of criticism or blame of any kind affects her peace. She is so good that she takes it all in silence."

- Friends, I've tried to make them understand that just because a child is quiet, it doesn't mean that nothing affects her. We do have a few cases where, by keeping their problems to themselves, they have reached a stage where they have attempted suicide!

- As for Sandeep, I've been explaining to his didis at Sunbeam that he is just seeking a few words of reassurance from them - that he is loved, wanted, accepted by them. Also, that he is not responsible for his mother's error; that he is right in loving her as he does, because he is right in stating that she has paid the price for her wrong act and she needs to be forgiven and loved. All that he is seeking from his didis is that his classmates be made to understand that he has a right to live in peace and not be blamed for anything that he is not responsible for.

5. Problem :Feeling of incompetence: "One thing that makes me very sad in life is when I don't stand first in class or when I fail in exams for circumstances beyond my control." "When I participate in sports, or dance and drama but do not win a prize, or lose a competition - that's the day when I feel very unhappy and disappointed."

Quite a few kids across the organisation – primary to the higher secondary ones - have expressed these sentiments in writing.

Solution : We need to let kids understand it's the effort that counts.

That : Academics, important as it is, has to be a joy and not a burden. One should always aim for good marks; but if circumstances do not permit one to study enough, then failure in a subject doesn't amount to failure in life. Not standing first in class doesn't mean not having performed well. Participation is more important than winning.

6. Problem : I'm very unhappy when it's a holiday or Sundays.

This problem could be indicative of problems at home front. In case our fears are proved right then, this is how we'd go about it.

Solution : Counselling parents.

Our counsellors talk to the children (individually) who've made this statement, and got to the root of the problem and suggested solutions. Alternatively, they visit the homes, and in a tactful, kind manner bring to the notice of the parents what effort on their part could make their child's life happier.

7. Problem : "I'm discontinuing studies because of monetary problems at home."

"I'm told it's my age to concentrate on studies. I'm in the 9th std. now. But I'm confused because I also believe I need to supplement my father's meager income - else I'll have no choice but to return to our village, and discontinue with my studies altogether. Can Sunbeam give me a job?"

Solution being worked upon: Vocational training for the next 6 months, direct SSC next year without attending daily classes, a full-time job next year with evening tuition for Math, Science, English.

These kinds of solutions will be more practical, and will work to the benefit of the child as well as the family. It's not as though child labour is being encouraged. He is a 17-year-old boy and as he himself feels responsible for his family's well-being, I believe this would be the best course of action in the given scenario.

On Issues that Need My Time and Attention

I believe it to be my prime-most duty to assist our staff in their efforts at meeting our organisational goals. Every day is a mission for our staff. They have to work hard to sustain the interest level of children towards formal education and their parents' cooperation in the same direction. Unfortunately, a few of them are unable to understand the emotional and psychological needs of our children. This is clear from the feedback I receive from the children from time to time at the different centers.

Taking pride in the positive academic results of our children is natural on my part. But I have to also look into matters that need urgent attention if we have to fulfill our mission of the holistic development of our beneficiaries. A center where the teachers are too lenient to bother about teaching ethics or values to a child, and focus only on the text book syllabus, also requires my attention.

Though the negative feedback from the children, especially if it's on Sunbeam, always pains me, I also profit by it. The shock of our children having to put up with unfairness or injustice at Sunbeam makes me understand that I haven't yet succeeded in sensitizing some of the Sunbeam family members. Labelling or beating children has never been acceptable to me, but what is even more disturbing is their stubbornness in their own belief system on how children should be moulded. In the given scenario, with quite a few of our field staff falling in that category, all I can do is put the power of love to its ultimate test by never giving up on myself and continuing with my attempts at making them understand their role.

Our child beneficiaries need to be treated with dignity and I leave no stone unturned to make that happen. Always calm and serene - is what I want to be, but can't, can't put up with the unfairness with which our children are treated, especially if it's at Sunbeam. In the slums, and on the streets where they live, it's a dark world. Sunbeam is meant to be a place where they feel secure, have a sense of belonging, and feel valued. It should never be the place to add on to their miseries in life.

The unfairness with which these children have been treated at home have made them seem well-equipped to handle challenges outwardly – when in reality, they are possessed with very little trust in themselves. At the staff meetings, when the problem cases are discussed, I request the teachers to recognise this tough exterior as a reflection of the children's efforts to cover up the hurt and pain they constantly go through. My request to our staff has always been to allow our children to feel and express their feelings instead of keeping them under check, or worse still, denying them altogether. Also, to explain to them that they need not put up a tough exterior all the time, they should feel secure enough with Sunbeam didis and bhaiyas to let their masks slip. That way, it would help them bond with the children better.

There have been a few field staff who have also erred and ended up hurting children. But their intention was not to do so. In such cases I've tried to handle them with care. Friends, it is all very simple to understand, yet emotionally taxing to carry it out. I'll not say that forgiveness comes to me easily. I confess, it doesn't. Yet, forgiveness, I've come to understand, is the key to bring about the best in such individuals.

The brighter side:

Also, I can never overlook the fact that children have been blessed with Sunbeam staff in whom I have often seen a reflection of God. I see that and I stand a little taller. I also see other staff becoming more sensitive to our children's needs. It makes me feel very reassured. I've never failed to express my appreciation towards a staff member (both individually and in a group) when they've taken that extra step to make our children feel loved and cared for – which almost all of them do every single day.

Taking a call:

There are also times when I'm left with no option but to terminate the services of a staff member, especially if I see our vulnerable beneficiaries being the target of their insensitivity. Our field workers are the ones in whose hands we have placed their destinies. The way our staff will mould them will have a direct effect on the kind of adults our children will grow into. Where the intention is to hurt a child's self-esteem, his emotional well-being, etc., I've not regretted taking corrective measures.

My dream in life is that the Sunbeam family leaves future generations a legacy of love and acceptance, for all children in need. My heartfelt prayer is to see the didis, bhaiyas and their adorable children grow and unfold as one family, united in love.

Positive responses from the staff are an indicator that they understand my role of having to direct them and instead of doubting my intention, they are able to step back and reflect. Instead of retreating, they absorb what I have to offer.

Though professional teaching skills are required, what is more important to make a person effective at field level jobs is a mother's heart that can listen to all the unspoken words of her child. The day I'm convinced that the staff turnover has become minimal and our existing staff – each and every one of them – are extremely nurturing individuals, I'll feel less guilty to work my way out of this job and spend time with children, simply bask in their love and innocent company. The day Sunbeam becomes completely independent of me, I know it will not leave an empty spot in my heart. On the contrary, it will fill my heart with pride at my own success in my extremely challenging role.

9

On My Role at Sunbeam as I See It 2007 Onwards

Introduction

As the founder and the managing trustee of the organization, I have several responsibilities. As also, I hold several expectations of myself. In the current scenario, I see myself not only as the CEO having a team of Functional Heads reporting to me, but also as a mentor, visualiser and implementer of numerous tasks and plans. There are four other areas where I feel my major contribution should lie over and above my already extensive, extremely vast role of managing all the aspects of the organization (including those that have been mentioned in the previous chapter):

1. Staff recruitment, orientation and retention
2. Sensitising children towards the needs of others as well
3. Absorbing interested and capable Sunbeam beneficiaries into our own system
4. Ensuring that our team aids all of our 1000+ children to reach their goals

Sunbeam and I are privileged to have support of our dedicated team members who've been largely responsible for the fulfillment of the above mentioned goals thereby resulting in the organization's mission being successfully accomplished.

I. Fostering the Foundation

Heading an organization is a monumental task, more so, when the enterprise in question is an NGO. As the managing trustee, the prime difficulties I've come across during the course of this eventful decade are staff recruitment, orientation and retention. There are people who've been with Sunbeam since its inception, giving the project proverbially their blood and sweat. They have virtually lived solely for the children all these years.

Reduced need for the counseling team:

Over the years the role of our community development team cum social workers has undergone a radical change, due to varied reasons:

- The primary focus of education shifted from non-formal to the formal one.
- The unrelenting work of counselors has resulted in the parents being empowered enough to estimate the value of sending their children to school. They also attend meetings regularly.
- The students themselves now understand that a sound education can lead to a better life. The attendance levels have shot up considerably.
- Whenever required, in some exceptional cases, the teachers themselves do not hesitate to visit their homes.

With little or no necessity for community work foreseen in the next few years to come, this calls for staff capacity building. Sunbeam would not be the same without the involvement of many of the people who form its core group, and thus, it would be unwise as well as insensitive on the management's part to let go of their indispensable services. Similarly, Sunbeam employs certain subject teachers who may not hold a B.Ed degree, but who are extremely motivated, focused, passionate and caring when it comes to taking care of the overall needs of the underprivileged children – emotional, social and psychological.

Measures undertaken:

A few innovative techniques involving internal capacity building have been put into practice to ensure maximum employee contribution, in order that the association may prove mutually rewarding:

- *Training:* Majority of the staff who are involved in conducting surveys, motivating the parents, and encouraging and counseling children to enroll into Sunbeam, are presently being given D.Ed. training within the organization by the trained faculty. This is to ensure that this set of dedicated workforce is absorbed as effective primary / secondary section teachers / supervisors. Fortunately, after a short initial phase of apprehensions and doubts, most of the staff has gracefully made the transition from community empowerment work to that of teaching their respective subjects.

- *Reinforcement:* Few of the existing teachers, though not holding a degree in education have acquired a vast deal of experience through the ups and downs faced by the institution over the years. These are, thus, retained owing to the deep reservoir of knowledge that they possess.

- *Salary restructuring:* The past three years have seen the staff salaries being revised twice. This is to honour their commitment to the organization, and their devotion of time and talents, despite the challenges they face as staff of an establishment that works for a section which is vastly different in its background – social and economical. They deserve a good pay in the least, though it is not at par with what the public sector could offer them. Giving due importance to the knowledge of the English language, its study has been made compulsory across the organization. Better packages ensure attraction as well retention of a qualified and committed workforce.

II. Offering the Beneficiaries a Perception of the Brighter side

Instilling moral values in children is as important as making them literate. One of the most significant ones is the virtue of compassion – for fellow human beings. And this is one of my prime areas of focus. Also, there has to be instilled in them a feeling of assurance and confidence in their own abilities, so that they may move ahead in life without any feelings of inferiority.

During my weekly visits to the centers, oftentimes I had sensed that some of the children either lacked self-confidence, or considered themselves to be the disadvantaged lot, or were simply apathetic towards problems faced by others.

That made me more aware that as their mentor, my prime duty should also be to mould them in a three-fold way:

- To get them out of their self-pity so that they stop considering themselves as less privileged than others simply on the basis of economic status; and to make them understand that there were people lesser privileged too – those that were physically disabled or mentally challenged.

- To inculcate in them a sense of acceptance of problems of people other than their own selves, such as of their siblings, classmates or the physically handicapped.

- To curb the high irregularity of attendance due to minor ailments such as a bout of flu, a slight headache or a stomachache, by making them aware that more critical conditions – like missing limbs or impairments – could never hamper one's progress if one really put his / her mind to it.

Personally, I haven't ever believed in sermonizing children. It has little or no effect on their minds. Hence, one of the best opportunities I got to sensitize their mindsets was the invitation from another NGO named 'Manthan', which works upon building the self-confidence and inborn talents of the physically disabled and the visually impaired children. While watching their beneficiaries perform at the program during early 2008, our Sunbeam beneficiaries underwent a change of heart and mind to a certain extent.

Being a witness to these kinds of events leaves a long lasting positive impact on them, as is evident from the responses of a few of the students who attended it:

"I learnt a few invaluable lessons from the visually impaired and the physically challenged children as they performed with confidence in front of a huge audience. It was a wake-up call to my inner voice of confidence in one's own abilities." – Pratik Nagotkar, 9th Std.

"It was memorable. That the handicapped could be so talented left me spellbound. I understood that if they, with a missing limb, can manage so many unimaginable feats due to their determination to excel, then we, with our physically fit bodies, can achieve anything that we set our minds to. This has increased my self-confidence, which I shall now channel in the right direction." – Akshay Gujar, 9th Std.

"It changed my attitude towards children with physical defects. I used to make fun of the visually impaired. But now, I have resolved never to mock the physically or the mentally challenged lot." Ashish Sonavane, 9th Std.

The aim is to not only make them able to read and write, and get them through important exams, but also to enable them to view their own selves on par with everybody – with their peers in college, or with their colleagues at workplace later in life. Otherwise, the purpose of giving them a respectable life, where they have decent jobs, shall be lost.

III. Incorporating the Beams

Part A

Just as the light of the sun spreads out through its rays, the growth of Sunbeam is largely due to the children that it caters to – they form the rays through which knowledge, enlightenment and love spreads. It was thus a matter of great pleasure and pride when one of the beneficiaries offered his services to the organization. Sunbeam got a dedicated employee, and the student in turn got an opportunity to exhibit his talents, gained work experience as well as benefit economically. The student in question is Ganesh and here follows his account.

Ganesh's Starry Eyes

One of our brightest pupils, Ganesh, secured a whopping 81 % at the SSC board exams. Currently, he studies in FYJC B.Com in the Hinduja College. When I offered him the post of an Office Assistant, he shared with me that he felt himself capable of contributing much more. "Didi, finance is my interest area and given a month's time, I'm sure I shall be able to handle the Accounts Assistant's role," he suggested one day. And so he was given voucher files, registers, MIS reports to study through the next few days, and in July'08, he joined us as a part time Accounts Assistant. Within a short span, he had proven himself true to his words. He is immensely capable, honest and hardworking as an employee. In a couple of months, he could handle most of the tasks independently!

The college being in the afternoon, he devotes 4 hours of his mornings to Sunbeam. After passing the Junior College, when he would be required to attend classes in the morning, he'll be able to work 6 hours a day and hence wishes to take up some of the Administration as well as Career Counselling work too.

"What makes you stay so committed to Sunbeam, Ganesh?" I inquired. He enumerated enthusiastically:

- "My immense pleasure it is that I was taken on by Sunbeam on merit.
- I receive full cooperation from all the staff, which is why to carry on with Sunbeam would be a unique experience in itself.
- By giving me this opportunity, didi has given me a chance to work in my own organization.
- I believe I can fulfill the need of keeping accurate and timely reports in Finance, so that donors would never hesitate to contribute to our cause.

I hope that in the future too, didi and my colleagues continue to support me, and accept me as a member of the Sunbeam family."

We are obviously more than happy and privileged to have him. There are certain more individuals who have expressed a similar desire, and Sunbeam shall make every effort to give them the training and the opportunity to lend of themselves to the organization they cherish.

Part B

When we thus took on Ganesh as an employee, it set me thinking. The problem of staff retention could be made manageable to a great extent if we could take willing students as staff – part time or as volunteers – while they are in college. This way, the beneficiaries could support us in extending a helping hand to the rest of the children too.

It is very difficult to obtain 100% results in the classes with 20% of the children being below-average performers, and needing individual undivided attention that is humanly not in the limits of a teacher. Having one tutor monitoring a handful of students is economically not feasible either.

In view of this, I suggested to the Higher Secondary classes in the beginning of 2008, if the excellent students would like to help the ones who have difficulty coping up with the syllabus. There were a few who volunteered whole-heartedly.

Though the 1st term response and result of this exercise was negligible, I feel proud to share now the impact this kind of a program had on the students:

Ankita, an 8th std. student, was the first to offer to arrive at the Worli education center an hour prior to her usual classes in order to teach English to 5 of her classmates. Vimal, another batch-mate of hers followed in her footsteps and started tutoring another batch of 5 class-mates in Maths. They found it interesting to teach their own syllabus, and felt it was easy to train fellow-students whom they knew well. Following their success, 3 more batches were started on similar lines.

A few months later, 18 of the bright performers have joined us now in our efforts. This is what the 13 year old students who teach, and the ones who are taught, have to say about their newfound experience:

- *"I decided to instruct my fellow students because I felt I could help them by doing so. I had myself expressed this desire to Swapnali didi. All the students should possess equal levels of understanding of the subject. If everyone makes the effort, it would bear fruit.*

I train them in basic English. I get angry at the students occasionally when they don't obey me. Their absence, even though on very rare occasions, makes me sad. Yet, watching the students study well even when once in a while when I'm late for the class, makes me glad. I feel privileged to have been given the opportunity to teach children; it was my desire that got accomplished. I hope to come across many more such prospects during my lifetime." ***Ankita Yelve***

• *"I had always wanted to teach someone, and my wish has got fulfilled. Sulbha didi used to say that serving people brings us blessings. I had always kept this in mind. I wanted all the children to secure good marks in Mathematics like me, so I decided to tutor them. This way I could be of assistance to didi too.*

I teach Maths and I enjoy it. At times I get irritated with the children who come late to the class. But then that hurts me and I apologise. When they accurately solve the sums given by me, I feel happy. When I tell all this to my parents, they advise me to train the children well, support didi, and learn a good deal in the process myself." ***Vimal Bhartav***

•*"We understand all that Ankita teaches, because she does it very well, explains every sentence. She comes early mornings for us, and tutors us without any charges. I'm happy, and hope to receive her assistance in future too. She can give full attention to each of us, which is not possible in a classroom of 32 students. I thank her with all my heart."* ***Hema Dalvi***

• *"Vimal is very nice and helps us a lot. I understand all that she teaches and am now able to solve sums* correctly on my own. I'm happy to receive help for my future."

Priyanka Kadam

None of them have been compelled to contribute their time and talent. Conversely, they love to utilize their potential during their free time and to help and give of themselves to the place they care so much for. These students too respect their teenaged teachers' contribution of their time. The proposition has been a big hit with them all.

The staff guides the 20 tutors on what is expected of them. The exercise has many benefits:

- Besides inculcating a sense of responsibility in the bright students, it made them realize their potential.
- Having been at the receiving end since long, they are happy to be contributors.
- Most of them would get an idea from this exercise whether they would like to continue as teachers later too, or would like to join Sunbeam in similar capacity in future.
- Slow learners developed confidence on receiving individual attention.

10

On Taking Our Mission Deeper

On Taking our Mission Deeper

I understood that real leadership was also about accepting what I could not do all by myself. So I invited, called for, drew, on all the goodwill there was for Sunbeam, and for me. Janaki Venkat and Pervin Varma were dear friends who had always stood by me in times of need, both at a personal and at an organisational level. And in January 2006, I once again sought their help. This time around, in assisting me in sensitising our staff on children's issues. To my joy and relief, Janaki and Pervin both assured me of their consistent, long-term support to Sunbeam. They offered to conduct monthly workshops with our teams. Via these workshops, they shared with them the values and principles of Sunbeam and sensitised them towards children's issues, and helped them understand their role beyond teaching. Their regular sessions with the teams meant a lot to me. No longer did I feel overwhelmed or lonely while facing challenging situations at Sunbeam. Before I move on to sharing with you the kind of support that I received from these 2 friends, and the extremely positive impact that their intervention had on our field staff, let me take this opportunity to pen my gratitude to each of them for their unique contributions in my life.

Janaki Venkat is someone whom I have turned to for support time and again, and I can say with conviction that Sunbeam could not have been blessed with a better facilitator for these kind of sessions. Janaki works as an Organisation Development Consultant. She is a consultant to Corporates. And from the time I've been with CRY, I've also known her to work with senior leadership. She had been involved in the Institution Building process for CRY during the period 1997 - 2001. That's how I had got to know of her.

Dear readers, Pervin Varma happens to be not only a friend who I have turned to in times of need for over a decade now, but also someone who loves children and has lived all her life for their betterment. She is the former CEO of CRY – Child Relief & You, now renamed Child Rights and You.

Janaki, my dear friend, has always shared her talents, time, and wealth with Sunbeam, without expecting anything in return. But what I need to thank her most for is her unique contribution to me as a person. She has assisted in making me a more compassionate person who now makes every attempt to awaken in one and all, the inherent goodness in them lying dormant, instead of giving up on erring staff members, especially if the lapses on their part have been unintentional. Moreso, when their seeming insensitivity towards our child beneficiaries has stemmed from their own conditioning in life. I reiterate that whenever I've felt angry or disillusioned with our staff members, she has helped me understand their behaviours and actions from their frame of reference, and in turn aided me in moulding them into more patient and caring human beings - more of friends to our children than teachers.

Janaki and Pervin helped take an organisational view of the process, without getting overly engaged with any one aspect that was not functioning properly. They aided me in stepping out and taking a larger view of the issues, thinking of solutions and coming back with realignment. They also helped me look at how the system was contributing to what was going wrong at Sunbeam, and what could be done about it.

Both Janaki and Pervin have been friends to our staff whom they appreciate, understand, and accept with love, while gently inducting them into our culture. Given that most of our teaching staff are new recruits and also appreciating that these individuals who have dedicated themselves to working for our cause can give just a year's commitment and no more, Pervin and Janaki have offered to hold these sessions on a regular and an ongoing basis.

In one session they worked on helping the staff members get to know each other better, bond together - and made them understand how, as a team, they could overcome so many obstacles that they faced at the field level. If they felt more distanced from one set of Sunbeam partners (colleagues, supervisors, donors, children, parents of the beneficiaries, formal school authorities, etc.) as compared to the rest, they helped them introspect and find out for themselves how they could work on those relationships.

Then in yet another session, they took our staff back to their childhood experiences – good and bad – and made each of them share the same within smaller groups. It enabled our staff to now see the link – rather - how their childhood experiences still affected their current behaviour. It also helped them understand their own strengths and all that they were sure of being able to offer our child beneficiaries. (Note I.) Surprisingly, our staff members were even able to come up with what, to their mind, could their children be afraid of, as regards themselves as their didis - be it teachers or community workers. (Note II.) It was such a revealing, enriching, learning session for all of us present there that I take this opportunity to share the same with you in our staff members' own words. It might be of help to some of the readers faced with similar situations as in not being able to understand a child's expectations or unspoken fears of them as parents or teachers.

I. As on date, what can the child expect of me (his / her didi) with guarantee?

(Staff feedback from across the organisation – Note I.)

- Proper guidance on studies
- Quality education
- They can trust us with their confidential matters
- General Knowledge sessions
- Games and story sessions
- Faith that if their health problems are shared, they will be taken care of
- Festival celebrations at their education centers
- Appreciation of good performance
- Average performers being motivated to perform better
- Building on a child's confidence
- Even if a child calls out to me at midnight, I'll be able to make time for him
- Provide a loving atmosphere at Sunbeam
- Teach them right from wrong
- They can count on me to guide them regarding their future
- Assist in building upon the leadership qualities in a child
- Mould them into becoming contributing members of society
- Effort to understand a child's feelings and help solve his problems
- Effort to find out the child's expectations of me and try to fulfil them
- Help them develop good habits, good manners and values in life
- Give children the space to share their problems / unburden themselves
- Give them a sense of belonging

- Keep our promises to our children
- Treat children with care and dignity
- Encourage children in their co-curricular activities
- Solve problems at his home-front by visiting his home

II. To our mind what kind of fears could the children possibly be having of us as didis?
(Staff feedback from across the organisation – Note II.)

Fear of being punished for the following reasons :

- Failing in exams
- Not getting good marks in the exams
- Not being able to put up with the pressure of studies and inability to perform well
- For not doing their homework
- If they haven't done their studies properly

These are the different kinds of punishment the children might be scared of receiving from us :

- Scolding
- Beating
- Harsh beating
- Being screamed at
- Being made to stand outside the class for not doing homework

Other fears that our children might have of us didis.

- The fear of rejection by didi if I go wrong / make errors
- If I share something confidential about my personal life, would didi humiliate me by discussing the same with me in another's presence?
- When I share something with didi, will she pay attention to what I'm saying, will she take me seriously?
- If I share something about my family or when I make mistakes at Sunbeam, would my didi complain about it to my parents?
- Does didi trust me?

- Can I trust didi?
- Am I as important to didi as she is to me?
- Would my expectations be fulfilled by didi?
- Would other children / adults make fun of me for my physical handicaps or for my poor academic performance, and didi not do anything about it?
- Fear of punishment when we do something we've been forbidden to do by our didis
- Fear of falling in the sight of my didi if I don't perform well or am unable to meet her expectations.

The above expressions proved to be an eye-opener for the field staff. They already knew the answers and began to work upon them. It was clear to them as to what steps, on their part, would lessen the distance between them and their children.

Oftentimes, some of our staff members were left feeling stressed out because others didn't cooperate. At other times, a staff member quit due to interpersonal problems. More often than not, when they couldn't resolve the issues amongst themselves, their anger and frustrations got passed on to our children. I shared with Janaki and Pervin these problems as well. Hence, in the workshops to follow, they decided that now that we had had our earlier sessions on Sunbeam and on the children, we could shift our focus on the problems of the staff members themselves, keeping in mind that the majority of them had to work directly with children.

Janaki and Pervin explained to the staff members that at a tender age, children could be moulded the way we wanted them to and that they'd imbibe the values and principles that we (as teachers) set by example, which in turn, to a large extent, would shape their destinies in the years to follow. A child who had grown with Sunbeam would reflect its culture and ethos – and it would be the field staff that would be largely responsible in creating the desired impact on the children, who were in daily contact with them. Despite the tremendous challenges that all of us at Sunbeam faced, we could help our children realise their hopes and aspirations. For this to become a reality, we needed to focus our efforts on the children who were at the heart of all our activities and programs. In the first session, the teams were made to discuss and put on paper what they believed would be the ideal situation amongst themselves. The session to follow focussed on the current scenario i.e. the reality at Sunbeam and the many reasons that prevented the ideal situation to take root.

Taking stock of both the sessions, all team members understood that in an organisation that was rapidly growing, inter-personal problems and issues were bound to arise. But those need not be allowed to become the focus of our attention, causing distraction from our main purpose i.e. the wellbeing of our children. It took courage to identify and acknowledge their limitations – but we're proud that our team members took that first step in the positive direction. All of us had the capacity to reduce the negative emotions that surfaced at regular intervals. We adopted measures such as :- Subduing the negative emotions, listening empathically, extending a helping hand to a co-worker, etc. - were sure to bring about the desired environment - free of friction and conflict, and one in which all members co-existed in harmony.

11

On My Motherhood – With My 4 Year Old Niece

Introduction

The chapter on Pearl, my sister Jasmine's daughter, is my way of cementing forever my memories of the months spent with her. Those 3 months in the company of my 4-year-old niece, were magic, and I was blessed with an opportunity to play the role of a mother. Her presence around me seemed to lift the stress off my life.

From the day she was born till she turned to a toddler, she had been at our place with Jasmine. My parents (and I) had had a wonderful time with her. Now, in mid 2003, Pearl had turned 4. And Jasmine was expecting another baby. So, she requested me to take charge of Pearl for a while.

"She is just 4. How will she take towards me in her mum's absence for the few days that she'll be away at the hospital?" Pearl settled those questions from the first moment, by expressing both in words and actions how thrilled she was at the prospect of staying with me. Every moment that she spent with me during that week, her face was beaming with joy. Now and then she'd walk towards me with arms open wide. Each time that she encircled me in a warm embrace, I felt like a proud parent. My trusting, loving, and vulnerable child loved being cuddled. A week later, she was back home with her parents and her baby brother, Jehan.

As days passed, Pearl became rebellious. She drove her parents to the limit of their patience. She grew more agitated and harder to handle by the day. In my presence, one day she declared to her parents, "It's a world for mummy, daddy and Jehan. I am nowhere to be seen in their world." It was the birth of a sibling that had made Pearl feel so insecure. Fortunately, her parents never brushed aside her feelings as unimportant. They requested me to come over and stay with them for a few months – to be a friend to Pearl.

I gladly took up that offer. In my own way, I explained to Pearl why Jehan needed full-time attention from their mum and at the same time that didn't mean that her mother's love for her had diminished. Still whimpering, she shook her head earnestly, tears flowing down her flushed cheeks. My role was just to make her feel secure in the midst of her chaotic life and to assure her that as mum was too busy to demonstrate her love for her in action, I was around to fill that gap - to provide for her emotional needs. My child was still trying to come to grips with the fact that her parents' love and attention was to be shared and not for her alone, as before. On her part, Jasmine demonstrated her love to Pearl very regularly to reassure her of the same.

Whenever I entered their house, I didn't go anywhere near Jehan's crib. Instead, I held out my arms and let Pearl run to me. Jasmine would feel too scared to allow Pearl to handle Jehan. But the moment she placed him on Pearl's lap (upon her insistence), she was elated. A smile of love would spread across her face and her eyes would twinkle with pride. Because the thrill of holding Jehan surpassed all her other joys.

Jasmine did most of the childcare work while I just watched the mother in her selflessly give of herself to the little darlings. And I have to give credit to Yezdi (her husband) who lent a helping hand at all the chores, including changing Jehan's diapers, dropping Pearl to preschool before leaving for office, and so on.

I normally reached their home by 8 p.m. after my day's work at Sunbeam. On my part, I simply played with Pearl, then with great difficulty managed to feed my fussy child, told her bedtime stories, held her in the middle of the night when she woke up after a nightmare or to clean her when she threw up due to fever or indigestion, bathed her and dressed her up for school.

Jasmine and Yezdi were wonderful parents who abided by the demands of parenthood at the cost of their sleep. I never once had to watch over the newborn. It was not my cup of tea. I needed a minimum of 6 hours of sleep (that Pearl would allow me), for me to be able to function energetically at Sunbeam throughout the day.

As Pearl's masi (mum's sister), I have many special and fond memories to share. Let me take you through some of them.

Children's Delightful and Magical Fantasyland

Sometimes I would tell her stories made up to fit her mood. At other times, it would be any other story from a storybook. As she tucked herself under my arm, she grabbed a storybook and held it in front of my face and said, "I can barely read beyond 3 letter words. So, what's the point in getting me these books if you're not going to read them out to me?" My long list of pending phone-calls and other work at Sunbeam haunted me. But I knew that my child's little wish (and my own need to be with an angel) surpassed Sunbeam work that could wait. I opened the book and began to read.

Getting utterly bored she stopped me halfway and pleaded with me to revert back to our old schedule. "O Masi, don't you remember those lovely stories you used to tell me? Stories where I used to be the main character!" Then, her eyes lit up in merriment as she added, "I remember the one in which I wore the monkey mask, your gift to me. How I climbed the treetop from where I'd pluck and throw mangoes and other fruits to the children passing by!" She continued with the same amount of enthusiasm, "And the other story as well – the one where we went snow-climbing and I put some snowballs under the collar of the naughty uncle who didn't let children play because he didn't enjoy their company! Ha, ha. I liked that one." Now with a wistful look on her face, she added, "Masi, also the stories when you took Jehan and me along with our cousins Farhan and Diana to stay overnight in the forest and we had joyrides - not like the ones in Essel World but of a different kind altogether- elephant rides, camel rides, horse rides and many more thrilling ones. O what fun, what fun we had moving in the jungles and living on berries and fruits and having the animals, including the wild ones as our friends!"

After this little speech from my dear child, I put aside the set of moral storybooks and once again took her back to her mischievous and innocent fairyland. After a few stories that she heard out in rapt attention (and even interrupted me to add on an incident or two of her own to make it sound more authentic!), I found myself drifting off to sleep. But she'd snuggle in for one last story, and I'd wake up to the call, happy to know that it brought joy to my dear child.

It was worth watching her eyes light up and hear her giggle as she imagined her pet parrot perched on top of the table of the student sitting behind her (hidden from the teacher's view) reading out the four and five letter words in her place! She was thrilled that her loyal pet saved her from embarrassment in class at her own inability to recite from the book.

And I don't know who was enjoying the bedtime stories more - Pearl or myself!

Pearl's First Letter to Her Mother

One day Pearl had been up to her usual pranks and she ended up thoroughly annoying her mother. In a defiant tone, she told me, "Masi, I'm sorry for what I did. But I'm also angry with mum, so am in no mood to apologise to her." "OK, would you find it easier to convey to her that you love her?" I asked of her. "Well, that's no problem," she responded with a smile. "Then what about writing a birthday note to your mum, wishing her all the best and also letting her know that you love her?" She was thrilled at the suggestion.

"Masi, you may help me with the spelling of the word 'birthday'. I know how to write the rest of the sentence of telling her, that I love her and wish her all the best on her birthday. As for the date that needs to be mentioned on the letter, I know how to write that as well since I do so on a daily basis at the school." So saying, my 4-year-old picked up a pen and scribbled, '30.9.4002'! And of course, the rest of the letter followed in her lovely scrawl. My child's shoulders squared with pride at the completion of her very first letter addressed to her mother.

I'm sure Jasmine may never have received a more loving letter in all her life. Knowing my sister as I do, I understand that she finds it difficult to express her love openly but I could see that her eyes were moist - and within moments mother and daughter were in each others' arms.

A Child's World of Innocence

It was always a herculean task to wake up Pearl and get her ready for school. At times, she would drag herself out of bed up to the bathroom. At other times, she'd just not budge and Jasmine had no option but to carry her to the bathroom and leave her there with me. She'd glare at me because she'd feel a burning injustice had been done to her. In a childish tone she'd threaten me with, "Just wait till I call up Pa (meaning my father, her doting grandfather) to tell him how cruel you can be." I always pretended to be scared by her threats and told her not to complain to Pa. Oh, it was so funny to again see her doze off in the bathroom and then, upon waking up before I could pour water over her, look petulant.

Pearl being a very mischievous child, could have got herself locked into the bathroom when she was by herself. One evening, that fear had made Jasmine send her off to the playground with me and in her absence she called upon a carpenter to remove the latch from the side of the door and fix it on the top where it would be out of Pearl's reach.

The next morning, I could see her eyes focussed on the latch, mouth agape. "Pearl, what is it?" I asked wondering what her little mind was contemplating. "Masi, are you seeing what I am seeing? The latch moved up of its own accord! But, can latches move?" she inquired more than a little puzzled, still sleep-blurred!

The Tortoise that Drowned!

Pearl's pleas over the months – always of a different nature - had burrowed into my heart like arrows. Fortunately, each time I had simple answers that satisfied her. This time around, it was once again the innocent selfless love of a child – love for life in the form of a tortoise.

"Masi, come fast, please come!" It was my child's voice calling out to me from the other end of the Taraporewala Aquarium at Chowpatty, where I had taken her for a visit. I turned in the direction from where the voice had come and so did many others. I was poised for action, ready for rescue. As I reached her, pointing out to a fish tank, she burst into tears. I turned to where her finger was pointing and found nothing amiss. It was a tank in which a tortoise lay quietly taking a nap. "Masi, had you reached in time, you could have perhaps stopped him from drowning. O, he was swimming so well and then right before my eyes he drowned," she wailed. To her consternation and anger, she heard everyone around laughing away and making light of a seemingly sad event. I gently explained to her that a tortoise was one of the few creatures that could live on land as well as in water. To prove my point, I tapped on the tank till I managed to disturb the tortoise enough for him to stop resting at the bottom of the water tank, and once again swim about as before.

As I drove my fledging home, I was in awe of her selfless spirit – a child's utter innocence and love that encompassed all living creatures.

Pearl's Confusion on who to Marry!

To add to one more astonishment to the day, Pearl declared out of the blue, "I'm confused as to who I should marry." Before I could think of a response, she continued in the same confused state. With her head tilted to one side, in a statement that only a child can think of. "Well, there are 4 of you whom I love equally. Should it be my brother Jehan who is 3-months-old? Or who should it be out of the two friends of mine - Kiran or his sister Rekha? (Here, she was referring to two of our Sunbeam kids with whom she had had a great time at the overnight yearly camp at Aksa, a camp that had been attended by about a hundred kids). And Masi, you too are equally dear to me."

She seemed so anxious to hear my answer that she shouted at me, "Masi, finish the suspense once and for all. Who can it be out of the 4 of you?" "None," I managed to get out despite the gales of laughter that I had no control over. When at last I could speak, I queried, "And what is it that marriage is all about?" In an exasperated tone, she said, "Wait a minute. I didn't know you were that ignorant." Running to her bedroom she brought 2 dupattas and tied the ends together, the other ends of which she placed over her and my shoulder. Then she said in a sad tone, "I'd have actually shown you how a marriage takes place had mum allowed me to light a fire in the hall. That's all that needs to be done and we'd have run around it a few times. Now is that clear? Perhaps you don't watch enough television."

She never failed to awaken in me love and adoration for her by her god-like innocence.

"My Cousin Sister's Bicycle has Grown small Enough for me to Ride it!"

"No, you can't have a two-wheeler cycle since you are not old enough to ride one," said her mother with finality in her tone. Disappointment filled Pearl's face. I knew how badly she wanted a 2-wheeler cycle; she had outgrown the 3 wheeler long time ago.

Her parents had her cousin sister's 2 wheeler cycle placed in their balcony but it was a bit large for Pearl to manage. As she sat next to me, every morning she stared wistfully at the cycle lying in the balcony. Then, one day joy sparkled in her eyes as she exclaimed in sheer delight, "Masi, the cycle has grown a bit smaller though I'm not growing up fast enough for me to have a ride on it!"

As I related this incident to Jasmine and Yezdi, Pearl's innocence provided yet one more memory that brought a smile on our faces each time that we dwelled upon it.

"Can You Please Tell the Fairy to Fix My Tooth?"

What seem like normal events to adults, could be heartbreaking ones for children and they need to be handled with utmost sensitivity. Once when Pearl found me in very low spirits and heard the cause of my trouble – my glasses having broken, she literally gave me a sound lecture. In a very bugged tone, she said, "Masi, how can you let a not-so-important event, such as losing a nonliving thing, affect your peace? Imagine my state. Have you even considered how sad and scared I'm feeling right now? I'm in the process of losing a part of my body!" I was concerned as to what she could be hinting at. Finding me in a puzzled state, she went on to clarify, "Any moment I might lose a tooth and that too a front one. It's got loose and once it's gone, I've no idea how I'm going to face my classmates. You've always told me that God exists. And I also believe in fairies who protect children. Masi, on my behalf, can you instruct, nay, request one of the fairies to see to it that I do not lose my tooth?"

Understanding how worried she was at the prospect of her classmates laughing at her, I sat and explained to her, on how the falling off of teeth was a natural event that couldn't be avoided by anyone. I added that she'd once again get new beautiful teeth to replace the lost ones. She seemed relieved and was off to bed with a smile. (This incident took place not in '03 but sometime in '06 when she was 6 ½ year old.)

Pearl's Bridge of Friendship

One day as I was travelling with Pearl by train, I noticed that she was shying away from a differently-abled child. She refused to meet her gaze because she was afraid of the strangeness of her apparent physical defects until I told her about what could be the possible background, and circumstances that could have led the child to be where she was today – fending for herself. Upon realising that despite a missing limb, this child could handle herself quite confidently in an overcrowded train, where she sold her wares to earn her livelihood, Pearl looked upon her no longer with pity but with respect. She turned to me and said that though she didn't need to buy any of the stuff that the little girl was selling, I could just purchase a hair-band, so that the girl might earn something and not move out of the compartment with empty hands and disappointment.

I looked at my child who initially had questions all over her face but now it held a smile of compassion as she extended a hand of friendship to her counterpart with physical deformities.

I had succeeded in helping my kid confront her fear and pity about the physically challenged children. She no longer looked upon the child in front of her as any different from herself.

"Who Says Cakes Contain Eggs, I Can't See Any!"

Pieces of cake lay all over her plate and Pearl was still busy breaking them into smaller crumbs much to my annoyance. "You either eat properly or allow me to take your plate away," I addressed her in an exasperated tone. Calmly, our child remarked, "Well, I'm searching for eggs in the cake. Masi, you claim that you can't share the cake with me because it contains eggs. I've been searching for it since the past few minutes. I've broken the cake into the tiniest pieces just to confirm for myself that there is no egg in it, so that you can share it with me."

Each word of hers came from the puzzled mind of a child, who, in a slightly hurt tone, sat justifying her behaviour so innocently. My anger at the little one evaporated into laughter.

My Child's Way of Reaching out to Sunbeam Beneficiaries

To some she may come across as a very mischievous child, always up to some prank or the other, and rightly so. But I've also experienced her as an extremely caring and affectionate baby.

Once, Pearl had come with me to spend a weekend at her grandparents' house. On Saturday evening, on our way home, just as we entered a cab, a few of our Sunbeam children (the ones dwelling on the pavements) came running to me. Each of them gave me a bear hug. She looked concerned at the way they were dressed - in faded, torn and unwashed clothes. Then she turned and looked the other way out of the window. As I turned to look at my child, I noticed that she had the strangest expression on her face that I had ever seen: a combination of confusion, fear and concern!

The moment our cab took off and the children were out of sight, Pearl mumbled to herself, "Mum has always taught me to be kind on the less fortunate by giving them alms." As an afterthought, she added, "But I never knew it's OK to hug them. I just saw all those children hugging you and you not objecting to it!" she blurted out somewhat embarrassed. "They're my children," I replied in soft tones. "O, then why are they so shabbily dressed? They're not like the ones whom I met at the Aksa camp where you had taken me." "These children's parents cannot afford to have a shelter. Nor are they able to provide their children with the bare necessities in life such as water and sanitation facilities. They dwell on the streets."

She looked at me contemplatively, not saying anything for a long time, then looked away, out of the window. When I had given up expecting any response from her, in a voice tinged with sadness, she said, "I wish I could do something for your children." Then, in a voice full of compassion, she added in a matter-of-fact tone, "I think 2 pairs of clothes should suffice for me to leave at your Forjett street house. I barely stay at your place overnight, at the most once a month or so. Then, why keep a cupboard full of clothes for me? Let's just pack everything and take a return cab back here to your kids who need it more than me." She was full of empathy for them and her suggestion made sense.

Her kind words and selfless spirit moved me to tears.

"Masi I Need You - Not Your Gifts"

Sometimes I wondered whether I had taken on more than I could handle. One evening, I was feeling cranky and was in no mood to take care of a 4-year-old who was a real handful. Sweet as she was, much to my irritation at my own feeling of exhaustion, she seemed to be bounding in energy that could keep her awake until way past midnight!

So, I conveyed to her over the phone my inability to visit her that night, stating that all the shops in my area had closed down and that I'd not be able to bring her any gifts. "Masi, I need you more than any gifts. So please come to me," beseeched my darling over the phone. The words conveying selfless love on her part left indelible impressions on my mind. I choked back the lump that rose in my throat. Little did my child know how many trying moments at Sunbeam the memory of her sincerely loving statement would carry me through, over the following months.

Daily I was in the habit of buying her favourite chocolates and other eatables. She had been a demanding child, not easy to please. So I was surprised at her words. That night when I reached her home, she needed no cheering up. On the contrary, she was comforting me, saying, "Masi, so what if all the shops have closed down. I've two chocolates. First I was planning to have one and give you the other. But I've changed my mind. You've been bringing me things almost everyday. So, today I've decided that you should have both the chocolates."

That was a tender moment and touched a chord. I was completely unprepared for such an overwhelming response. I glanced over at my little darling and she was beaming. I could summon that look of delight merely by coming home night after night to give her company. Each time that her face shone with joy, it doubled my own joy of being her much-needed friend.

"Masi, I can see you're very tired. Today, you need not tell me any stories. Just your presence is enough. You may go to bed immediately and I'll lie quietly without disturbing you, I promise." She smiled her angelic smile. And her body language said it all, as she huddled up to me and was fast asleep within seconds - content in the knowledge that she still had me around!

"I'm so Happy You're Unwell!"

"O Masi, I'm so happy that you are unwell!" Her statement took me by surprise. Joy sparkled in her eyes and she seemed all excited. I was a little puzzled at her strange behaviour but only until I heard her next sentence. "That means you won't be going to work today. Am I right? If so, then neither do I have any plans to go to Sheni mummy's place (she meant the creche). Instead, we can spend an entire day together. Can we play at home, then do some cooking together and rush to the playground in the evening?" I agreed. Pearl was visibly elated at the prospect of spending an entire day doing what she loved to. Sunbeam and our children would have to wait.

My child and I shared a secret smile. Making a child responsible for chores builds independence and self-reliance. So, Jasmine was right in instructing Pearl to do her own small jobs instead of telling the maids to do the same. But the very idea of our naughty little Pearl being allowed to get anywhere near the gas stove, let alone cooking, would have horrified Jasmine. So both of us waited till she left for work. The minute she was out of sight, Pearl ran to the kitchen and plopped herself on the kitchen platform. "Masi, what shall we cook for lunch today?" "Noodles," I replied. She was amazed and thrilled that she could actually prepare a dish for lunchtime.

If I allowed my 4-year-old to cook, I also made sure that she didn't hurt herself in any manner. I looked at her trusting eyes resting on my face when she broke the noodles into tiny pieces and poured them into boiling water or when she added salt, pepper and butter to it. Later, she leaned back in her chair and gave me her most bewitching smile. "Isn't it tasting better than what it does when you or mum prepared it?" she asked, her face beaming with pride. I couldn't keep from smiling the way she had said that. Today, the food seemed most delicious to her, and why not? Hadn't it been the very first meal independently prepared by her? She even fed me with her own hands. Little did she know that she was feeding my heart with her unconditional love.

That evening at the park, we both had a wonderful time. Watching her on the swing in a happy mood, my heart rejoiced - no longer feeling guilty at having taken a day off from my hectic schedule at Sunbeam.

Jasmine's Expectations

Pearl made academic progress but hardly enough to be at par with her classmates. She still wasn't reading or writing as per senior KG syllabus. No doubt, she needed to have a strong academic foundation but as parents, Jasmine and Yezdi were clear on how that could be possible. So they requested the Principal to allow her to repeat the class instead of promoting her to the 1st std, since their child found it difficult to cope with studies.

As a mother, Jasmine's expectation of Pearl was never for her to outdo others in academics, but just to perform her best. She also had the humility to accept that with working parents and the birth of a sibling having affected her child's emotional state, it wasn't Pearl who was responsible for her below average performance but the many factors that had contributed to the same. So when report time came around, Pearl never became fearful of receiving less-than-perfect academic results. To be honest, she wasn't even aware that she hadn't fared well!

Jasmine's decision was the right one. It did a world of good to Pearl. From then on, our child flowered because both Jasmine and Yezdi put into action, their resolution to devote time to their child's studies despite their gruelling schedules at work. Hence, Pearl's true capabilities began to find expression. She gained self-confidence and was able to score commendable marks when she reached the 1st std, a year later.

There is nothing children cannot make of themselves with the right encouragement. When they see others believing in them, they begin to believe in themselves. (Today 5 years later, i.e. after repeating a class in senior KG, Pearl has now put her best effort year after year.) Our child has performed remarkably well in her yearly exams in April'06, actually scored 93 %! What explains her success? Constant encouragement and trust that her parents have placed in her has resulted in a high sense of self-esteem and self-confidence. The same has translated into sterling academic performance.

One evening before her 1st std. results were declared, she called me up, "Masi, I've got minus 10 marks in one subject. Ask me why? Because I was helping the girl sitting next to me frame the sentences that she couldn't on her own. My parents and you have always taught me to help others. Well, I do not understand what minus 10 means, but mum and dad are planning to go and apologise for my act of helping my classmate! They have explained to me that during exam time I'm not supposed to help others because that amounts to cheating, whatever cheating means."

(Later, Jasmine shared with me that Pearl's teacher informed Yezdi that if she had put –10 on her exam paper it was only to make Pearl understand that she couldn't help others during their exams, and not because she actually wanted to deduct her marks.)

"I'd Prefer to have a Fair Competition Even if it Means I'll not Get a Prize."

All children need to be given an opportunity to discover what they are good at. And after discovering their hidden talents, the same needs to be nurtured at a young age. One also needs to compliment children who win a prize in a school competition or perform well on stage. Not only would that motivate them to perform better but also would increase their self-confidence.

I can recall a day when Pearl had come to spend a week-end at our home and dad had taken her along to his office. To keep her busy with something fruitful so that she'd spare us and let us do our work, I requested Meenakshi (a teacher at Sunbeam), who was then present, to participate in a drawing competition with Pearl.

For a long time, she painstakingly worked on her drawing. Then she walked up to me with two drawings in hand. One could easily make out a child's drawing as compared to the one made out by an adult. But so as not to disappoint her, to her amazement, I called out her name as that of the winner.

"Had I written my name on the front side of the page, as my masi, you might have felt tempted to choose my drawing over Meenakshi aunty's. So that it should be a fair competition, I had written my name at the back." Pearl addressed me in a victorious tone. Beaming with pride she turned over her drawing paper to show me her own name scribbled on the back of it.

It was a natural action on her part, in keeping with the integrity with which she was brought up by her parents and the others in the family.

"I have Mum, Dad and You to Take Care of me. Who'll Look After the Street Child Living on his Own?"

One day, Pearl and I were travelling by train. I tried to stop her, but she tugged hard, broke free from my hand and went running to the street urchin who was sweeping the compartment and then asking the passengers for alms. Suddenly, she turned around and ran back panting. "Masi, the biscuits that Pa gave me are more than what I need," she said. I recall being extremely moved watching her search for her favourite packet of biscuits, and wanting to offer it to that child in need. "Masi, his appearance scares me. So do you mind going and handing it over to him? He might be hungry."

The train incident was erased from my memory by the time we went to bed. "Masi," I could hardly hear her whisper. Panicky thoughts filled my sleep-dazed mind as I woke up for the 3rd time in 2 hours. She was clutching her stomach and again throwing up. Sleep still fogged my mind, and I attempted to fight back the panic. My baby was very ill.

"Masi, what time of the night is it? And how many times have I thrown up by now?" "Thrice. And it's 2.30 in the night.

But why do you ask me for the time each time that you wake up?" "Mum is fast asleep. At times when I'm awake, I've noticed that she wakes up with Jehan on and often during the night. I don't want to disturb her further by letting her know of my health problem just yet." As I looked upon her, selfless love filled the air around her.

I had never seen my child so sick. By 3 a.m. she was drained of all energy, barely able to sit. Jasmine and Yezdi sat next to her, coaxing her to have electral water in order to avoid dehydration. "I think her illness is due to food poisoning. Perhaps her problem has to do with something that she ate tonight." (Jasmine was referring to the chicken dish that they had had for dinner.)

Her tortured sobs drew my attention. I was moved and totally unprepared for what followed. "It's my fault," she said over and over. "I shouldn't have offered him the biscuit packet," she wailed. Our explanation on food poisoning seemed to have increased her agony. In a barely audible whisper she added, "He's all alone. I have mum, dad and you. Now who'll take care of him?" The muffled voice came from under the covers. On top of the nightmare of the gastroenteritis problem that she was faced with, she was trying to deal with her guilt.

Again, I wondered what to say to calm her down. I held her hand and heard myself say, "God will take care of him by sending him caring individuals whenever he is in need. And as for food poisoning, your mum meant the chicken that you ate and not the biscuits that you had or shared with that boy." My explanation seemed to satisfy her.

Pearl recovered within a day or two, but I'll never forget the anguish expressed by her out of genuine concern for the little urchin at a time when she was herself so unwell - thereby exemplifying the most selfless love I'd ever known.

The Negative Impact of Television on Children

In those few months of being a mother to Pearl, one more incident stands out for me.

"Masi, don't leave me alone, not even to go to the toilet. I've never slept on my own. I get very scared of robbers barging into our house." I began to wonder what had prompted her to make such disturbing statements. She'd want me to keep patting her back till she went to sleep. This was her way of ensuring that I myself never went off to sleep prior to her or with my back turned to her!

I tried to reassure her that with tight security in her building premises, no robber could enter her home and rob her of her toys or other belongings. Figuring I had solved her dilemma, I turned and went to sleep only to find Pearl tugging on my arm. "The robber won't rob me of my toys. He'll stab me with a knife. There'll be blood all over and I'll never be able to stand up again," she stammered. She was scared and wouldn't release her grip on me.

I put my arms around her and sat assuring her that she was secure. God was there to protect her and children the world over. She prayed along with me. It was as if faith in an all-protective God had found its way into my child's heart.

I drifted back to sleep. A moment later, a tug at my arm and an urgent appeal from a terrified Pearl shattered the silence. I saw her ashen face and streaming eyes as I switched on the light. She was distressed. My eyes followed her trembling finger pointing at the door. "The robber will enter the house and there will be blood all over me." My child whimpered. She then mentioned that in a television serial she had seen someone stab a child to death. The impact of television on her young mind was certainly not positive. But I had to find a way out to help her outgrow her fear of murderers. On a night like this, she needed the comfort of a calm, reassuring voice that she could trust.

It is only normal for children to worry about things, real or imaginary. And Pearl was no exception. By hearing her out, consoling her and reassuring her of God's constant protection, I had helped lessen her fear, but she was yet to overcome it. She seemed to be having fears that she couldn't conquer. And I had to find a way out to help her overcome them. Silently praying to God, I fabricated a story that would be soothing to her ears. I assured her that the robber had decided to give up his bad habits and was now working in an office next to mine, living a decent life - one of hard labour. She believed every word of my story. "Oh, is that so?" she asked and her eyes again closed in slumber.

"Masi, the robber is a changed man, isn't he? He no longer causes any harm to anyone, does he? He continues to work in your next-door office?" She looked me right in the eye and waited for my reassurance. It was almost a week since I had fabricated the story!

I was dumb in the face of her complete innocence and faith in my word. In the middle of the night if I were to sit explaining to her that the robber had never existed in the first place, and it was a story in the TV serial that she had taken too seriously, I would have made too light of her fears. On the other hand, I didn't feel it right to now say that the robber turning over a new leaf was a story made up by me just to pacify her for the moment. So I assured her that she was right in her surmise and that he was indeed a changed man. That sometimes people did end up doing wrong things in life and hurt others but God's love brought them back to the right path. (Today, when I pen these lines, Pearl is almost 9, and understands that whatever she watches on television does not come true in real life; that these are just stories and the characters in the television are simply playing their roles. She also understands and appreciates that the world comprises of the good and the not-so-good individuals, but that her parents are there under whose shelter and protection she's growing up.)

The Anguish of Separation from My Child

The months passed happily. But I sensed her growing attachment to me. One day she placed 4 mobiles in a row – her mum's, dad's, mine and her own (hers was a toy one). She picked up Jasmine's and Yezdi's cellphones and kept them aside. Then, pointing out to mine and hers, she said, "That's my mum and myself. That's my family. Masi. You're my mum. I want you alone." Her words hit me with such force that I couldn't respond. "Here it comes. My time to move on before my child gets too attached to bear with separation from me," I thought, steeling myself. With the time approaching to put my resolve into action, I braced myself for the separation.

Pearl had melted my heart during my few months' stay with her. She had been brought into my life for a reason. I cannot remember ever having watched and experienced a child's innocent fairyland so closely. While in the past 4 - 6 months Jasmine had been busy with diapers, bottles, bibs, injection doses, timely feeds and the endless chores with Jehan, she had, with full faith, handed over Pearl's responsibility in my hands. Letting go of her was wrenching, and yet I had to accept that she was not my child. She had come in my life temporarily to give me an opportunity to experience deeply all the joys of motherhood.

"Now Jasmine's life is settled. Jehan is around 6-months-old and Jasmine too will be back to work soon, leaving her kids with Shehnaz, the caring lady at the crèche, under whose loving umbrella Pearl had been since the past 2½ years. Between Jasmine, Yezdi, Shehnaz and the maids, they'll be able to manage the two kids well. It's high time that I move on to be full time at Sunbeam (12 hours a day instead of the present 6 - 8 hours that I managed to put in)." I consoled myself with this little speech and in the next few days, slowly brought Pearl to understand that I had no choice but to leave because there was no one to take care of my Sunbeam children. I promised her that I'd continue to spend the weekends with her though.

Finally, the day arrived and I took their leave. The moment Pearl was out of sight, my heart longed for her. And I wept in anguish, unable to come to terms with the fact that my child's presence would no longer fill my life as before. I felt as though an important part of my life was missing. It wasn't until several hours later that I could bring myself to call her up, but only to deeply regret it. Because I ended up traumatising her by not acceding to her request to continue to spend the nights at her place. A few days passed with her calling me up every evening, her voice pleading over the phone, "Masi, please come back. Who will tell me bedtime stories? I miss you."

With Pearl not being a daily presence in my life, I felt I had lost a vital part of myself. None would know how much it hurt to move away. Being back home, I missed her more than she missed me. I missed her voice that would plead with me to tell one more story and how I'd carry on till sleep overcame me and she'd wake me up with protest. I missed her holding on to me and asking if robbers (she meant murderers) did exist in real life or just in TV serials and whether God was really there to watch over her. Also, missed her early morning threats of complaining about me to her grandparents for disturbing her sleep and placing her in the bathtub to get ready for school! O, life became so lonely without her. My heart ached to see her, to hold her in my arms.

I soon recovered from the separation pangs and found solace in Sunbeam beneficiaries. But, even today, 5 year later, the uplifting, familiar, most loving voice, calling out 'Masi' continues to bring joy to my heart when I spend a few hours with her on week-ends, or stay overnight with her.

Today's Scenario with Pearl who is 9 Years Old

Now, when I see my confident girl, happy with friends of her age, I wonder if it's my same little girl who used to cuddle up to me for bedtime stories.

Today, Pearl's sense of security rests where it should – with her mother. I wonder how Jasmine managed with 2 full time jobs up until recently. One at the State Bank of India Capital Markets Ltd. where she was employed (she resigned last year) and the other being a mother to 2 doting children. But I can say with conviction that Pearl no longer feels second to her younger sibling. She feels secure in the knowledge that her parents are there for her. Once a fortnight or so, when I stayed over at their place, I was in awe of how Jasmine managed to handle her - just watched the ideal mum rush home, spend time cooking, and yet still find time to talk, play and laugh with her children, and of course ensure that Pearl completed her homework under her loving but stern gaze.

Whenever I still go to Pearl's house and she opens the door, nowadays with Jehan (nearly 5 years old) too running after her, I feel again the same sense of belonging combined with an overwhelming love that's still mutual and has not in the least bit diminished. In my child's company, it is always magic. Every so-called ordinary day is filled with unique experiences that move me to the core. Her company is His divine gift to me, one that makes my life enchanting.

In May'05, my parents and I moved to our new residence at Andheri, a few blocks away from Pearl's house and she was thrilled at the idea of having her Pa, Ma and Masi so close to her.

As she entered our home, she looked up with a smile. Then, to my delight, with her arms around my neck, she said, "You come and stay with me for a few days and then I'll come over to stay with Pa and Ma in this home for a day or two. I know you can't stay with me forever. You've got Pa and Ma to take care of. You've also got to stay with aunt at times. And of course, there are so many children of yours who must be waiting for you."

It felt strange but somehow correct. Pearl knew she could trust me to be around once in a while. Jehan was now almost 5-year-old and her best friend.

The beautiful phase of 5 years ago was gone. Those days that I had lived with Pearl were different. My child now has friends and other activities to look forward to, so she generously gives me concessions to take care of my 1000+ children for most of the days and requests me to keep aside just a few days a fortnight for her!

Index